Guide to Edinburgh Monuments

John N. Amoore

To Kathleen

Text and the photographs of monuments by John Amoore

The right of John Amoore to be identified as the Author of this work has been asserted in accordance with the Copyrights, Designs and Patents Act of 1988

ISBN-13: 9781794100657

First Published: 2018
Revised and Updated: June 2024

.

CONTENTS

Note: The number of monument sections in each of the first six chapters are shown in brackets after its title. There are 113 sections.

ACKNOWLEDGMENTS

The material for this book was researched from many sources. Quotes are acknowledged by endnotes detailed in the References and Bibliography at the end of the book. The help of staff in the Edinburgh Room at the Central Library and at the Scottish Poetry Library is gratefully acknowledged.

Whilst acknowledging their help, the author remains responsible for the material in the book and for any errors, grammatical or factual, that may remain. The author has attempted to correct all errors in the text, but would be grateful if readers could let him know of any errors. The author would also be grateful for suggestions for improving future editions of the book.

Foreword

Why do we erect monuments in towns and cities? What images of the city do the monuments convey? What images would we like them to convey? And who are all these men (and it is mainly men) cast in bronze or carved in stone standing high above our streets?

Many monuments recall those mighty in power (monarchs, politicians and leaders, military and civilian) and, as we shall see, appropriate for a City of Literature, those mighty with the 'pen'. But it is not only the mighty that are remembered. Plaques on benches remember loved ones. The simple memorial in James Court to Susannah Alice Stephen (*4.12*) who died in her prime recalls a friend sadly missed. (The monuments are numbered sequentially by chapter; each monument or group of monuments is accorded a section within its chapter. Thus *4.12* refers to the 12th monument discussed in Chapter 4.) And a wife mourning her husband remembers, with words that remind us of our own mortality and immortality (*5.10*):

> *How long is a man's life finally? Is it a thousand days or only one?*
> *One week, or a few centuries? How long does a man's death last?*
> *A man lives for as long as we carry him inside us,*
> *Holding memories in common a man lives.*
> (From Brian Patten's 1946 poem 'So many lengths of time')

Edinburgh has been enriched by many. Our understanding of the city is enriched by understanding its monuments and those they honour.

The monuments are arranged by location. Chapter 1 covers Princes Street and its gardens, the Mound that divides the gardens into two and the North Bridge erected at the east end of the Nor Loch that once filled the valley. Chapter 2 focuses on the New Town, George Street and its subsequent developments in the East and West Ends. Chapter 3 covers Calton Hill. In general monuments in cemeteries are excluded, with the exception of a few monuments in the Old Cemetery on Calton Hill, primarily to include the towering obelisk to the Friends of the People (*3.8*), known also as the Martyrs' Monument. Chapter 4 takes us along the Royal Mile, from the Castle and its Esplanade down to the Canongate and Palace of Holyrood. Chapter 5 looks at Leith and Chapter 6 briefly explores some statues and memorials around other parts of the city. Many who have lived in the city or enjoyed visits to the city are remembered by the benches in the city's parks, some of which are shown in Chapter 7.

Chapter 8 draws the monuments together, exploring what they have in common and what they tell us about Edinburgh, its history, what shaped its soul and its future. This concluding chapter also gives an opportunity to raise questions about who should be honoured with monuments. Physical monuments are not the only way we remember people and events and Chapter 8 discusses this.

Not all monuments within the city boundaries are included. Those in cemeteries are generally excluded. Those inside buildings, museums and art galleries are excluded as are memorials in many of the city's suburbs. The many allegorical statues and statuettes on the outside of buildings are excluded as is urban art.

Most plaques on the walls of buildings are excluded. There are a few exceptions. One of these is a plaque in the New Town to James Craig who laid out the design for its development, the 250th anniversary of which was celebrated in 2017 (for plaque see Chapter 2, *2.8*). Three large plaques at the base of Calton Hill are mentioned at the end of Chapter 3 because they had intrigued me, and I had wondered who and what they represented.

But the plaques to which I want to draw the reader's attention are those to Dr Elsie Inglis. There are two wall plaques to her at 219 High Street on the heart of Edinburgh's Royal Mile, the heart of the Old Town and indeed of the city. Her innovative leadership and contribution to the city and to the wider community beyond this country is briefly discussed in Chapter 4 (*4.23*). It was at 219 High Street that Dr Inglis set up a maternity clinic providing a much needed and appreciated service. The photograph in this section shows the two plaques with people below in the street. How many of those people, of the visitors and indeed residents of Edinburgh, look up to see these plaques, or, if they do, have any knowledge of 'Dr Elsie Inglis'; who is she and what did she do to deserve to be included among the 'Women of Achievement'? Updating this book in 2023 it is heartening to report that agreement has been reached to erect a statue to her, scheduled for 2024.

This is one of the reasons for writing this book: who are these people? When I walked past observing the many monuments as I enjoyed the sites of this grand city of many contrasts, I did not know who the people honoured were and what they had done. Residents of the city whom I asked did not know either – and in most cases were not really interested! So, this book began as a venture of exploration for me, seeking to uncover the lives and contributions of those to whom monuments had been erected. This venture of exploration will continue for me personally. I hope that, through this book, others will come to a deeper appreciation of the monuments and the city.

The book includes most of the monuments that are likely to be encountered while meandering around the city streets. The monuments are arranged in sections, some sections discussing more than one monument. Examples include the 30 statues on the exterior of the National Portrait Gallery (*2.10*) and the 12 Scottish Poets (*6.12*). There are 112 sections. The Index provides a quick way of finding the monuments, pointing to about 180 memorials included in the book. The Index does not link to the many memorial plaques on park benches and flower beds listed in Chapter 7.

This 'Guide' is a sequel to '*101 plus Edinburgh monuments*' with added monuments and improved text. It is a companion to '*A Journey with Edinburgh's Monuments*', the colour version. This black and white version is smaller, easier to carry whilst exploring the monuments.

I hope you enjoy reading about and, more importantly, going to see these monuments and, through them, gain a deeper appreciation of Edinburgh, Scotland's Capital. This is a guide, inviting the reader to explore Edinburgh through its monuments, reflecting on what they tell us about the city.

Chapter 1:
Princes Street, its Gardens, The Mound and North Bridge

Princes Street and its Gardens date from the 18th and 19th century New Town developments, the city extending northwards, freeing itself from the confines of the Old Town. What is now Princes Street was a pathway on the northern banks of the Nor Loch. Over the centuries the loch became dirty and polluted, with calls for it to be drained. Gardens were laid out in the 19th century.

Edinburgh's landscape was formed millennia earlier. Glacial ice age carved away soft rock, exposing a volcanic plug, now called Castle Rock, leaving a narrow ridge sloping down eastwards, valleys on either side. Fortifications were built on Castle Rock and dwellings on its eastward ridge. The ridge forms what we call the Royal Mile. The developing city was vulnerable to attack from the north, prompting the creation of a defensive loch. In the mid-15th century a burn, fed by springs at the foot of the castle, was dammed up, creating the Nor Loch. The loch extended eastwards from St. Cuthbert's church to an earthen dam wall, built to the east of where the North Bridge now spans the valley.

Besides protecting the city from attack, the Nor Loch helped deter, but not prevent, the smuggling of wine and other goods into the city. The Forth coast shoreline was the entry point, smugglers encouraged by the profits from avoiding the high excise duties.

The loch and its banks were also used for recreation, boating and fishing. The minister of St. Cuthbert's had fishing rights on the loch (eel was the principal fish). Wild duck lived on the loch and swans were introduced. The 'green path' or 'lang gait' north of the loch provided a pleasant footpath. Ice skaters enjoyed the frozen winter waters, perhaps a foretaste of the winter ice-rink of the early 21st century Winter Wonderland.

However, the loch, largely fed by the spring, became a stagnant pool. The habit of throwing rubbish and remains of livestock into the water left it very murky. Allegedly it became a place of punishment: 'dookin' (ducking) involved strapping those accused to a ducking chair and ducking them in the foul water. Legend reports that it was used to test whether those accused of witchcraft were in league with the devil. If the accused floated when thrown into the Nor Loch they were declared guilty of witchcraft. This has probably been exaggerated, but there was a vicious campaign against those alleged to be guilty of witchcraft. Hundreds of women were burnt at the stake on Castle hill - a memorial on the Esplanade remembers those who suffered this fate (Chapter 4, *4.9*).

The silting of the stagnant water and its use as a refuse dump turned the Nor Loch into an unpleasant marsh. By the 18th century protection from attack and smuggling became less important than opening access and expanding the city to the north. Consequently, proposals were made for draining the loch and developing easy access from the Old Town to the opportunities in the north. At the east end the North Bridge was built. A clothier, George Boyd, in 1783 laid stepping stones across the marsh from below Bank Street. Others added to the crossing which became known as Geordie Boyd's Mud Brig. Earth excavated during the development of the New Town was dumped over the crossing,

1

forming the Mound. By 1793 some 1.3 million cart loads of earth had been dumped, dividing the valley. But it was criticised: *'One of the greatest mistakes .. was the erection of the earthen mound across the beautiful valley of the loch. It is simply .. a clumsy enormous and unremovable substitute for a bridge which should have been there.'*

Progress was slow. Despite the Town Council proposing in 1787 to drain the loch as quickly as possible, Lord Cockburn in 1816 described the area as 'a receptacle of many sewers and drowned dogs'. But eventually it was drained and gardens were laid out by James Skene. What is now East Princes Street Gardens was the last to be drained, but by 1844 it had become a public park. Access to the area to the west of the Mound was initially restricted to private New Town landowners, but by the late 1860s it too was opened to the public.

This chapter covers Princes Street and its gardens, the Mound and the North Bridge. It has 3 parts: 1-1, the Western section to the Mound; 1-2, the Mound; 1-3, the Eastern section up to and including the North Bridge.

Part 1.1 - West Princes Street and its Gardens

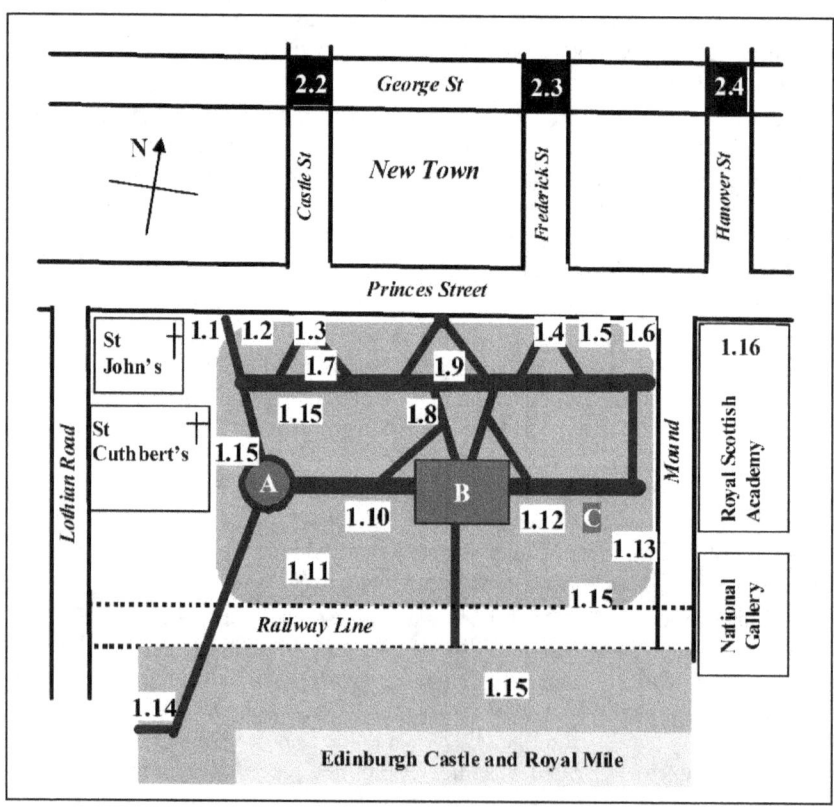

Map 1-1: West Princes Street and its Gardens

Map 1-1: Monuments of West Princes Street and its Gardens

1.1	1.2	1.3
Dean Ramsay	**Sir James Young Simpson**	**Dr Thomas Guthrie**

1.4	1.5	1.6	1.7
Royal Scots Greys	**Allan Ramsay**	**Floral Clock**	**Wojtek**

1.8	1.9
Falklands Memorial Garden	**Scottish American War Memorial**

1.10	1.11	1.12	1.13
Norwegian Boulder	**RL Stevenson**	**Babies' Ashes**	**The Royal Scots**

1.14	1.15
Canine Connection	**Commemorative Plaques on Rocks and Trees**

Urban Art and Landmarks

A	B	C
Ross Fountain	**Ross Bandstand**	**Genius of Architecture**

Notes

- *1.15:* Plaques on rocks and trees; approximate positions shown

- George Street is the central axis of the New Town. Statues at its intersections with Castle, Frederick and Hanover Streets are (see Chapter 2):
    (*2.2*) Dr Chalmers;   (*2.3*) William Pitt;   (*2.4*) King George IV

- Drs Guthrie (*1.3*) and Chalmers (*2.2*), early leaders of the Free Kirk, look at each other along Castle Street, Guthrie looking north and Chalmers south

- Queen Victoria (*1.16*), atop the Royal Scottish Academy at foot of Mound, looks north up Hanover Street to King George IV (*2.4*) looking south

- Three prominent landmarks, though not monuments, are indicated for clarification

  A. Ross Fountain: gifted to the city by Daniel Ross, a city philanthropist, who saw it at the 1862 Great Exhibition in London and had it shipped as a gift to Edinburgh. Its 2018 restoration saw new colour schemes, a new water pumping system and repairs to allegorical figures, notably Art and Science.

  B. Ross Bandstand: created in 1877, gifted to the city by William Henry Ross, Chairman of Distillers. Plans were underway in 2018 for its redevelopment

  C. Lady with two children sculpted by William Brodie, a prolific 19th century sculptor. This work of art is known as 'The Genius of Architecture', the lady crowning the two children representative of the theory and practice of architecture.

1.1 Dean (Edward Bannerman) Ramsay, 1793-1872

Popular respected clergyman, author

The Celtic cross celebrates Dean Ramsay. He was priest-in-charge of the nearby St John's church for 40 years and for over 30 years was Dean of the Episcopal Diocese of Edinburgh. A popular clergyman and Edinburgh personality, he was sociable, fond of music and an accomplished flautist. Elected as a Fellow of the Royal Society of Edinburgh aged 34, he served as its Vice President for 3 years. He founded the Scottish Episcopal Church Society in 1838 and, in 1846, helped establish Trinity College, Glenalmond.

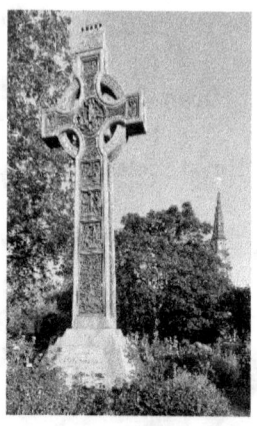

His 1858 book *'Reminiscences of Scottish Life and Character'* described *'features of national life and character'*. Its objective was to preserve the memory of the ways of life and manners that were changing. Chapters include: *'Scottish religious feelings and observances'*, *'On old Scottish Conviviality'*, *'On the old Scottish domestic servant'*, *'Scottish Judges'* and *'On Scottish stories of wit and humour'*.

Description: Granite Celtic cross, 8m high, bronze panels of Biblical scenes
Design by: Rowand Anderson. Bronze panels by F.A. Skidmore
Produced: Farmer & Brindley, London. Erected: 1879

The book ran to 22 editions in his lifetime. It used anecdotes to illustrate Scottish life and character. The changes in the life and character of the people *'comprise much that is interesting and amusing. But they also contain much matter for serious thought and reflection to the lovers of their country. The Christian, when he looks around him on society, must observe many things which, as a patriot, he wishes might be permanent, and he marks many things which, as a patriot, he wishes were obliterated.'*[1] Ramsay hoped that the *'abiding attributes of Scottish character should be associated amongst all men with truth and virtue with honour and kindly feelings with temperance and self-denial with divine faith and love with generosity and benevolence'*.

He helped initiate and raise funds for the statue of Dr Thomas Chalmers (*2.2*).

Born in Aberdeen, the son of Sir Alexander Ramsay, he grew up in Yorkshire, attending school in Durham and then Cambridge University. He returned to Scotland, curate at St George's York Place, then to St John's where he is buried.

1.2 Sir James Young Simpson, 1811-1870

Obstetrics & Anaesthetics pioneer

Simpson, medical pioneer, demonstrated the anaesthetic properties of chloroform in 1847, transforming surgery. He introduced it as an anaesthetic agent in obstetrics and surgery at the Royal Infirmary of Edinburgh (RIE) where he had been Professor of Midwifery since 1840. His use of chloroform was initially opposed by the medical establishment. Its use by Queen Victoria (*5.1*) when giving birth to her son Prince Leopold helped its acceptance. The ability to anaesthetise patients revolutionised surgery, winning him world-wide fame as

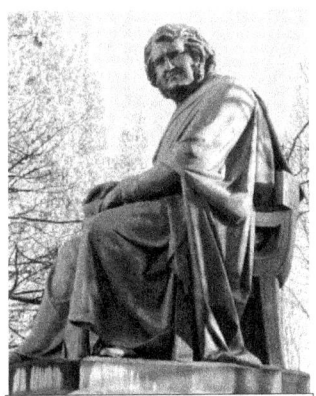

Description: Simpson robed, seated, open book in his hand
Sculptor: William Brodie
Cast: Masefield & Co. London.
Unveiled: June 1877

In 1847 in a pharmacy on this site
Duncan Flockhart & Co
made the chloroform used by
Sir James Young Simpson
in the historic experiments on the relief of pain.
This plaque was erected on the occasion of the
Third World Congress of the International Association
for the Study of Pain held in Edinburgh 1981.

Location: Wall of Balmoral Hotel on North Bridge (see Map 1-3)

the anaesthesia pioneer. He was knighted in 1866, the first knighthood for services to medicine.

His name lives on in Edinburgh's maternity hospital, Simpson wing at RIE, Little France – prior to 2002 at the Simpson Memorial Maternity Pavilion at the Lauriston Place site.

His pioneering chloroform experiment took place in a dining room in November 1847 in his home, 22 Queen Street. Simpson and two colleagues inhaled the gas and were rendered senseless, to the concern of his watching wife. Recovering, he was jubilant, hailing the ability to conquer surgical pain.

A plaque on the North Bridge wall of the Balmoral Hotel commemorates the pharmacy where he obtained chloroform.

Born in Bathgate, his father the baker, his mother devout and nurturing him with a cheerful positive personality. At the village school the 'wise wean' outshone his peers. His mother encouraged his further education; sadly, she was to die when he was 9. Entering Edinburgh University at 14, enrolling in medical school at 16, he passed his final exams with honours at 19. Too young to graduate, he worked as a junior assistant and travelled. Graduating in 1832 he obtained a hospital appointment. Marriage followed and later, aged 29, he became midwifery Professor. He quickly attracted appreciative patients.

Buried in Warriston Cemetery in Edinburgh, about 1700 joined his funeral procession, with over 100,000 lining the route.

1.3 Reverend Dr Thomas Guthrie, 1803-1873
Preacher, Ragged Schools Founder

Dr Guthrie strove to offer a better life for the Old Town's 'ragged' children. Touched by children begging and stealing amidst its poverty and squalor, he sought how to turn them from a life of crime and punishment. He developed the Ragged School: basic education including Christian instruction combined with regular meals and skills developments opening work opportunities. His appeals for funds to transform the children's lives gained support, including that of Edinburgh's Lord Provost, Adam Black, (*1.20*). He appealed: '*their faces tell how ill they are fed; their fearful oaths tell how ill they are reared.*'[2].

Food was provided; cleanliness, godliness, reading and writing, with job-promoting skills, cobbling, tailoring and cooking were taught. Carrying out tasks for local shops was encouraged, linking work with earning money. His transforming zeal cleared the streets of young beggars, reducing the number of children in prison to a quarter.

There is a story[2] of pub drinkers noisily criticising clergy when one drinker interjected:

'I'll tell you a gude man, a really gude man.'
'Wha's that!?' 'That's just Tam Guthrie.'
'Ay! you've said it now.' 'I believe Dr Guthrie to be as a gude a man as ever waggit his head in a poopit.'
'He's different fare the ithers a'thegither; he practices mair than he preaches.'

He discouraged drinking, supporting abstinence and legislation to close pubs on Sundays. He was a member of the Royal Infirmary's Board and supported refuges for women and the blind. Like Dr Chalmers (*2.2*) he was an early leader of the Free Church of Scotland, elected Moderator in 1862. To promote the Church's work, he helped provide manses throughout Scotland through the Manse Fund.

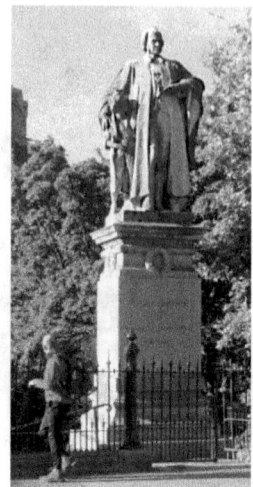

Description: Guthrie, Bible in hand, protects a young 'ragged boy'. Stone, on Peterhead granite pedestal
Sculptor: Frederick W. Pomeroy
Unveiled: October 1910

Thomas Guthrie was born in Brechin, Angus, the 12th child of David and Clementina. His father was for many years Provost of the town. He entered Edinburgh University aged 12, studying literature and philosophy, divinity, surgery and anatomy. Licensed as a minister, he developed popular Sunday evening sessions for young people in his parish near Forfar. His talents led to him being invited, in 1837, to Old Greyfriars Kirk where he also proved a popular preacher. Conflicts in the Church of Scotland were in progress; Guthrie became a supporter of Chalmers (*2.2*) and other leaders, joining the seceding ministers who formed the Free Church in the 1843 Disruption. Guthrie established the Free St John's Church on Johnston Terrace, now the St Columba's Free Church of Scotland.

He died in 1873 surrounded by his wife and 8 of their 10 children. His funeral was in Edinburgh with the procession watched by 30,000. At his graveside 230 children from his Ragged Schools sang *'There is a happy land, far, far away'*. A little girl remarked: *'He was all the father I ever knew.'* [2]

1.4   The Royal Scots Greys
In Memory of those who died in the Boer War 1899-1902

The monument was erected to honour the Royal Scots Greys who died in the Boer War. The regiment saw action from the Cape to Pretoria, the relief of Kimberly, the advance to Bloemfontein and Pretoria, the fall of Pretoria and in the increasingly guerrilla warfare. After the 1902 Boer surrender the regiment remained to help garrison the country till 1905. The plaque lists those who died. It shows the Eagle, the Regiment's symbol adopted after the Battle of Waterloo where the Eagle of a French regiment had been seized by Ensign Ewart (*4.4*).

Commemorative plaques were later added to honour those who died in World Wars I and II and subsequent conflicts.

Formed in 1678 to suppress the Covenanters (*6.3*), the Royal Scots Greys name derives from a nickname from their grey horses. Its motto: '*Nemo Me Impune Lacessit*' - *No one provokes me with impunity.*

At the time of the Anglo-Boer War its Colonel-in-Chief was Tsar Nicolas II, Emperor of Russia, appointed by Queen Victoria (*5.1*).

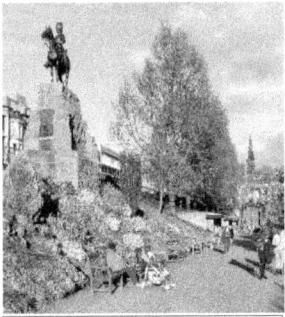

Description: Bronze Royal Scots Greys soldier mounted on a horse on a rock plinth.
Sculptor: William Birnie Rhind.   Models: Sergeant Major Anthony Hinnigan and his horse 'Polly'
Unveiled: 16th Nov 1906 by Lord Rosebury

1.5   Allan Ramsay, 1686 - 1758
Poet, publisher, helped establish a new golden age of Scottish literature

Allan Ramsay arrived in Edinburgh to find a lively literary environment, clubs meeting in city taverns, in which he thrived. He went on to play a leading role in 18th century Edinburgh literary circles. His promotion of Scottish literature revived Scots vernacular poetry, paving the way for Fergusson (*4.25*) and Burns (*3.9; 5.2*). He founded a book market near St Giles.

He came to Edinburgh as a wig-maker's apprentice, in 1712 opening his own wig shop in the Grassmarket. Commercially successful, but his interest lay in literature, finding support from the city's literary clubs, where he recited his poetry. An early presentation in 1712 was '*The most happy members of the Easy Club*' to the club of that name. The 1715 Jacobite rebellion curtailed the clubs' activities; Ramsay, a Jacobite sympathiser, kept his views secret.

He published single page poems at a penny, much sought after by the women who sent their children to buy 'Ramsay's last piece'. In 1721 plans for publishing a book of his poems advanced his literary career, his easy-going nature endearing him to leading members of

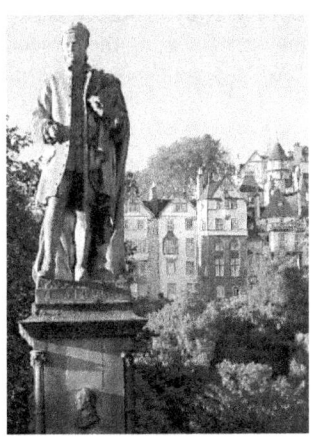

Description: Ramsay, 10ft high stands, book in left hand, pencil in right, plaid is over his shoulder, wearing a silk night-cap. The plinth has medallions of the Ramsay family
Sculptor: Sir John Steell from 18 ton Carrara marble block
Unveiled: 25th March 1865 by Sir John McNeil

society. Single sheet poems on pastoral life led to the verse-play the 'The Gentle

Shepherd'. Written in the Scots dialect this 5-act poem describes 18th century pastoral life through the lives of shepherds and shepherdesses who have a *'homely yet poetic reality, a humour and archness, at moments a tone of passion'*[3].

He established the first lending library in Britain. He built a playhouse in Carruber's Close, but opposition from the city's puritanical authorities forced its closure within a year. Financially successful, he moved to an octagonal villa on the north of Castle Hill overlooking the Nor Loch. Nicknamed the 'goose pie', it is part of what is now known as Ramsay Gardens, re-developed by Patrick Geddes (*4.11*) (Ramsay Gardens is visible in the photo behind the statue).

At the age of 26 he married Christian Ross, the daughter of an Edinburgh writer. Their first child, the portrait painter Allan Ramsay, was born a year later, seven more children following. He died in January 1758 and was buried in Greyfriars churchyard. A headstone on the external south wall of the church, erected in the mid-19th century, contrasts the burial of Ramsay's mortal remains with the enduring legacy of his written work: here *'was interred the Mortal Part of an Immortal Poet'*:

> *'Tho here you're buried, worthy Allan,*
> *We'll ne'er forget your canty Callan;*
> *For while your Soul lives in the Sky,*
> *Your Gentle Shepherd ne'er can die.'*

Lord Murray, a descendant, paid for the statue, but died before its completion, his wife finishing the project. It was unveiled by Sir John McNeil on 25th March 1865 at a dual ceremony with the unveiling of John Wilson's statue (*1.19*).

1.6   Floral Clock   *Floral clock with commemorative theme*

At the eastern corner of West Princes Street gardens, below Allan Ramsay's statue (*1.5*), is the popular floral clock, locals and visitors marvelling at its horticultural craftsmanship and intricate floral designs. Believed to be the world's first floral clock, its inspiration came from a floral display in 1902 in the gardens commemorating Edward VII's coronation. John McHattie, Edinburgh's Park Superintendent, teamed up with the Edinburgh clockmakers, James Ritchie and Son, to create a floral clock. The clock mechanism was installed in the base of the Allan Ramsay monument. The cuckoo house was installed in 1953.

Since 1946 the floral arrangement has commemorated anniversaries and events, recently: 2008 - World War II; 2009 - Bicentenary of Royal Caledonian Horticultural Society; 2010 - century of Girl Guiding; 2011 - Royal National Institute for the Deaf; 2012 - London Olympic Games; 2013 - Edinburgh Zoo Centenary; 2014 - Edinburgh Fair Trade; 216 - centenary of Royal Incorporation of Architects in Scotland; 2017 - bicentenary of 'Scotsman', the founders commitment to *'good sense, courage and industry'* proclaimed in flowers; 2018 - 1914-1918 Great War and the continuing charity work of Poppy Scotland that grew out of that war and its 2018 fundraising 'The 1918 Poppy Pledge' (see also Earl Haig *4.10*); 2019 - centenary of 'Save the Children', formed by sisters Eglantyne Jebb and Dorothy Buxton in response to the poverty of children in post-war Europe, exacerbated by the continuing post-war blockade by the victorious allies; 2020 - the response to Covid-19 and theme '*Stay Safe*' and '*Edinburgh thanks all key workers*', the display without clock hands; 2021 – the 2020 350th anniversary of the Royal Botanic Garden Edinburgh started as a 'physic garden by Robert Sibbald and Andrew Balfour in 1670; 2022 - Platinum Jubilee of Queen Elizabeth; 2023 - centenary of Flying Scotsman. 2024 – Bicentenary of the RNLI.

In 2015 it celebrated 10 years since Edinburgh was declared, in 2004, UNESCO's first City of Literature. This honoured Edinburgh's rich literature

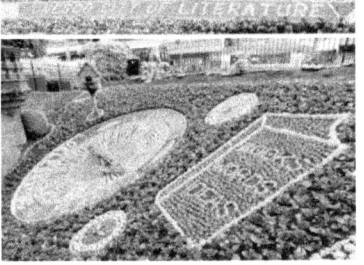

tradition: leading authors over many centuries; a tradition of publishing and making available literary works; Edinburgh's Book Festival, occurring annually during August, the largest in the world. The 2017 book festival presented over 1000 authors from 50 countries, with over 250,000 visits to its Charlotte Square and George street grounds.

Description: A garden of flowers forming a clock. A cuckoo calls out each quarter hour. Created anew each year, representing a different anniversary
Original design: John McHattie, Edinburgh Parks Superintendent. Clock by Messrs James Ritchie & Sons Ltd from the old parish church clock of Elie, Fife.
Unveiled: 10th June 1903, the clock electrified in 1977. But in a real sense it is new every year, new commemoration, arrangement and pattern of flowers.

1.7   Wojtek (1942- 1963) **and Polish Army Unit**
Contributions of the Unit and Wojtek, the bear, to World War II

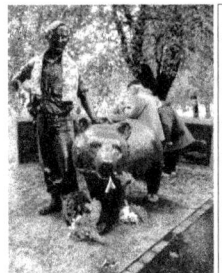

Description: Syrian bear & Polish soldier in peace and unity, on Polish granite. 4 metre relief panel depicts 6 scenes from Wojtek's life.
Sculptor: Alan Beattie Herriot
Unveiled: 7th Nov 2015

Soldiers of a Polish military corps training in Iran (then called Persia) in 1942 were approached by a starving boy, alone and ragged, carrying a bag; he wanted to exchange it for food. Opening the bag, the soldiers saw a baby Syrian bear, only a few days old.

The Polish soldiers had themselves had a long hard journey. Taken from Poland to Siberian labour camps, Allied-Russian agreements led them to be moved to join a new Polish Army being formed in the Middle East. They warmed to the boy's plight and to the tiny cub for which they gave the boy food. Hiding the cub, the soldiers cared for and fed it. Initially hidden from the officers, this became impossible as the bear grew and, given the name Wojtek (little warrior), the bear was accepted into the army transport unit. Growing big and strong he became a hero when he surprised a thief in the ammunition compound, leading to the thief's capture. Wojtek enjoyed his reward of a bottle of beer.

Preparations were being made for the Polish Army's move to Italy; what to do with Wojtek? The navy insisted that only enlisted soldiers could be transported on naval ships. But the men had become attached to Wojtek. A solution was determined: enlist Wojtek with his own pay book, rank and army number.

Across in Italy, Wojtek and his 2nd Polish Corp were deployed to help overcome the Germans who, at Monte Cassino, had fortified themselves in a former monastery on a strategic hill. This hill had been the target of an earlier campaign by the Allies, partly described in Section *2.16*, the 'Manuscript of Monte Cassino'. The fortification guarded a strategically important major road which the Allies wished to capture to open the road to Rome. The fighting was bitter and Wojtek helped move crates of ammunition to the artillery firing line. Wojtek was not frightened by the sounds of battle and after the successful conclusion of the battle the 22nd Transport Company adopted as its official badge Wojtek carrying an artillery shell.

After the war ended in 1945 the Polish troops were sent to Berwick upon Tweed and demobilised. Wojtek was moved to Edinburgh Zoo where he died in 1963.

Wojtek became a symbol of Polish wartime struggles, of pride to the Polish soldiers. They had lost their country, first to the Nazis and later to the Communists and looked forward to the day when their homeland would be free. The Wojtek Memorial Trust campaigned for a memorial to him and the Polish soldiers. Edinburgh City Council granted permission in 2013. The Trust's secretary spoke of its objective of erecting '*a monument fitting to Polish veterans of the Second World War, and to the many men, women and children displaced as a consequence of the war and its aftermath, as told through the story of Wojtek, the Soldier Bear*'.

A fundraising campaign raised £300,000 to pay for the monument which was unveiled on the Saturday before Remembrance Sunday, 2015. At the event Edinburgh's Lord Provost spoke of Wojtek the Soldier Bear and the statue making a '*statement about fighting for freedom and showing support and comfort to those who are suffering*' and celebrating ties with Poland.

1.8   Falklands Memorial Garden, 1982
Memorial to those who died in Falkland War

> Description: A sheltered garden with white heather remembers the men and women who died in the 1982 Falkland War
> Dedicated: 28th November 1982

The 74-day Falklands war followed Argentina occupying British territories in the South Atlantic: Falkland Islands, South Georgia and the Sandwich Islands. Britain reclaimed the islands after heavy fighting; sea and land battles left nearly 650 Argentinean and 255 British dead. The conflict was associated with patriotic fervour in both Britain and Argentina. Whilst relations between the two countries were restored in 1989, the islands' sovereignty remains in dispute. In a March 2013 referendum the islanders voted to retain links with Britain.

1.9   Scottish American War Memorial, The Call

A tribute from men and women of Scottish blood and sympathies in the United States of America to Scotland

Erected in 1927 to celebrate the World War I comradeship between Scotland and the USA, it was sculptured in bronze by Dr Robert Tait McKenzie. The strong links between Scotland and the USA are symbolised by two shields, one with the Stars and Stripes, the other with a St Andrews Cross. Dr McKenzie is honoured by a plaque on a park bench nearby; plaques on other benches remember links between USA forces and Scotland – see Chapter 7.

The relief behind the statue shows Scottish miners, shepherds, farmers and fishermen being led off to war by a regimental band of pipes and drums. Below the relief are words from the poem 'A Creed', written at Vimy Ridge in 1916 by Lieutenant E. Alan Mackintosh M.C. of the 5th Seaforth Highlanders: '*If it be life that waits, I shall live forever unconquered, if death, I shall die, at last, strong in my pride and free.*'

The plinth includes a Biblical inscription (Judges Chapter 5, verse 18): '*A people that jeoparded their lives unto death in the high places of the field.*'

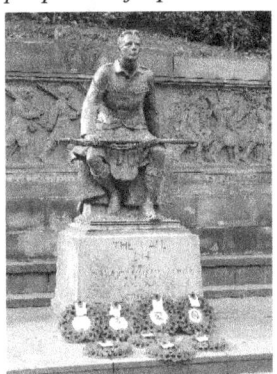 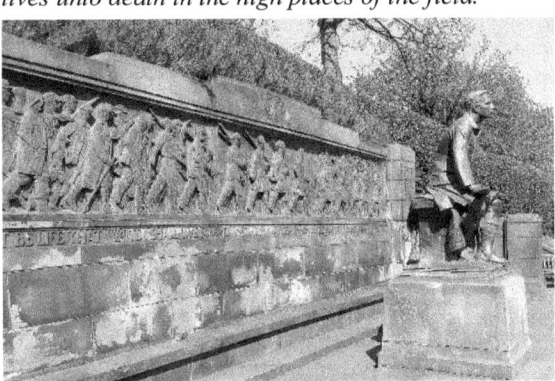

Description: A young soldier in a kilt, leaning forward, gazes intently, rifle across knees. Behind, a 30-foot bronze bass-relief of the call to arms, with Scottish working men led off to war by a pipe and drum band.
Sculptor: Figure and relief by Dr Robert Tait McKenzie.
　　　　　Setting by Reginald Fairlie
Unveiled: 1927, by Alanson B. Houghton, U.S. Ambassador to Britain

1.10 Norwegian Memorial Stone

Commemorates Scottish Norwegian links

During World War II 7000 Norwegian men and women served in the Norwegian Brigade raised in Scotland. In gratitude the Norwegians presented this massive gneiss boulder in 1978. Scottish Norwegian links remain strong, visible in the Christmas Tree at the Mound donated each year by Norway.

The boulder's south and north sides are inscribed:

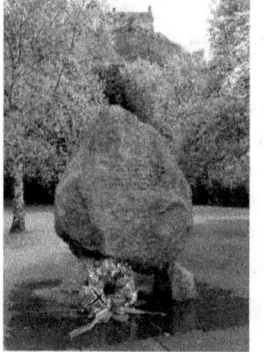

South side: '*During the War Years 1940 – 1945 The Norwegian Brigade and other army units were raised and trained in Scotland. Here we found hospitality, friendship and hope during dark years of exile. In grateful memory of our friends and allies on these isles this stone was erected in the year 1978.*'

North side: '*This boulder was brought here from Norway where it was worn and shaped for thousands of years by forces of nature, frost, running water, rock, sand and ice until it obtained its present shape.*'

Description: 8 ton, 900 million year old Gneiss boulder inscribed on north and south sides
Presented: 18th Sept 1978 by Norwegian Army

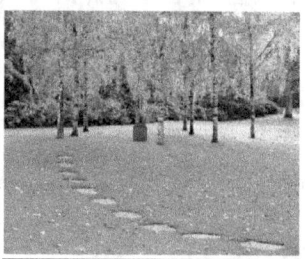

1.11 Robert Louis Stevenson,
1850-1894
Author, novelist and adventurer

Robert Louis Stevenson (RLS) achieved fame and fortune as a writer during his lifetime. His works ranged from poetry to travel and adventure, including 'A Child's Garden of Verse', 'Treasure Island', 'Kidnapped' and 'The Strange Case of Dr Jekyll and Mr Hyde'.

The Princes Street Gardens memorial combines a sense of adventure, the paving slabs leading onwards, his tranquil nature in a peaceful spot, and his sense of fun enjoying a summer's day.

Description: Base of stone column inscribed '*A man of letters / R L S / 1850 – 1894*'. Within birch tree grove approached by paving stones
Design: Iain Hamilton Finlay.
Unveiled: 1989, Muriel Spark

Edinburgh born into a family of leading lighthouse engineers, Robert Lewis Stevenson (he changed his middle name to Louis when 18) started engineering studies before switching to law, qualifying as an advocate in 1875. Suffering from lung disease, travel to warmer climates was recommended, so summer holidays from Edinburgh University were spent in France with artists and writers. He developed a love of travel that continued throughout his life and was to inspire much of his writing.

A canoe trip through Belgium and France with the son of Dr James Young Simpson (*1.2*) provided information for his book '*Inland Voyage*'. Marriage took him to California. During a cold and rainy holiday back in Scotland, he and his stepson drew a map of an imaginary treasure island, triggering '*Treasure Island*', which was published in 1883. His writings brought wealth and subsequent travels took the family to the South Pacific, settling in the Samoan Islands where he was known as Tusitala, the weaver of tales. He died in Samoa. Edinburgh has several other memorials to him and his work.

Within **St Giles Cathedral** a large plaque honours Robert Louis Stevenson.

Drummond Street plaque: A plaque on a wall in Drummond Street, near what used to be Rutherford's pub (now the Hispaniola) tells of Stevenson recalling his Edinburgh student days in a letter to his friend Charles Baxter in September 1888 [4]. The plaque reproduces Stevenson's words, encouraging future students: *'And when I remembered all that I hoped and feared as I pickled about Rutherford's in the rain and the east wind; how I feared I should make a mere shipwreck, and yet timidly hoped not; how I feared I should never have a friend, far less a wife, and yet passionately hoped I might; how I hoped (if I did not take to drink) I should possibly write one little book. And then now – what a change! I feel somehow as if I should like the incident set upon a brass plaque at the corner of that dreary*

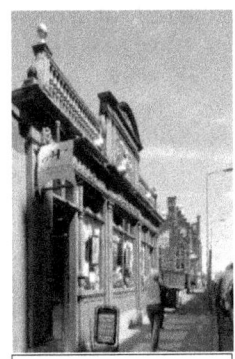

Hispaniola, formerly Rutherford's, in Drummond Street

thoroughfare, for all students to read, poor devils, when their hearts are down.''

A nearby plaque on Drummond Street recalls other literary figures meeting in the same pub. George Davie (author of 'The Democratic Intellect') in 1934 introduced Hugh MacDiarmid (see 'Stones of Scotland', *3.10* and 'Poets', *6.12*) to Sorley Maclean (*6.12*, author of Gaelic poems).

Paving slab, Makars' Court: A paving slab in Makars' Court, near the Writers Museum (containing a collection of his works) is inscribed: *'there are no stars so lovely as Edinburgh street lamps'*. The quote is from 'The Silverado Squatters', his memoir of his two-month 1880 Californian honeymoon. The paving slab was unveiled in 1998, one of the first 12 inscribed in Makars' Court. See Chapter 4, *4.13*.

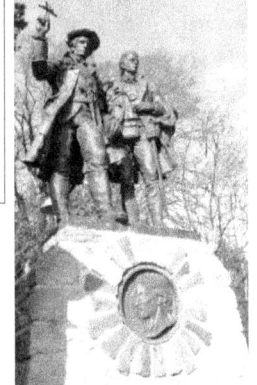

Description: Alan Breck Stewart and David Balfour, from 'Kidnapped' with a medallion of Stevenson. It is inscribed: *'This memorial to Robert Louis Stevenson depicts the two characters from 'Kidnapped'*
Sculptor: Alexander (Sandy) Stoddart
Unveiled: 2004 by Sir Sean Connery
Location: Glasgow Road, below Corstorphine Hill

Statue of two characters from 'Kidnapped': He wrote 'Kidnapped' in 1886, initially published over three months in the magazine 'Young Folks'. An adventure story based on the aftermath of the 1745 Jacobite uprising, it tells the adventures of Alan Breck Stewart and David Balfour. The book's full title summarises the theme: *'Kidnapped: Being memoirs of the adventures of David Balfour in the year 1751: How he was Kidnapped and cast away; his sufferings in a desert isle; his journey in the West Highlands; his acquaintance with Alan Breck Stewart and other notorious Highland Jacobites; with all that he suffered at the hands of his uncle, Ebenezer Balfour of Shaws,* *falsely so-called'.*

At the end of the book Stewart and Balfour part on Corstorphine Hill: *'We came by-the-way over the hill of Corstorphine, and when we got near to .. Rest-and-be-Thankful, and looked down .. over to the city and the castle on the hill, we both stopped, for we both knew .. that we had come to where our ways parted'.* The statue depicts their parting. Walkers still stop to admire the views from Corstorphine Hill, a sign-post marking 'Rest-and-be-Thankful'

George Square: On 7 George Square a plaque is inscribed: *'In honour of Robert Louis Stevenson, 1850 – 1894. Poet, author of Treasure Island, Kidnapped, Dr Jekyll & Mr Hyde, alumnus of the University'* (of Edinburgh).

Colinton: Robert Louis Stevenson as a boy with his dog – see Chapter 6, *6.11*

1.12 Babies' Ashes

Inscribed: *'In memory of our precious babies, gone but never forgotten.'*

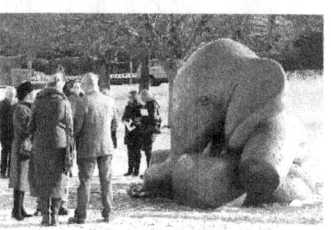

Remains of babies cremated at Edinburgh's Mortonhall Crematorium (and at other crematoria around Scotland) were not returned to parents but disposed of in unmarked graves over a period of several decades. After this was discovered in 2012 the reasons were sought and crematoria practices improved. Edinburgh Council, in consultation with the parents of the babies, decided to erect a memorial in Princes Street Gardens to remember those who had died.

Description: Bronze baby elephant embossed with 'forget-me-not' flowers.
Design: Andy Scott
Funded: Edinburgh City Council, £250,000
Unveiled: 2 Feb 2019

The sculptor, Andy Scott, described his design [5]: *'Elephants never forget. I wanted to do something that will capture the imagination. It was quite a daunting thing to take on because of the emotions and the terrible loss the parents had suffered. ... I wanted the idea of something of a lost toy, maybe being left behind and the feeling of sadness and loss. But also something that would resonate with siblings. I hope the parents respond well to it.'*

1.13 The Royal Scots

The Royal Scots, 'The Royal Regiment', the oldest regiment in the British Army

The Royal Scots (The Royal Regiment) was

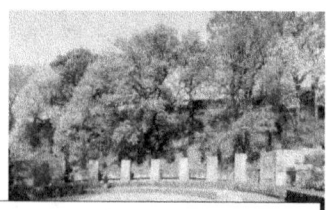

Description: Arc shaped Doddington stones depict regimental uniforms, with monarchs from Charles I to George VI between, the regiment's motto and a quote from the Declaration of Arbroath.
Design: Sir Frank Mears (architect); sculpture by Pilkington Jackson
Bequest of: Campbell Smith, S.S.C, friend of regiment
Unveiled: 1952, HRH Princess Mary, The Princess Royal, Colonel in Chief

the oldest Regiment in the British Army and, in honour of this, has the title of Senior Infantry Regiment of the Line. It was raised in 1633 when Sir John Hepburn, under a royal warrant from King Charles I, recruited 1200 men in Scotland. The regiment gained its first battle honour in Tangier in 1680 followed by 148 battle honours in almost every British Army campaign, including the 1991 Gulf War. The arc shaped monument portrays in stone and bronze the regiment's history.

It merged with other Scottish regiments, remembered in a plaque unveiled in 2007 by HRH Princess Anne, The Princess Royal: '*On 28 March 2006, 373 years to the day since its formation, The Royal Scots merged with the other surviving Scottish Infantry Regiments to form The Royal Regiment of Scotland.*'

An extract from the declaration of Arbroath is inscribed on the monument:
> '*It is not for glory or riches, neither is it for honour that we fight, but it is for the sake of liberty alone, which no true man loseth, but at the cost of his own life.*
> *Given at Arbroath by the Barons, Free Tenants and the whole community of the Kingdom of Scotland in the year 1320*'

1.14 Canine Connections
Celebrating city dogs: Bum, San Diego; Edinburgh's Greyfriars Bobby (6.4)

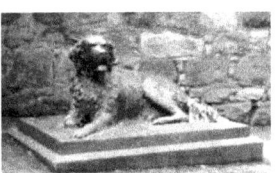

Bum became an unofficial mascot of San Diego in the 1890's. A St Bernard-Spaniel, he arrived as a stowaway on a steamer from San Francisco in 1886. With an independent spirit he preferred to roam the streets, resisting all attempts by families to adopt him. Restaurants and butchers fed him as he went around looking for handouts – hence his nickname. Some even displayed signs: 'Bum Eats Here'. He

Description: Bronze statue of the dog, Bum
Sculptor: Jessica McCain, USA
Date: 19th July 2008

hung around bars, developing a taste for alcohol. Whilst Bum and a bulldog were fighting on a rail track they were struck by a train, killing the bulldog. Bum survived but with a damaged right foot. An 1891 bylaw required the registration of all dogs and Bum, in recognition of his popularity, was exempt from registration for life by the City Council. His picture was imposed on dog licences. Injury to his rear leg from a kick by a horse in 1894 and arthritis curtailed his movements and he died in 1898 aged 12 years.

Edinburgh twinned with San Diego in 1978, leading to the exchange of statues of the city dogs. A statue of Greyfriars Bobby (*6.4*) was presented to San Diego and this one of Bum, the San Diego vagabond, to Edinburgh. The plaque on the wall behind the statue of the dog records that the shared statues '*represent the spirit of the twinning link friendship, loyalty and shared experience*'.

1.15 Plaques in West Princes Street Gardens

Trees and plaques commemorate people, events and organisations. They include:
Anne Frank. Anti-Jewish programmes in Nazi Germany forced Anne with her family to flee to Amsterdam where they hid from the German invasion forces. In hiding for 2

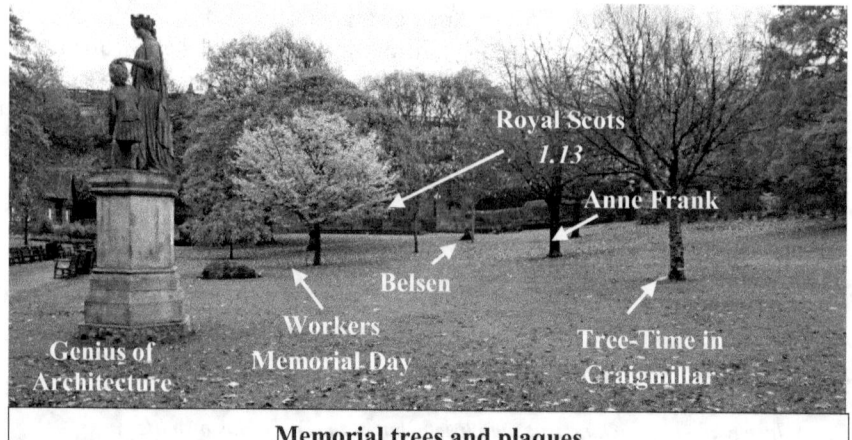

Memorial trees and plaques
Some of those in the south-east corner of West Princes Street Gardens.

years, Anne kept a diary. The family was betrayed. All but Anne's father died in concentration camps, Anne, aged 15, in Bergen-Belsen in 1945. He returned to Amsterdam after the war and found her diary that recounted their experiences. Its publication has been an important record of life under the Nazi occupation.

The **Bergen-Belsen** plaque was erected in 1995 to commemorate the concentration camps liberation in 1945. Scenes of horror greeted the British Army, 60,000 emaciated captives and over 10,000 unburied corpses.

Tree time in Craigmillar was recognized by a tree that was planted in the garden to mark the campaign to improve **Craigmillar**'s physical environment by planting trees.

Edinburgh Trade Union Council marked **International Workers Memorial Day** with a tree (28th April): safe working lives, remembering the dead, fighting for the living.

Tree honours **Sri Chimnoy**, Indian spiritual teacher, philosopher and his 'Peace Runs'.

The Burmese peace campaigner and Nobel Laurette, **Aung San Suu Kyi,** was honoured by a plaque on a stone inscribed 'Freedom of the City of Edinburgh 18 June 2005'. The honour was withdrawn by the City in August 2018 following controversies about refugees who had fled Burma. The plaque had been removed earlier in the year.

Trees planted to mark the Golden Jubilee of the **National Association of Round Tablers of Great Britain and Northern Ireland** are remembered by a plaque on a stone to the north of the Norwegian boulder (*1.10*)

A tree planted near St Cuthbert's church remembers **John 'Jocky' Mulgrew** (1957-2008) and his life of commitment to public service.

On the north side of the railway line is a tree in memory of **Carol Brattey**, a plant virologist who died in 2000, born in 1960; the plaque honours a 'Treasured friend' with the words '*Time passes, memories stay. Missed and remembered every day.*'

Also on the north side of the railway a tree was planted in 2011 to celebrate the 400 years of service of the '**High Constables of Edinburgh**'. The plaque recounts: '*In 1611 the Privy Council of King James VI ordered the Burgh to appoint constables to impose law and order on the streets of Edinburgh. This function was taken over by a regular police force in 1805. 'The Society of High Constables of Edinburgh' now provides a ceremonial bodyguard to The Lord Provost and Council of the City.*'

On the upper path in West Princes Street Gardens, near Simpson's statue (*1.2*), is a commemorative plaque on the fence rail that was presented by the **Consular Corps in Edinburgh & Leith** on 8th March 2013 to mark their 70th anniversary.

Part 1.2 – The Mound

The Mound divides Princes Street gardens, the valley to the north of the Royal Mile, into west and east sections. Created from sand and rubble excavated from the New Town, it is now a major north-south link across Edinburgh.

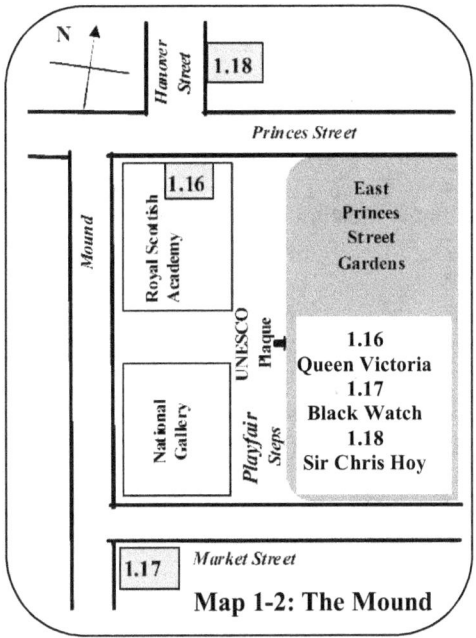

Map 1-2: The Mound

The National Gallery and the Royal Scottish Academy, both art galleries, are on the Mound. By William Henry Playfair (*6.2*), they contribute to Edinburgh's 'Athens of the North' accolade.

The plaza on the Mound provides a venue for open-air entertainment, much made use of, particularly by street performers during the Edinburgh Fringe Festival, but also by occasional showing of open-air films, by dance groups and by groups exhibiting and advertising their products and services

UNESCO World Heritage Site: A plaque on the plaza's east wall (Map 1-2

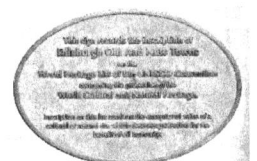

shows the approximate position) records the award, in 1995, by UNESCO of World Heritage status to Edinburgh's Old and New Towns, both of which are visible from the Mound and linked by the Mound. *'This sign records the inscription of Edinburgh Old and New Towns on the World Heritage List of the UNESCO Convention concerning the protection of the World Cultural and Natural Heritage. Inscription on this list confirms the exceptional value of a cultural or natural site which deserves protection for the benefit of all humanity'*. A large paving slab in Caithness stone on the plaza is inscribed with the logo, with 'World Heritage' in English, French and Spanish.

Further details of the award are on the UNESCO website[6] from which the following are copied: *'The remarkable juxtaposition of two clearly articulated urban planning phenomena. The contrast between the organic medieval Old Town and the planned Georgian New Town of Edinburgh, Scotland, provides a clarity of urban structure unrivalled in Europe. The juxtaposition of these two distinctive townscapes, each of exceptional historic and architectural interest, which are linked across the landscape divide, the "great arena" of Sir Walter Scott's Waverley Valley, by the urban viaduct, North Bridge, and by the Mound, creates the outstanding urban landscape.'*

1.16 Queen Victoria, 1819 – 1901
British Monarch

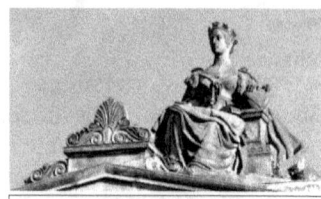

Queen Victoria ascended the throne aged 18 in 1837, reigning for 63 years and 7 months, a period known as the Victorian era, the longest reign of a British monarch till exceeded by Queen Elizabeth II in September 2015.

Queen Victoria, from the Royal Scottish Academy, looks north along Hanover Street and across the Forth to Fife. At George Street her gaze will meet that of King George IV (*2.4*).

Description: Queen Victoria, in regal robes, seated on the Royal Scottish Academy rooftop
Sculptor: Sir John Steell;
Erected: 1844

But is she looking further north to Balmoral, her Scottish holiday home?

William Henry Playfair designed the building, till 1911 called the Royal Institution. Its first phase was completed in 1826. The statue of Queen Victoria was added in 1844.

Queen Victoria is also remembered by a statue at the Foot of Leith Walk where she looks southwards up the road to Edinburgh (*5.1*). Her husband, Prince Albert, is remembered by the mounted statue in Charlotte Square (*2.1*).

1.17 Black Watch
In memory of the soldiers of The Black Watch who fell in the South African War, 1899-1902

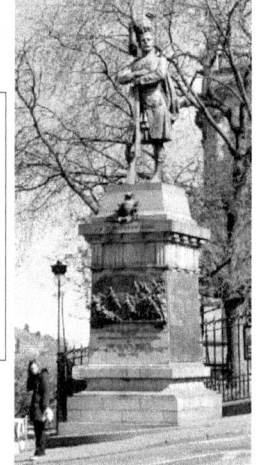

Description: 11 ft Black Watch soldier in dress uniform standing on a 17 ft red granite pedestal with Queen's and King's South African Medals. A bronze relief depicts a battle scene of khaki-clad Highlanders in war uniforms.
Sculptor: William Birnie Rhind
Unveiled: 1910; ceremony cancelled out of respect for Edward VII's death, shortly before its planned unveiling
Restored: 2008, bayonets & other accoutrements repaired – see photo below

It commemorates General Wauchope and the Black Watch soldiers who died in the 1899 – 1902 South African War, also known as the Anglo-Boer War. The Black Watch suffered heavy losses, both from direct military action and from disease. The monument lists, on its right-hand panel those who died in action or from battle wounds; on its left the nearly 80 who died from disease.

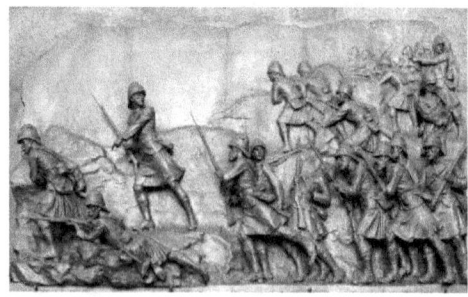

The regiment suffered heavy losses when it attacked Boer positions at Magersfontein in the early stages of the war; amongst the dead was General Andrew Gilbert Wauchope. The regiment was caught in open ground after a long night march.

The Black Watch is an infantry battalion of the Royal Regiment of Scotland, known as 'The Black Watch (Royal Highlanders)' at the time of this war. The regiment dates to the Jacobite rebellion when King George II authorised General George Wade to form six 'watch' companies to patrol the highlands of Scotland, to disarm and hinder the highland rebels. The soldiers wore a uniform of dark tartan which might have led to the name. In Gaelic it is Am Freiceadan Dubh, the Dark or Black Watch.

1.18 Gold Post Box: Sir Chris Hoy
Commemorates his gold medal at 2012 Olympic Games

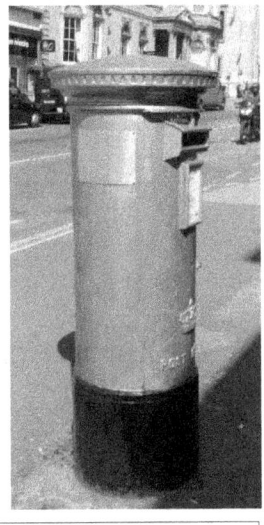

Sir Chris Hoy won two cycling gold medals at the 2012 Olympics, the first for Team Sprint and the second for Kierin. A plaque on the post box details the event in English and in Braille.

Declared Britain's most successful Olympic athlete, Chris Hoy won 6 Olympic golds and a silver during his career. Voted the 2008 BBC Sports Personality of the Year, he was knighted in 2009. He won his first Olympic gold at the 2004 Athens games, three further golds at the 2008 Beijing Olympics and two at the 2012 London Olympics after which he retired from competitive cycling.

Sir Chris Hoy was born in Edinburgh where he was educated at George Watson College and then graduated with a BSc (Honours) in Sports Science from Edinburgh University. An early interest in cycling led to him taking up the sport competitively, achieving the 2nd top ranking in UK BMX in his early teens.

To celebrate gold medal achievements by UK athletes in the 2012 London Olympic and Paralympics the Royal Mail painted one of its red post boxes gold for each athlete winning a

Description: Royal Mail post box painted gold, honouring Sir Chris Hoy's first gold medal at the 2012 London Olympics.

He won a second gold, honoured by a gold-post box in Hunter Square off the Royal Mile (Chapter 4)

Location: Hanover Street

gold medal at the Olympics. Over 100 UK post boxes were painted gold, Sir Chris Hoy's two being the only ones in Edinburgh. The Royal Mail also produced a set of special postage stamps recognizing the successes in the 2012 Olympics.

Part 1.3 – East Princes Street, its Gardens and North Bridge

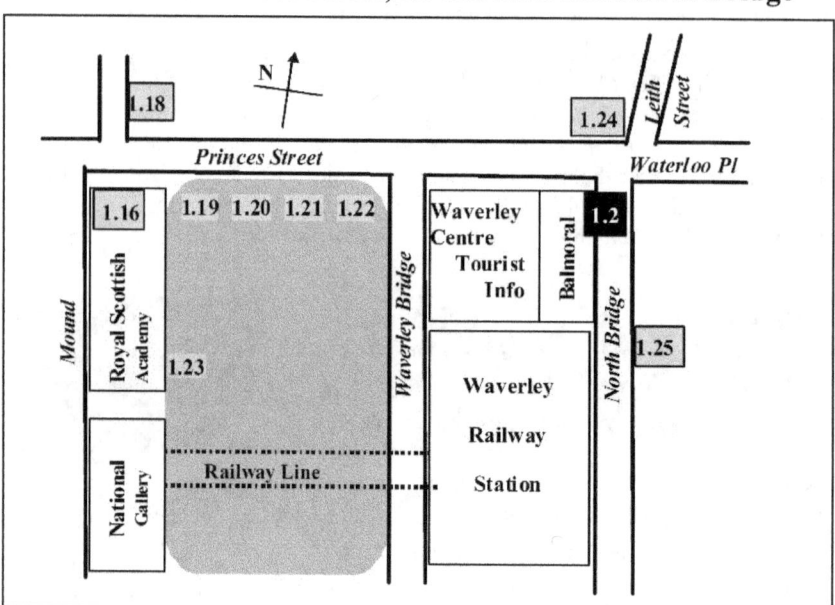

Map 1-3: East Princes Street and its Gardens and North Bridge

1.19	1.20	1.21	1.22
John Wilson	Adam Black	Sir Walter Scott	David Livingstone

1.23	1.24	1.25
Spanish Civil War	Duke of Wellington	Edinburgh Regiment

1.2
Chloroform (Simpson – see Section _1.2_ earlier in this Chapter)

This Eastern part of Princes Street Gardens is separated from the Western by the Mound. It has the imposing monument to Sir Walter Scott (*1.21*). The gardens end at Waverley Bridge, named after Scott's Waverley novels, under which the railway line leads to and from Waverley Railway Station, Edinburgh's main railway station, also named after the novels. Around the railway station are many quotes from Sir Walter Scott.

To the east of the railway station is the North Bridge, originally constructed in the 18th century to span the valley between the Old Town and the developments of what was to become the New Town. On the North Bridge is the monument to the Edinburgh Regiment (*1.25*). Near the junction between the North Bridge and the east end of Princes Street a plaque on the wall of what is now the Balmoral Hotel remembers the pharmacy where Sir James Young Simpson (*1.2*) obtained chloroform for his famous experiment that revolutionised surgical practice.

At the East end is the statue of the Duke of Wellington (*1.24*) astride his horse Copenhagen, situated in front of the Register House, the statue looking south along the North Bridge.

1.19 John Wilson, 1785 – 1854
Author, Lawyer, Publisher, Professor of Moral Philosophy

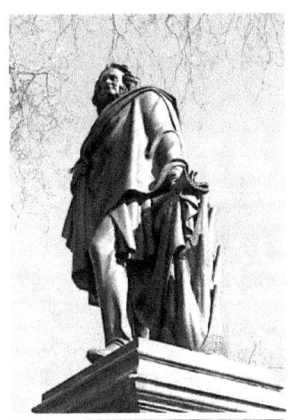

John Wilson contributed to Edinburgh's literary development by his writing and publishing.

He was born in Paisley, one of 9 children to a wealthy manufacturer who died when John was 11 years. He enrolled at the University of Glasgow and later at Oxford, winning the Newdigate poetry prize and graduating in 1807. Benefiting from inherited income, he moved to the Lake District to pursue his literary interests. He settled near Windermere, associating with literary figures such as Wordsworth, Southey and Coleridge.

While living the life of a wealthy landowner, he wrote and published poetry, including, in 1812, '*The Isle of Palms and other poems*'. But his idyllic life in the Lake District ended after much of his fortune was lost by his uncle's speculation. He was forced to move to Edinburgh to live with his mother, earning a living as a lawyer. Fortunately, his literary work prospered, devoting his attention

Description: Wilson standing on pedestal, manuscript in left hand
Sculptor: Sir John Steell. Pedestal by David Bryce
Commissioned by: Wilson Statue Committee that was formed after his death
Unveiled: 25th March 1865

to it. He continued to publish including, in 1816, '*The City of the Plaque*' a 3-Act drama. He became principal writer for Blackwood's Magazine, writing under the pseudonym 'Christopher North'.

John Skelton described Wilson in the introduction to '*The Comedy of the Noctes Ambrsoianae*' [7]: '*John Wilson was an immense man, physically and mentally, and yet his nature was essentially incomplete. He needed concentration. Had the tree been thoroughly pruned, the fruit would have been larger and richer. As it was, he seldom contrived to sustain the inspiration unimpaired for any time; it ran into shallows, and spread fruitlessly over the sand. In many respects one of the truest, soundest, honestest men who ever lived*'.

Wilson, under the pseudonym Christopher North, wrote most of the 'Noctes Ambrsoianae', 71 imaginary colloquies, published in 'Blackwood's Magazine'. Typically set in Ambrose's Tavern (hence title), a pub, now demolished, on Gabriel's Road, Register House. Blackwood's was a monthly magazine publishing satire, reviews and critical thought, much of it written by Wilson. The title page featured George Buchanan (c16[th] Scottish intellectual, see *2.10*, Scottish National Portrait Gallery).

He became Professor of Moral Philosophy at Edinburgh University in 1820, largely through political connections. Initially he knew little of the subject, relying on a friend for lecture notes, but his knowledge developed and he proved a competent lecturer, inspiring his students. He and his wife Jane Penny had five children. He was greatly saddened by her death in 1837; he died in Edinburgh and was buried in the Dean Cemetery.

1.20 Adam Black, 1784 – 1874
Publisher, Lord Provost of Edinburgh, Member of Parliament, liberal politician and reformer

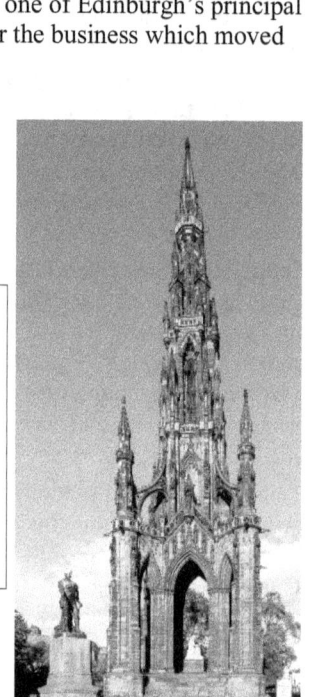

Description: Bronze on sandstone plinth, Adam Black in robes of Lord Provost of Edinburgh
Sculptor: John Hutchison   Unveiled: Nov 1877

Adam Black founded the publishing firm A and C Black which became one of Edinburgh's principal booksellers. His publishing firm published the Encyclopaedia Britannica and acquired the copyright of Sir Walter Scott's Waverley Novels. A Liberal, he was twice Lord Provost (1843–1848) and then Member of Parliament (1856-1865).

Edinburgh born, a builder's son, he was educated at the Royal High School and the University of Edinburgh. After an apprenticeship to an Edinburgh bookseller he began his own business becoming recognized as one of Edinburgh's principal booksellers. He retired in 1865, his sons taking over the business which moved to London in 1895.

1.21 Sir Walter Scott, 1771 – 1832
"Scotland never owed so much to one man" [8] *Author, pioneer of the historical novel, author of Waverley novels, patriot, lawyer, revived Scottish pride and self-respect*

Description: 200ft high Gothic steeple adorned with figures (68) from his books plus others, in total 93. Within it Scott is seated with his deerhound Maida. A 287-step spiral staircase to the top provides spectacular views of Edinburgh. A museum is on the first floor.
Designer: George Meikle Kemp
Dates: Foundation stone laid on anniversary of Scott's birth, 15th Aug 1840. Monument inaugurated 6 years later, also on anniversary of his birth.
Note: Livingstone's (**1.22**) statue dwarfed by Scott's.

Sir Walter Scott, a romantic poet and author of the Waverley novels, pioneered the historical novel that blended fictional characters in an historical setting. A patriotic Scot, he revived Scottish national identity. His monument, the tallest to an author world-wide, dominates central Edinburgh. He published from his early 30's, starting with poetry and collections of traditional ballads, writing for both the Edinburgh Review and its rival, the Tory Quarterly. His narrative poems,

'The Lay of the Last Minstrel' (1805), 'Marmion' (1808) and *'The Lady of the Lake' (1810)* were all commercial successes. He then wrote historical novels, initially anonymously, nicknamed the 'Great Unknown'. His first novel, 'Waverley', was set during the 1745 Jacobite uprising. Its central character Edward Waverley wavered between the two sides, the Stuart claimants to the throne and the Hanoverian monarchy, then King George II. The supplemental title 'Tis sixty years since', takes the reader 60 years back from 1805 to 1745 when *'Waverley, the hero of the following pages, took leave of his family to join'* his regiment [9]. Further books by 'The Author of Waverley' followed.

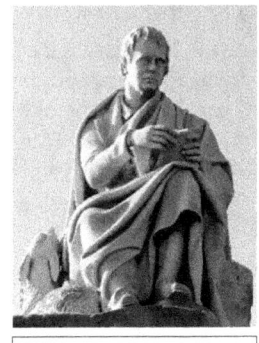

Description: Scott, manuscript in hand, with his deerhound Maida
Sculptor: Sir John Steell (carved from a 30-ton Carrara marble block)
Unveiled: 1846

Politically Scott was a conservative patriot, proud of his Scottish heritage. However, Scotland had in 1707 lost its Parliament and, a century earlier, the seat of monarchy to London with the Union of the Crowns. The enlightenment was changing peoples' outlook and libertarian fervour was fanned by the American war of Independence and the French Revolution. The house of Stuart had been defeated at Culloden and many Scots lived in poverty.

The country sought a new identity; Walter Scott, Scottish patriot, sought to restore Scottish pride. The Dress Act' of 1746, introduced after Culloden to break the power of the clans, forbidding the wearing of Highland dress had been repealed in 1782 and he was to encourage its use. He was later to argue successfully for the retention of the right of Scottish banks to print their own banknotes, a right still enjoyed. His inclination favoured the restoration of a Scottish Parliament, though he believed in the benefits of the Union between England and Scotland – his Waverley novels cleverly linked Scottish patriotism with support for the Union, and he helped revive Scottish self-respect.

Fame from his literary work led him to be asked to search Edinburgh Castle for the Honours of Scotland (Scottish Crown jewels). They had been hidden, buried for protection in the castle during Cromwell's rule. For finding them he was knighted in 1818. He was then asked to manage George IV's state visit to Scotland, the first visit of a reigning monarch since the 17th century. The visit was stage managed to strengthen the Union. It is commemorated by the King's statue in George Street (*2.4*). The event encouraged the wearing of Tartan.

Scott is also remembered for the 'Radical Road' below Salisbury Crags in Holyrood Park. Social unrest culminated in the 1820 strike, its leaders severely dealt with. Scott encouraged deploying unemployed weavers to build the path.

Scott lived in North Castle Street in the New Town (Chapter 2) from 1802 to 1826 when he wrote the Waverley novels. In 2017, as part of the celebrations of the 250th anniversary of commencing building the New Town, various historical sites were illuminated, with Scott appearing in the windows of his New Town house. One

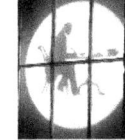

scene depicted Scott writing at his desk, quill in hand.

Born in Edinburgh, the son of a prominent lawyer, his ill-health prompted his parents to arrange for him to spend his early years in the Borders, whose fresh air was hoped to be of benefit. Not only did it improve his health, though the polio contracted at 18 months left him with a permanent limp, his early childhood there gave him a passion for Scottish folklore and writing. But his parents wished him to enter law. He returned to Edinburgh, studying at the Royal High School and Edinburgh University, before starting a legal career. Whilst writing he continued his legal career, including a part-time position as sheriff of Selkirkshire linking him back to the Borders.

A prominent establishment figure in Edinburgh, he served as President of the Royal Society of Edinburgh. His attachment to the Borders led him to purchase land there developing the romantic Abbotsford mansion, a project that proved financially costly. However, it was his links with a publishing company that went bankrupt that led him into heavy debt in his later years. Determined to clear the debt, he wrote industriously during the last years of his life – royalties in the early years after his death finally clearing the debt.

After Scott's death it was decided that '*a Public Memorial should be created in the metropolis of Scotland to the memory of Sir Walter Scott, on a scale worthy of his great name, and fitted to convey to future times an adequate testimony of the estimation in which he was held by his contemporaries*'. Most of the funding was raised by public subscription and such was his popular acclaim that a national holiday was declared for the foundation-stone laying in August 1840. The gothic steeple was designed by George Meikle Kemp, who sadly died during the construction, slipping into the Union Canal and drowning. The monument was completed in 1846 at a cost of £16,000. Its restoration in 1999 cost £2million, requiring re-opening the Binnie quarry in West Lothian to ensure matching sandstone for replacing eroded and damaged stone.

The nearby Waverley Railway Station and Waverley Bridge are named in his honour. The station celebrates Scott and Edinburgh's 'City of Literature' with quotations from his works; for example: '*Life is too short for the indulgence of animosity*'; and '*Life is dear even to those who feel it as a burden*'.

Corstorphine Hill Tower
Description: 20m tall square tower amidst the trees. Gifted by: William Macfie celebrating the centenary of Scott's birth Erected: 1871

Corstorphine Hill Tower was erected in 1871 by William Macfie to commemorate the centenary of Scott's birth. Situated on the wooded top of Corstorphine Hill to the west of the city, it is a 20m tall square tower, five storeys high, with a castellated square and round top. An internal spiral staircase of about 100 steps provides access to the top with panoramic views of Edinburgh and the surrounding countryside. It is sometimes opened to visitors in the summer by The Friends of Corstorphine Hill.

1.22 David Livingstone, 1813 – 1873
Medical missionary, explorer, anti-slavery campaigner

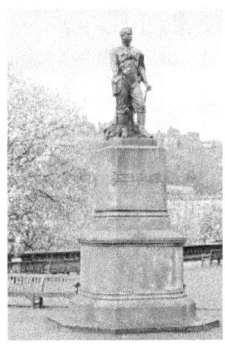

Description: Livingstone, Bible in right hand, wears a cloak and haversack, pistol and compass at his waist. The lion skin recalls his survival from a lion attack
Sculptor: Amelia Robertson Paton Hill;
Cast in bronze by R Masefield and Co of London
Commissioned by: Livingstone Memorial Committee
Unveiled: August 1876

The statue shows Livingstone offering a Bible in his right hand, symbolising the missionary calling and Christian beliefs that led him to Africa. His motto 'Christianity, Commerce, Civilisation' is inscribed on his monument at the Victoria Falls which he was the first European to see. Known primarily as an explorer, he undertook pioneering travel in much of central Africa, inspiring other missionaries and explorers. He sought to abolish the slave trade.
He is remembered by Stanley's greeting when finding him in Africa in 1871: '*Dr Livingstone, I presume?*'

One of 7 children, his father was a Sunday School teacher, and David started work at age 10 in the cotton mill in Blantyre, working a full day to support his impoverished family and attending the local village school. Attracted to an appeal for medical missionaries to China he studied in Glasgow and London. After meeting a London Missionary Society member from Kuruman in South Africa his vision turned to Africa where he hoped both to support the abolition of the slave trade and to spread Christianity. After arriving in Africa he explored deep into central Africa, becoming the first westerner to travel across the continent, traversing from Luanda at the Atlantic Ocean in the west to Quelimane, near the mouth of the Zambezi River, at the Indian Ocean.

He died in Africa from malaria and internal bleeding. His loyal attendants removed and buried his heart. They carried his body 1000 miles across Africa to the coast for shipping to London where he was buried in Westminster Abbey.

The monument was designed by Ameila Hill (nee' Paton), one of the few women sculptors in 19th century Edinburgh and wife of photographer David Octavius Hill. She designed 3 of the stone figures on the Scott Monument, and the figures of 'Painting' and 'Poetry' on the ornate entrance to the Albert Buildings in Shandwick Place.

1.23 Spanish Civil War, 1936 – 1939
To honour the memory of those who went from Lothian and Fife to serve in the War in Spain
The Spanish Civil War attracted volunteers from across the United Kingdom who rallied to support Spain's leftist Republican Government threatened by General Francisco Franco's army-led coup. It was a bitter campaign in which

nearly a million were killed, ending with the surrender of the Republicans in March 1939.

<table>
<tr><td>

<u>Description</u>: Plaque on a rough-hewn boulder
<u>Commissioned by</u>: Friends of The International Brigade Association
<u>Date</u>: Late 1980s
Photo taken: 2009, the 70th anniversary of the end of the war

</td><td>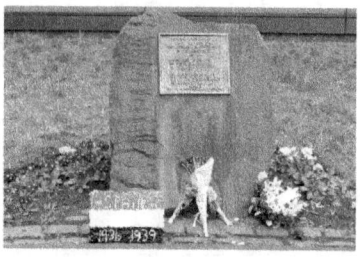</td></tr>
</table>

Franco had been supported by Germany and Italy, whilst the Republican side was supported by the Soviet Union and an International Brigade formed from volunteers from many countries – including the UK. This is one of many memorials to UK volunteers who joined the International Brigade. Franco became dictator of Spain, ruling until his death in 1975. The plaque is inscribed with the poem:

> *Not to a fanfare of trumpets*
> *Nor even the skirl o' the pipes*
> *Not for the off'r of a shilling*
> *Nor to see their names up in lights*

> *Their call was a cry of anguish*
> *From the hearts of the people of*
> *Spain*
> *Some paid with their lives it is true*
> *Their sacrifice was not in vain.*

1.24 Arthur Wellesley, Duke of Wellington, 1769 – 1852
Victor of Waterloo, leader, Anglo-Irish aristocrat and politician

<table>
<tr><td>

<u>Description</u>: The Duke mounted on Copenhagen
<u>Sculptor</u>: Sir John Steell; cast in bronze at a foundry in Grove Street, Edinburgh
<u>Unveiled</u>: 18th June 1852, anniversary of the Battle of Waterloo. Wellington was not able to be present and died shortly afterwards

</td><td>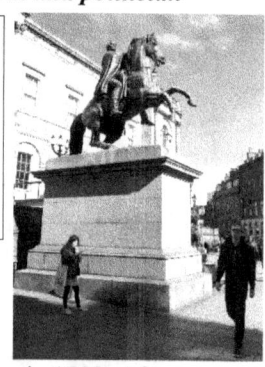</td></tr>
</table>

A military leader, Arthur Wellesley, defeated Napoleon Bonaparte at the Battle of Waterloo.

Arthur Wesley was born in Dublin into an aristocratic Anglo-Irish family who changed their name to Wellesley in 1798. After studying at Eton he joined the British Army aged 18. He fought against the French in Flanders before serving with distinction in India.

Returning to England he was knighted and became a Member of Parliament and chief secretary for Ireland. He returned to active military service against the French, and in 1808 assumed control of the British, Portuguese and Spanish forces in the Peninsular War, forcing the occupying French to withdraw from Spain and Portugal. Napoleon abdicated and was exiled in 1814. Wellesley returned to a hero's welcome and was created Duke of Wellington.

However peace didn't last. Napoleon returned, determined to recover his power. War followed. Wellington, commanding the allied armies, defeated Napoleon at the Battle of Waterloo on 18th June 1815. The Battle was fierce, taking place over a relatively small area, less than 4 miles by 2 miles, with nearly 70,000 allies and 71,000 French troops, of whom about 22,000 and 37,000 respectively were to die. The afternoon arrival of Prussian reinforcements under Marshall Blucher proved decisive and the French were routed.

In 1827 Wellington became commander in chief of the British Army. In 1828 he reluctantly accepted the post of Prime Minister. Believing in a strong, authoritative government he opposed parliamentary reform, becoming unpopular and nicknamed 'Iron Duke' when he erected iron shutters on the windows of his London home to prevent them being smashed by angry crowds. His government fell in 1830, but returned in 1834. Wellington declined the post of Prime Minster and briefly served as foreign minister in Robert Peel's government.

Wellington died in 1852 and was given a state funeral.

Copenhagen, a chestnut stallion, faithfully carried Wellington at Waterloo. Copenhagen died in 1836, age 28 and was buried with full military honours.

1.25 Kings Own Scottish Borderers (The Edinburgh Regiment) *Honouring those who died between 1878 and 1902.*

In memory of the officers, non-commissioned officers and men who gave their lives for their country serving with the Kings Own Scottish Borderers during the following campaigns: Afghanistan, 1878-1880; Egypt, 1888-1889; Chin Lushai, 1889-1890; Chitral, 1895; Tirah, 1897-1898; South Africa, 1900-1902.

The regiment was raised in 1689 by David Melville, 3rd Earl of Leven, to defend Edinburgh against the Jacobites still loyal to the exiled James VII/II. It was recruited within 2 hours by 'beat of drum' down the High Street, men flocking to join to defend their city.

Its first action was at the Battle of Killiecrankie in July of that year at which battle the regiment killed 'Bonnie Dundee', John Graham, 1st Viscount Dundee.

Description: Four soldiers in Anglo-Boer War campaign uniform; one of whom is wounded
Sculptor: William Birnie Rhind
Subscription: Private subscriptions
Unveiled: 4th October 1906 by Lt-Gen Sir E P Leach, VC, KCB

Early successes led the regiment to continue its privilege of recruiting in the City of Edinburgh by beat of drum, without prior permission of the provost. It is the only regiment allowed to march in the city with bayonets fixed.

The inclusion of 'Scottish Borderers' in its name derives from its recruiting area which was moved to the Scottish Borders in 1805.

Chapter 2:
New Town including East and West ends and Lothian Road

Before the late 18th century Edinburgh was largely confined to the ridge running eastwards from the volcanic Castle rock down to Holyrood Palace. The Nor Loch protected from northern attacks; it also prevented northwards expansion of the growing medieval city. To the south King David I had, in the 12th century, gifted to the city part of Drumselch forest, as the common muir, 'Burgh Muir', (muir is Scottish for moor); it stretched southwards from the South Loch (now Meadows) (Smith, 1978). But the thick forestry prevented habitation. Threats from the English led to the erection of a southern protective wall, enlarged after the terrible defeat of the Scottish army by the English at Flodden in 1513.

The result, a protected city, enclosed by wall and Nor Loch. Within its confines the city accommodated more by adding to the High Street tenements, medieval skyscrapers, increasingly overcrowded, dirty and smelly.

Pressure for expansion grew. The 1746 Jacobite defeat promised peace and the city freed from its confines. Lord Provost George Drummond, a keen advocate of a northern new town, envisaged a '*splendid and magnificent city*' on the fields to the north. Determined to expand the city, he laid, in 1763, the foundations of the North Bridge to provide access, bridging the valley, slightly to the west of the loch's dam wall. A new town was proposed, a design competition held. Won by James Craig in 1766, the design was modified by the Town Council (1767) presenting an elegant, orderly town based on a rectangular grid, a square at each end. Whilst crediting Drummond's leadership of the new town's proposals, Youngson[1] in 'The Making of Classical Edinburgh' cautions against singling out individuals:

"The New Town may thus be seen as a product, not of several separate minds, but of the times in which it is conceived, that is to say of the Enlightenment. Those who planned it, like those for whom it was planned, were '*citizens of the world, looking out upon a universe seemingly brand new because so freshly flooded with light* [2]', a universe in which everything seemed far more intelligible than before, and in which everything could be improved by reason. [1]"

The plan emphasised the union of England and Scotland. Harris (pg. 425, Bibliography) describes the origins of its street names. The southern street, along the former Nor Loch was to be named St Giles after Edinburgh's patron saint. King George III objected because of a then unfashionable Giles street in London. It was re-named Prince's Street after the Prince of Wales, becoming Princes Street by the 1830s. The central street became George Street after the King. Queen Street was the northern border. The squares were to be named after the Scottish and English patron saints, each with a church. St Andrew Square was created to the east, but that to the west became Charlotte Square, honouring the King's wife – avoiding confusion with the already developed George Square. The king's ancestry was Hanoverian, hence Hanover street. Rose and Thistle Streets recognize the national flowers of England and Scotland.

Neither square now has a church. A church was built in Charlotte Square, named

St George's. However, in the 20th century, unable to afford the maintenance, the building was transferred to the state, becoming West Register House. The church merged with St George's West in Shandwick Place, which later, in the early 21st century, became the home for the Charlotte Chapel Baptist church. The church at St Andrew Square was never built, its proposed site having been taken by a member of the Dundas family for his home. It is now the magnificent Royal Bank of Scotland at St Andrew Square. A church was later built along George Street, now the active church of St Andrew and St George.

The First New Town's ('first' distinguishes it from subsequent developments) orderly grid and genteel housing contrasted with the Old Town's adhoc tenements. Chambers wrote [7] of it making Edinburgh "*a double city - first an ancient and picturesque hill-built one, occupied chiefly by the humbler classes; and second, an elegant modern one, .. possessed .. by the more refined portion of society*". It rapidly became very fashionable leading to expansions to north, west and east, with magnificent crescents and wide, open streets. The contrast between Old and New was recognized by UNESCO granting them joint World Heritage status (Chapter 1, Part 1.2, logo and plaque on Mound).

Part 2.1 of this chapter discusses the statues in James Craig's First New Town. Part 2.2 describes monuments in the expanding New Town areas, concluding with the bridge over the Calton ravine, begun in the 'ever memorable' year of 1815, known as The Regent Bridge (*2.18*).

Works of art (e.g. 'The Dreaming Spires' (two giraffes) at Picardy Place) are excluded. Also excluded are the allegorical statues on the buildings, several associated with the enterprise of the building that they adorn. Thus, excluded are both sets of 'Wise and Foolish Virgins', the 19th- and the 20th century sets. These are placed high up towards the skyline on a financial institution on the north-east of George Street, symbolic of the need for wisdom in investments. The figures on the top of the former Bank of Scotland in St Andrew Square representing Art, Agriculture, Commerce, Manufacture, Science and Navigation are not included. Nor is St Bernard's Well along the Water of Leith in Stockbridge included. Statues inside buildings are not included in this book, but mention should be made of the statue of King George III in the General Register House at the East end of the New Town, at the entrance to which is the statue of the Duke of Wellington (*1.24*).

Plaques abound in the New Town, many described by Berry (see Bibliography). Whilst plaques are outside this book's scope, some are worth noting. A Manor Place plaque honours Scotland's first woman doctor, Sophia Jex-Blake who began her practice there in 1878. She is also remembered in St Giles. She led the 'Edinburgh Seven' pioneering women studying medicine at university, facing verbal and physical abuse from male students. 4 Years into their study the rules allowing women access were overturned. She persevered, studying in Switzerland and Ireland, finally registered in Britain. Dr Jex-Blake practiced as a doctor and in 1887 opened the Edinburgh School of Medicine for Women which Dr Elsie Inglis (*4.23*) attended. A plaque in Walker Street, nearby, marks Dr Inglis's New Town clinic. Rooms at the University's Medical School in its new (since 2003) Little France site are named after Dr Jex-Blake and Dr Inglis.

Plaques depict Edinburgh's importance as a City of Literature. In Castle Street a plaque recognizes the birthplace of Kenneth Grahame in 1850, writer of 'The Wind in the Willows'. There is also poetry along Rose Street, such as the verses of George Mackay Brown's 'Beachcomber', illustrated by Astrid Jaekel. It is part of the celebration of the Rose Street poets who met in pubs along the street. A plaque to Sir Henry Raeburn is on the house in Queen Street where he painted from 1798 to 1805. The telephone's inventor, Sir Alexander Graham Bell, was born in South Charlotte Street, a plaque on the wall.

This description of the 18th century northerly development should not be seen as ignoring the important southward growth, which was slow, hampered by thick forestry, difficult access across the southerly valley (now Grassmarket and Cowgate), and fear of attack and hence crowding into high tenements near the Castle for protection. Mention should be made of the development of George Square from 1766 (named after George Brown, brother of the developer), where Sir Walter Scott (*1.20*) lived part of his early life. Further description is beyond this book's scope; see 'Historic South Edinburgh' by Charles J. Smith.

Part 2.1 – Craig's First New Town

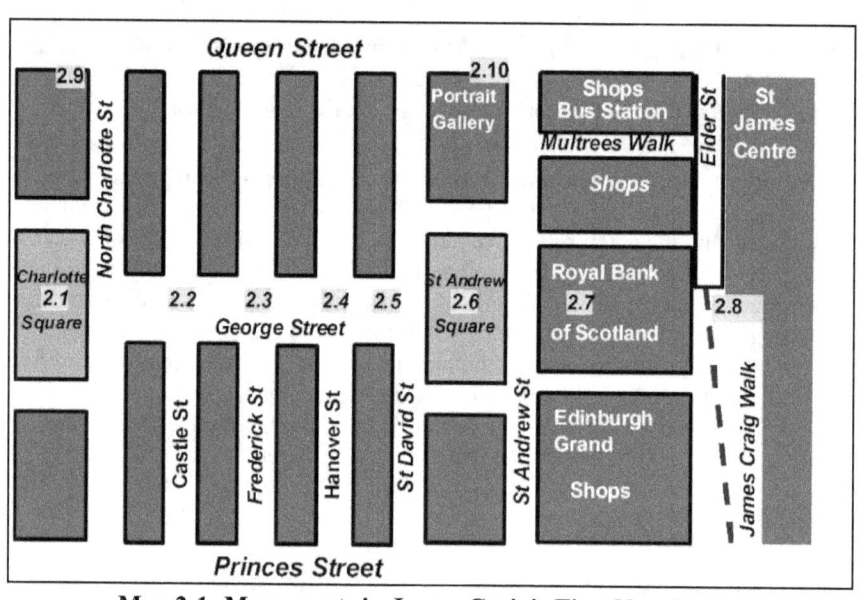

Map 2-1: Monuments in James Craig's First New Town from Charlotte Square to St Andrew Square

2.1	2.2	2.3	2.4	2.5
Prince Albert	Dr Chalmers	W. Pitt	George IV	Maxwell

2.6	2.7	2.8	2.9
Henry Dundas	Earl of Hopetoun	J. Craig	Catherine Sinclair

2.10
Statues on the exterior of the Scottish National Portrait Gallery

Note: Not shown for the sake of simplicity are Rose Street, between Princes and George Streets, and Young and Thistle Streets, between George and Queen Streets.

2.1   Prince Albert, 1819 – 1861
Beloved Consort of Queen Victoria

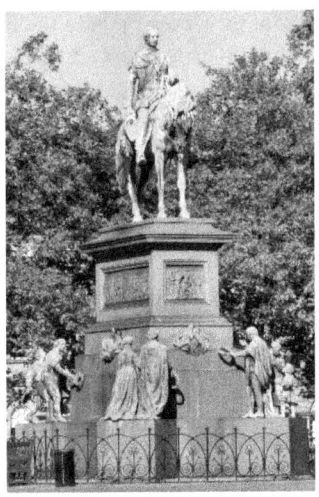

'*Prince Among Men*' is how The Times described Albert at the 2019 bicentenary of his birth [3]. His reformation of the monarchy had '*rendered it an institution still revered today*'. '*He deserves to be remembered with honour.*'

The young Queen Victoria (*1.16, 5.1*) was determined to marry her first cousin Prince Albert Francis Charles Augustus Emmanuel. Her mother was the sister of Albert's father and of Leopold, King of Belgium, both wishing the cousins to marry. But it was not supported by the British establishment, nor, when he was alive, by her uncle, King William IV, to whom she was next in line as he had no direct heir.

Two years after she became Queen, Victoria proposed to Albert and they married in February 1840. Deeply in love, they had 9 children, with Albert an important support to the Queen throughout their marriage.

Albert was born in Bavaria, the younger son of the Duke of Saxe-Coburg-Saalfeld. The young prince was initially educated privately at home, followed by studies in law, politics, philosophy and art history at Bonn University.

Though both Albert and Victoria were deeply in love, Albert was initially unpopular in Britain because of anti-German sentiment, with disdain for his dukedom of a small German state. The British government wanted to exclude him from any political role. He had to wait till 1857, 17 years after their marriage, to be given the title Prince Consort. Gradually, and with tact, he

Description: Prince Albert in Field Marshall's uniform on horseback. 4 groups of figures around the Peterhead granite base represent: 'Nobility' (sculptor William Brodie); 'Army and Navy' (Clark Stanton); 'Labour' and 'Science and Learning' (D.W. Stevenson).
Sculptor: John Steell, knighted after the statue's unveiling by Queen Victoria, who was delighted with it. Memorial designed by David Bryce
Unveiled: Queen Victoria on 17th August 1876. Paid for by public subscription

gathered support. He encouraged and helped his wife as queen and was her private secretary. He advised that the monarch be politically neutral.

Albert supported welfare reform, raising the minimum working age and extending the abolition of slavery world-wide. He called for better schooling and, as Chancellor of the University of Cambridge, campaigned successfully for university curriculum reform. Interested in the arts, science and industry, he helped lead the Great Exhibition of 1851 to celebrate British industry, using the profits to establish the south Kensington museums in London. He campaigned for army modernisation, and guided strategic planning which helped win the Crimean War. His diplomatic skills helped avert conflict between Britain and the USA in 1861. Astute modernising of the royal finances released money for the purchase of a private residence for the large family, Osborne House, Isle of

Wight. It is now open to the public through English Heritage, still mostly furnished as it was when the royal couple lived there.

An early visit to Scotland by Victoria and Albert was to Loch Laggan in the west of Scotland, but that summer of 1847 was a rainy holiday. Learning of dry sunnier days spent by their doctor's son at Balmoral Castle and, soon afterwards, that the tenant had died, Albert negotiated a lease of Balmoral in May 1848, and the family stayed there in September 1848, starting a traditional Scottish holiday for the Royal family at Balmoral.

Albert died suddenly of typhoid in Dec 1861, Victoria overwhelmed with grief.

2.2 Dr Thomas Chalmers, 1780 – 1847
Scotland's greatest 19th century churchman

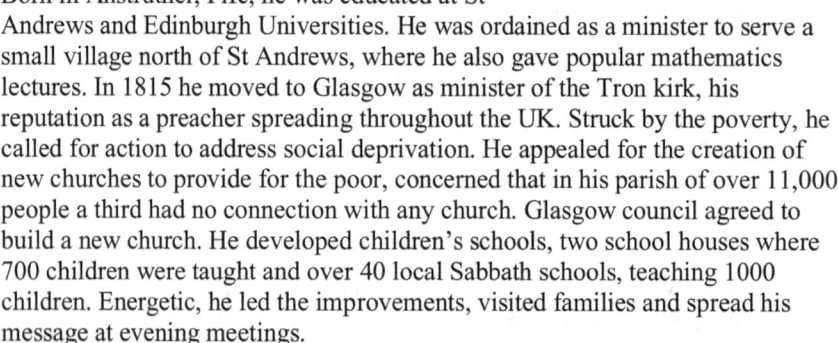

Description: A 12-foot high statue of Chalmers, standing with an open Bible in his hand. Bronze statue on polished red granite pedestal
Sculptor: Sir John Steell
Unveiled: July 1878, paid for by public subscription

Leader of the Church of Scotland and of the Free Church of Scotland, Thomas Chalmers was a Professor of Theology, educator, political economist and mathematician. He was Professor of Moral Philosophy at St Andrews, then Professor of Divinity at Edinburgh, and then Moderator of the General Assembly of the Church of Scotland.

Born in Anstruther, Fife, he was educated at St Andrews and Edinburgh Universities. He was ordained as a minister to serve a small village north of St Andrews, where he also gave popular mathematics lectures. In 1815 he moved to Glasgow as minister of the Tron kirk, his reputation as a preacher spreading throughout the UK. Struck by the poverty, he called for action to address social deprivation. He appealed for the creation of new churches to provide for the poor, concerned that in his parish of over 11,000 people a third had no connection with any church. Glasgow council agreed to build a new church. He developed children's schools, two school houses where 700 children were taught and over 40 local Sabbath schools, teaching 1000 children. Energetic, he led the improvements, visited families and spread his message at evening meetings.

From Glasgow, he moved to St Andrews as Professor of Moral Philosophy, influencing many. He then became Edinburgh's Professor of Theology. Highly respected, he was elected a fellow of the Royal Society of Edinburgh.

He became leader of the evangelical section of the General Assembly, calling for church expansion and leading a successful appeal that led to 220 new churches. He was outspoken against church patronage, calling for separation of church and state, leading the 'non-intrusionism' movement that argued that no minister should be imposed on a parish against the will of the congregation.

Whilst it was accepted by church and state that the Church of Scotland had independence in ordering its spiritual affairs without royal or parliamentary interference, the right of patronage, whereby wealthy patrons could install a minister in the church without the approval of the congregation, remained. This right was upheld by the courts and government. Those arguing against this held that Jesus Christ and not Parliament was head of the church. The dispute led, in 1843, to the 'disruption', over a third of its ministers leaving the Church of Scotland to form the Free Church of Scotland with Chalmers as moderator.

He published extensively. Sermons discussing astronomical discoveries in relation to Christian revelation were published in 1817, with 20,000 circulated within a year. He investigated how soil fertility affected the social condition of local communities. His 'Political Economy' argued that people's economic condition depended on them having the right moral condition.

His experience dealing with the poverty in Glasgow made him an influential thinker on poverty. He argued for public charity rather than public expenditure to relieve poverty, but critics argued that this was not workable in large cities.

2.3   William Pitt, 1759 – 1806
Britain's youngest Prime Minister (at 24)

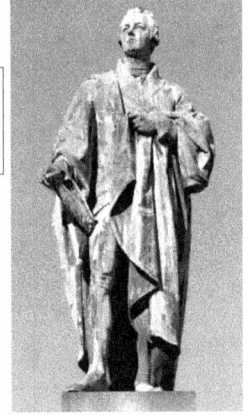

Description: Pitt wearing cloak; bronze, on ashlar pedestal
Sculptor: Sir Francis Leggatt Chantry
Commissioned: Edinburgh Pitt Club;   Unveiled: 1833

Aged 24, William Pitt became the youngest British Prime Minister when he took office in 1783, ruling till 1801 and then again from 1804 to his death in 1806. He is also known as William Pitt the Younger, his father, William Pitt the Elder, having been Prime Minister. His early popularity with the public led to the nickname 'Honest Billy', contrasting with the dishonesty and corruption of other leading politicians. It was said of him: '*For personal purity, disinterestedness and love of this country, I have never known his equal.*' [4]

He is regarded as one of Britain's greatest Prime Ministers, particularly for his leadership during the Napoleonic wars. He managed the economy astutely, developing and consolidating the office of Prime Minister. A man of integrity, hard work and strong character, he helped stabilise British political life, managing political turmoil in Europe and, at home, steering the country through the constitutional crises arising from the ill health of King George III.

He proved an outstanding administrator, reforming and improving efficiency. In military matters he relied on Henry Dundas (*2.6*), but Dundas was to oppose some of his reform attempts.

He was Chancellor of the Exchequer as well as Prime Minister. As Chancellor he inherited a massive public debt (£243 million, with annual interest payments of £24million) arising from the Napoleonic Wars, exacerbated by the cost of fighting the American War of Independence. He was successful in managing and reducing the debt through policies based on the ideas of Adam Smith (*4.22*) and by introducing Income Tax.

Smuggling constituted a fifth of imports and Pitt's reduction of import tariffs encouraged honest traders, increasing the customs revenue by nearly £2million.

Legislative acts included his work on the Act of Union of 1800 between the Kingdom of Great Britain and the Kingdom of Ireland, developed partly to ensure that Ireland would not side with France in the Napoleonic wars. But his attempts to ensure the extension of civil rights to Roman Catholics were unsuccessful, leading to his resignation as Prime Minister in 1801. He re-organised the British East India Company through the India Act of 1804, creating a Board of Control to oversee its affairs and seek to stop corruption.

Domestically he sought to introduce parliamentary reform and extend the franchise, but was unsuccessful. He was also unsuccessful in abolishing the slave trade, supporting his friend William Wilberforce. It was abolished with the Slave Trade Act of 1807, a year after his death.

He was born in Kent, the 2nd son of the Earl of Chatham. After early education at home due to poor health he studied at Cambridge before entering Parliament aged 21. He did not marry and died in London.

2.4 King George IV, 1762 – 1830
Commemorates 1822 state visit to Edinburgh

Description: Bronze on ashlar pedestal, the King in a long cloak, sceptre in his right hand, his right foot forward,
Sculptor: Sir Francis Leggatt Chantry
Unveiled: 26th Nov 1831

The State Visit of King George IV in 1822 was the first visit of a reigning monarch to Scotland since 1650. Orchestrated by Sir Walter Scott (*1.21*), it was arranged partly to distract attention from political pressures, including those arising from the French revolution. These pressures led to what has become known as the Radical War or the Scottish Insurrection of 1820, a period of strikes and unrest in Scotland with demands for political reform.

George IV, the son of George III and Queen Charlotte (after whom a New Town street and square are named), ascended the throne in 1820, crowned in 1821.

Sir Walter Scott, already well known and popular from his novels and his exploration of Scottish history, had met George IV when heir to the throne. Edinburgh's city council, at the king's request, invited Scott to manage the proposed state visit. This he did with pleasure, creating a spectacular pageant lasting several days. Scott saw this as an opportunity to welcome the new king, to celebrate Scottish traditions, renewing and re-invigorating them and in so doing to help heal the divided Scottish people. Recommending that the King wear Highland dress befitting his ancestry as a Stuart prince, a bright red Royal

Tartan, the Royal Stuart, was designed.

The king sailed to Scotland, a journey of 4 days, arriving in Leith on 14th August 1822 in torrential rain, welcomed and greeted by Sir Walter Scott. The following day, in sunshine, the king disembarked at Leith and entered Edinburgh, greeted by cheering crowds along decorated streets. He was driven to Holyrood Palace and presented with the Honours of Scotland. However, the Palace was not in a fit state to accommodate a royal visit and the king stayed in Dalkeith Castle on the outskirts of Edinburgh, guest of the 16-year old Duke of Buccleuch (*4.19*).

Events to greet the king had been arranged: a performance of Sir Walter Scott's 'Rob Roy' in the Assembly Rooms; a Caledonian Ball; a service at St Giles Cathedral; a civic banquet in Parliament House; a military review of cavalrymen at Portobello; a reception for the Scottish aristocracy at Holyrood Palace.

Dressed as a Field-Marshall he greeted the crowds from the Castle's half-moon battery, standing in rain and wind, reportedly saying [5]: '*Good God! What a fine sight. I had no conception there was such a fine scene in the world, and to find it in my own dominions; and the people are as beautiful and as extraordinary as the scene. And Rain? I feel no rain. Never mind, I must cheer the people.*'

After a visit to Hopetoun House the King departed from Scotland, leaving from South Queensferry on the 29th August 1822.

Besides the statue on George Street (named after his father King George III), the visit also led to the name 'George IV' Bridge being given to the street and bridge built to traverse the Cowgate south of the Lawnmarket.

2.5   James Clerk Maxwell, 1831 – 1879
One of 3 Physics 'Greats'; Mathematical Physicist; described the theory of electromagnetism and relationships between electricity, magnetism and light

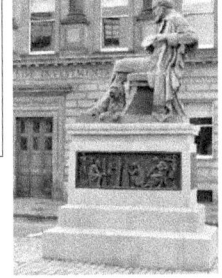

> Description: Maxwell in bronze, seated on an ashlar pedestal, a colour wheel symbolising his pioneering understanding of electromagnetic fields and the relationships between electricity, magnetism and light. His dog, Toby, is at his side.
> Sculptor: Alexander Stoddart
> Unveiled: 25th Nov 2008 by Scottish Parliament Presiding Officer

Maxwell developed the basis of modern physics and is one of the three Physics 'Greats' (with Newton and Einstein). Einstein described Maxwell's work as the most profound since Newton's. His theories of electromagnetic radiation and the relationships between electricity, magnetism and light changed the understanding of physics. The relationships were defined by equations named in his honour (Maxwell equations – on plaque at foot of monument), linking electrical and magnetic fields. He described the electromagnetic spectrum and the wavelike nature of light leading to prediction of radio waves. His theories underpin current electrical and communication technologies.

The statue shows Maxwell holding a 'colour top', a device that shows that any colour can be made by combining Red, Green and Blue. This is the basis of colour in TV monitors, printing and digital photography.

The bronze reliefs pay tribute to the three Physics Greats. On the south panel Apollo, god of the sun, shoots a light beam which is split by a prism held on an obelisk by the seated Newton. A board and second prism directs red light to the foot of Eos on the far right, standing on a rising sun, roses around her head.

On the north panel Einstein demonstrates that bodies are subject to gravity, the weak force. The mighty god Apollo, on the left, is struck by an arrow fired by Eros, the god of love, whose power, even though but a boy, can't be resisted by even the greatest god.

James Clerk Maxwell was born in 14 India Street in the New Town on 13th June 1831. (The International Centre for Mathematical Sciences has offices there.) But he spent much of his early years in Dumfries and Galloway in south west Scotland where he was educated at home, initially by his mother who sadly died when he was only 8. His father and an aunt continued his education. Aged 10 he left the countryside for the Edinburgh Academy. Ironically for someone so clever, he was nicknamed 'daftie' because of his country accent and rough homemade clothes. His intellectual prowess extended beyond the school syllabus, writing his first scientific paper at age 14. His work 'Oval Curves' was presented to the Royal Society of Edinburgh on his behalf by Professor James Forbes as Maxwell was considered too young to present. He entered Edinburgh University at 16, then Cambridge when 20 having submitted significant papers to the Transactions of the Royal Society of Edinburgh. Appointed Professor of Physics at Aberdeen at 25, he moved to King's College London and then, in 1871, to Cambridge to direct the new Cavendish Laboratory.

Dying from abdominal cancer in Cambridge at the young age of 48, he was buried in Galloway near Castle Douglas.

2.6 Henry Dundas, 1st Viscount Melville, 1742 – 1811
Leading Scottish politician; Lord Advocate; 'uncrowned King of Scotland''

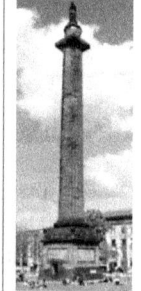

Description: Dominating St Andrew Square, a 26m high fluted column, acanthus leaf decoration at base with eagles at each corner, with statue of Viscount Melville.

Sculptor: Column: by William Burn, based on Trajan's column in Rome. Robert Stevenson, lighthouse builder, advised on foundations and the column's structure.

Statue: 4.2m high, carved out of yellowish grey sandstone by Robert Forrest from model by Sir Francis Chantry; not initially part of design.

Unveiled: 1823; subscription raised from Royal Navy; commissioned by naval officers

Edinburgh born and bred, Dundas trained as a lawyer, was admitted to the Faculty of Advocates at 21, appointed Solicitor General for Scotland at 24 and, at 33, Lord Advocate. Holding the important Scottish posts gave him unrivalled power, hence nicknamed 'Harry the Ninth, the uncrowned King of Scotland'.

His influence was UK-wide. He entered Parliament in 1774 as Member for Midlothian, joining the cabinet in 1791 as Secretary of State for the Home

Department. The wars with France saw him initially become Minister for War and then, from 1794 to 1801, War Secretary under Prime Minister William Pitt (*2.3*). From the late 1790's he wished to resign his parliamentary duties on health grounds, but Pitt, who relied on him heavily, refused, appointing him First Lord of the Admiralty in 1804. He sought to expand British influence in India to advance trade, at that time dominated by the East India Company (c.f. **4.8**). Locally he advocated reform of the governing of Ireland and relief for its Catholic majority, but was opposed by the king, George III.

It was said that he had outstanding talents, quickness of mind, oratorical gifts, comprehensive understanding, moderation of opinion and exceptional powers of administration.

Dundas led the case in the Court of Session for freeing James Knight, a slave, from his owner, Wedderburn. He called slavery unjust, eloquently arguing that slavery was incompatible with Scots Law. James Boswell wrote: '*I cannot too highly praise the speech which Mr. Henry Dundas generously contributed to the cause*'. The majority of 8 to 4 judges agreed, ruling in 1778 that slavery was not recognized in Scots law.

But the slave trade continued. Wilberforce introduced an abolition bill in the UK Parliament in 1791. It was severely defeated. Re-introduced in 1792, Dundas, who had been ill in 1791, sensed the opposition. He suggested amending to gradual abolition to ensure it passed. It passed in the Commons but not the Lords. Within weeks Dundas pressed on to limit the implication of 'gradual', eventually agreed to be by 1796. However, opposition in the Lords and international conflicts stopped progress till abolition passed in 1807.

Dundas married Elizabeth, daughter of the owner of Melville Castle in 1765, but the marriage ended in divorce after which he married the daughter of John Hope, 2nd Earl of Hopetoun (c.f. 4th Earl's statue, *2.7*). In 1802 Dundas became a peer, taking his title as Viscount Melville from Melville Castle which he had acquired from his father-in-law from his first marriage. He also became Baron Dunira of Dunira, Perthshire.

During the early 1800s concern was raised about financial management of the Admiralty where he had been Treasurer from 1782 to 1800. A commission of inquiry was appointed and in 1806 Dundas was impeached in the House of Lords for misappropriation of public money. Acquitted he retired from active politics, declining an earldom in 1809, though he did resume his membership of the Privy Council.

He had great influence in Scotland for 40 years, positively helping guide the governance of Scotland, particularly with no Scottish Parliament.

Much of his power derived from the nature of the franchise in Scotland. There was no universal vote: Edinburgh, for example, elected 3 Members of Parliament, but there were only about 33 voters per MP. Dundas clashed with advocates of franchise reform, notably those now known as the Political Martyrs whose monument is on Calton Hill (*3.8*).

Dundas died in Edinburgh in 1811, but his name lives on in monuments and in the names of streets, towns and areas from Canada to Australia.

In 1802 the Edinburgh Weekly Journal (27/10/1802) called for the erection of a statue in his honour: '*While England is taking the most public and spirited measures to commemorate the services of Mr Pitt, the inhabitants of Scotland can not forget, that there is another public character, to whom the Empire at large is left indebted and who had done more for his native country, than any Scotsman who has preceded him. It is therefor proposed that a statue shall be erected in the city of Edinburgh, as a memorial of the gratitude of Scotland to Mr Dundas.*' Controversy ensued about its site, at one stage suggested as Melville Street, where later the statue to his son Robert was erected (*2.12*).

2.7   Sir John 4th Earl of Hopetoun, 1765 – 1823
Army officer, Scottish politician, Governor of the Royal Bank of Scotland, 1820 – 1823

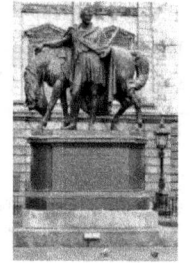

Description: Sir John, robed as a Roman general, with horse
Sculptor: Thomas Campbell;
Commissioned by the Town Council of Edinburgh
Unveiled: 1829, originally in Charlotte Square. Placed in St Andrew Square in 1834

John was born in Hopetoun House (West Lothian), the only son of the 2nd Earl of Hopetoun and Jane Oliphant his second wife. She died when he was only a year old. He succeeded his elder half-brother as 4th Earl in 1816.

Joining the army aged 19, he was commissioned as an officer in the 10th Light Dragoons. His distinguished military career included successful operations in the West Indies from 1796 to 1797. He was posted to the Netherlands in 1799 as Deputy Governor and in 1801 sent to Egypt to accept the French garrisons' surrender. He took part in campaigns during the wars with France, serving under the Duke of Wellington (*1.24*). He was appointed as Commander-in-Chief, Ireland and admitted to the Irish Privy Council in 1812.

He entered parliament as MP for Linlithgow (1790 to 1800) and was Lord-Lieutenant of Linlithgowshire from 1816 to 1823. In May 1814 he was created Baron Niddry of Niddry Castle, Linlithgow and two years later succeeded to the earldom of Hopetoun. He married Elizabeth in 1798. After her death he married Louisa Dorothea Wedderburn. He died in 1823, aged 58 and is buried at Abercorn in West Lothian outside Edinburgh.

The statue is in front of the Royal Bank of Scotland, sometimes known as Dundas House. The original plan for this site was for a church dedicated to St Andrew (see *2.8* for Craig's design). However, Sir Lawrence Dundas, relative of Viscount Dundas (*2.6*), acquired the site, building his mansion on it before a church could be built. The church was later built along George Street.

The plinth's citation links him with famous military leaders:

'*To John, Fourth Earl of Hopetoun, erected by the gratitude of his countrymen, who loved and reverenced in his person the assembled virtues of distant periods of history; the unshaken patriotism of the ancient Romans; the spirit of honour, and gentleness, and courtesy proper to the age of chivalry; together with skill in the art of war, worthy of the companion of Abercrombie, Moore and Wellington*'.

[Abercrombie, also spelt Abercromby, is General Sir Ralph Abercromby (statue on the north-west turret of the Scottish National Portrait Gallery, *2.10*). Wellington has a statue at the east end of Princes Street (*1.24*). Sir John Hope succeeded to the command of the British forces after the death of Sir John Moore at the Battle of Corunna during the Peninsular War with France in 1809. Under Sir John Moore's leadership the British won a decisive victory against the French, but he was killed when struck in the chest by cannon shot. There is a monument to Sir John Moore in Glasgow's George Square, his funeral is remembered in Charles Wolfe's poem whose first verse has the lines:
'Not a drum was heard, not a funeral note, As his corse to the rampart we hurried. Not a soldier discharged his farewell shot, O'er the grave where our hero we buried.']

2.8   James Craig, 1744 – 1795
Planner of the New Town; transformed 'Auld Reekie' to 'Athens of the North'

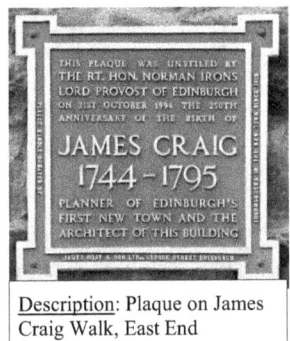

Description: Plaque on James Craig Walk, East End
Unveiled: 1994
Similar plaque is on Craig's House on Calton Hill where he lived.

From the early 18th century Edinburgh, confined to the ridge running down from the Castle, was not able to contain its increasing population. The wealthy, seeing the prospects of the open countryside north of the Nor Loch, wanted to move from the Old Town's increasingly crowded, filthy and noisy tenements. By the mid-18th century the Jacobite uprising had been crushed, peace and prosperity were blossoming and Edinburgh was leading the Scottish Enlightenment with influential thinkers like David Hume and Adam Smith.

A competition was held to design a New Town, fit for the new era of peace, prosperity and elegance. The 1766 competition was won by the relatively unknown young architect, James Craig, then 22. The original design, based on the Union Flag, responding to the patriotic mood at the time, was modified leaving the classic design we know today. It provided the canvas for architects, in particular Robert Adam, to develop the elegant New Town. The opportunities for a more elegant lifestyle led the wealthy to move from the crowded squalor of 'Auld Reekie' to the elegant 'Athens of the North'.

The design was based on a central wide street, to be named after King George III, with squares at either end, to be named after the patron saints of Scotland and England, St Andrew (to the East) and St George (to the West). To avoid a clash with the existing George Square (near the Meadows) St George's Square was renamed Charlotte Square in honour of George III's wife. Charlotte Square was developed by Robert Adam in the late 18th century and is considered his finest townscape. To the North the wide Queen Street was named to honour the queen. To the south another wide street would be created fronting on the drained Nor Loch. Originally it was to be named St Giles, after the patron saint of Edinburgh. However, the King objected, associating the name with a less than elegant London street and it was renamed Princes Street after the King's two sons. Political considerations led to other street names such as Thistle and Rose Streets after the emblems of Scotland and England, whilst Hanover Street honoured the royal family, the House of Hanover.

2.9 Catherine Sinclair of Ulbster, 1800-1864
Philanthropist and Author

> Description: Ornate 60-ft high stone Gothic spire modelled on the Eleanor Crosses erected by Edward I of England in honour of his wife. Its resemblance to the Scott Monument reflects her contribution of funds to erect that monument.
> Designed by: David Bryce   Sculptor: John Rhind
> Unveiled: 1868; public subscription

Catherine Sinclair became a prolific and popular author, her parents encouraging their 13 children. Her first book sold out its 9,000 print-run within months and was reprinted. A later book sold 100,000 copies. She used her wealth for good: founded Volunteer Brigade for Leith boys; founded a school where girls could learn domestic work; gave pensions to the elderly; erected Edinburgh's first public fountain; started a food kitchen to serve a dinner of broth, bread and potato for the poor. Her monument is inscribed: '*She was a friend of all children and through her book 'Holiday House' speaks to them still. Her Volunteer Brigade for the boys of Leith was the first of its kind.*'

Born in Edinburgh, one of 13 children, from aged 14 she worked for her father, Sir John Sinclair a prominent politician, as his secretary till his death in 1835. Amongst her books was the popular '*Holiday House, A Book for the Young*' (1839) telling of two lively children Harry and Laura. It was full of humour and included tales of fairies and giants. Witty dialogue recounts Harry bemoaning his elder brother Frank's obsession with reading instead of playing. "*I wish everybody who wrote a book was obliged to swallow it. .. Frank sat mooning over a book for two hours. .. I am sure some day his head will burst with knowledge.*" His uncle replied: "*You have a head and so has a pin; but there is not much furniture in either.*" The book was reprinted running to 14 editions.

She erected a water fountain originally placed at the junction of Princes Street and Lothian Road. Designed to provide water for dogs and horses as well as humans; it was inscribed '*Water is not for man alone: A blessing on the giver: Drink and be thankful*'. Removed to allow road works, part was placed along the Water of Leith path at Gosford Place in Leith in 1983.

She died in England and is buried in St John's Episcopal Church, Edinburgh.

2.10 Statues on the external walls of the Scottish National Portrait Gallery. *Scottish Historical Figures*

> Description: 30 Statues of Scottish Historical Figures on the North St Andrew Street and Queen Street external walls of the Scottish National Portrait Gallery
> Sculptor: various sculptors
> Donated by: John Ritchie Findlay and others;   Erected: from 1891 to early 1900s

The Scottish National Portrait Gallery opened in 1889 as the world's first purpose-built portrait gallery, its aim to explore '*aspects of the story of Scotland and her people, told through a wealth of imagery .. of famous historical figures and .. pioneers in science, sport and the arts*' [6]. It was '*dedicated to the illustration of Scottish History .. the gift to his native country of John Ritchie Findlay*'. (From Queen Street dedication plaque.)

The building by Sir Robert Rowand Anderson was generously funded by John Ritchie Findlay, proprietor of the 'Scotsman' newspaper. David, 11th Earl of Buchan, an enthusiastic collector, had amassed a considerable number of images that provided a good foundation for the collection.

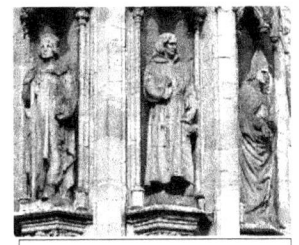

The many images, paintings, photographs and sculptures within the gallery provide graphical historical stories of Scotland, but are not subjects of this book: though inside is the statue of Robert Burns by Flaxman, originally placed on Calton Hill (see Chapter 3, *3.9*). Instead, the focus here is on the statues of historical characters on the building's external wall. Above the main entrance are allegorical statues, not discussed in this book.

Three of the four figures on the South East Tower: Barbour, Dunbar, Douglas

At the south-east tower on North St Andrew Street are John Barbour (poet – 14th century), William Dunbar (poet – 15th century), Gavin Douglas (poet and Bishop of Dunkeld – 15th & 16th century) and Sir David Lyndsay (poet and Lyon King of Arms – also spelt Lindsay). A quote from John Barbour's poem, 'The Brus', about the life of Robert 1 (Robert the Bruce, King of Scots) is inscribed on a paving slab at the Makars' Court (*4.13*) as is a quote from a poem by Lyndsay.

In the centre of the east wall Mary Queen of Scots is flanked by two supporters, John Lesley (on her right, our left, author and Bishop of Ross) and William Maitland (politician, secretary to the Queen).

On the north-east tower along North St Andrew Street are: geologist James Hutton (*6.8*); surgeon John Hunter; portrait painter Sir Henry Raeburn; James Dalrymple, 1st Viscount Stair (17th century statesman and lawyer); and John Napier of Merchiston who in the early 17th century invented logarithms and after whom Edinburgh's Napier University is named.

On Queen Street, to the east of the Main Entrance, are several kings of the Scots: Alexander III; James I; James V; the Regent James Stewart (regent for the infant King James VI, his half-nephew); and James VI.

The main entrance has statues of King Malcolm III and his wife Margaret. The saintly Queen Margaret founded the Benedictine priory of Dunfermline and is remembered for her patronage of the ferry across the Forth to take people to the Abbey. Her name is also remembered by the name of the two towns South and North Queensferry on either side of the Forth. She is also remembered by the chapel at Edinburgh Castle. Below the king and queen are statues of Sir William Wallace (see also *4.2*) and King Robert the Bruce (see also *4.1*).

To the west of the main entrance is Sir James Douglas, valiant supporter of Robert the Bruce. He fought many successful battles against the English, including an important role at Bannockburn for which Robert the Bruce knighted him on the field of battle. His exploits led to his nicknames: 'The Good Sir James' amongst Scots; 'The Black Douglas' to the English. He died fighting the Moors in Spain whilst on a crusade attempting to take Robert the Bruce's heart to the Holy Land. The heart and Douglas's body were carried back to

Scotland, the heart being buried in Melrose Abbey.

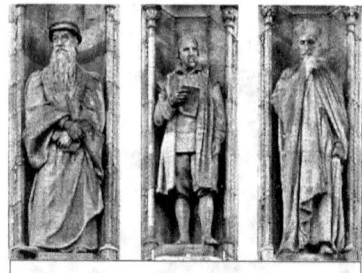

Knox, Buchanan and Beaton

To the west of Douglas are three religious: two of protestant reformation in Scotland (John Knox – *4.14*; George Buchanan); the third the Roman Catholic Cardinal Beaton who bitterly opposed the reformation.

George Buchanan (1506-1582) was the 'most profound intellectual' of sixteenth century Scotland. A scholar, particularly in Latin which he wrote as it were his native language, he travelled in continental Europe, occupying important university positions. Though clashing with the church for which he was briefly imprisoned in a monastery, he remained Roman Catholic during the early reformation, only becoming a Calvinist in his fifties. Aged 60 he became Moderator of the Church of Scotland, though a layman. Earlier he had tutored the young Mary Queen of Scots who he was later to vigorously oppose. He was later to tutor Mary's son, the future James VI, reputedly turning him against his mother.

His scholarship included much writing, perhaps his most important 'De Jure Regni apud Scotos' (the law of kingship among Scots), completed towards the end of his life. A quote from it is on a Makars' Court paving slab (*4.13*). In it he argued that ultimate power is vested in the people. A consequence was the legitimacy of deposing kings who fail to respect the people. This was a revolutionary idea, contrasting with the then established concept of the divine right of kings. The book was banned but its influence persisted. It was re-published in 2006, the 500th anniversary of his death.

Cardinal David Beaton (1494-1546) had political ambitions, including supporting the alliance with France, but it was his opposition to the reformation that was to dominate his later life. He arranged for the reformist preacher George Wishart to be tried and executed. Wishart's supporters retaliated, seizing St Andrews Castle, capturing the cardinal there and killed him.

Completing this western section is the statue of Field Marshall John Campbell, 2nd Duke of Argyll. Campbell was a senior commander of the British Army during the first decades of the 18th century, serving in continental Europe and leading the government army against the Jacobites during the 1715 rebellion.

The north-west tower honours Admiral Adam Duncan, 1st Viscount Duncan of Camperdown, who in a significant naval battle defeated the Dutch fleet off Camperdown, north of Haarlem in October 1797. Next to Duncan is General Sir Ralph Abercromby who did much to restore the discipline and order of the British Army in the late 18th century. He commanded the British forces in the West Indies, capturing Saint Lucia, Saint Vincent and Trinidad. He was mortally injured at the Battle of Alexandria in 1801, dying a week later. He had served under the Duke of York (*4.5*) who paid tribute to Abercromby's military leadership. Completing the north-west tower are two leaders of the Scottish Enlightenment, David Hume (*4.15*) and Adam Smith (*4.22*).

Many of the 30 statues on the external walls of the Scottish National Portrait Gallery are of monarchs (8) but also included are scientists (Hutton and Napier), poets, religious leaders and military men.

Part 2.2: Extensions to the First New Town: West End, Haymarket, Lothian Road, Picardy Place, and East End

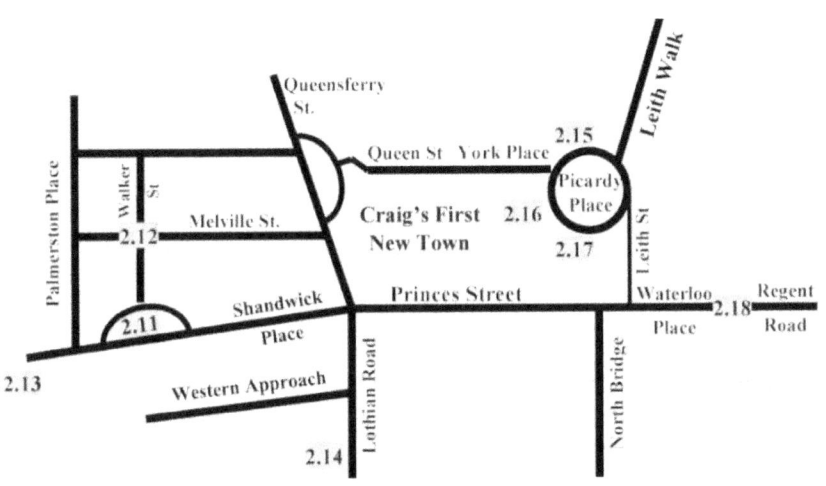

Map 2-2: Schematic showing location of Monuments of the extended New Town

2.11	2.12	2.13
William Gladstone	**Robert Dundas**	**Heart's War Memorial**
2.14	2.15	2.16
Woman and Child	**Conan Doyle**	**Manuscript of Monte Cassino**
	2.17	2.18
	Ken Buchanan	**Regent Bridge**

Note: The Heart's Memorial is at Haymarket, to the left (west) of the schematic. The statue to Robert Dundas, 2nd Viscount Melville, is at the centre of Melville Crescent, the intersection of Melville and Walker Streets, north of the statue to William Gladstone in Coates Crescent Gardens, along Shandwick Place.

2.11 William Ewart Gladstone, 1809 – 1898
Prime Minister, Chancellor; Midlothian MP

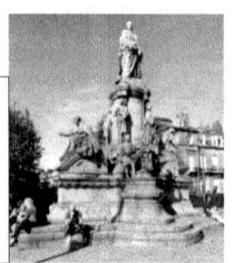

Description: Gladstone, robed as Chancellor of the Exchequer, high on a plinth; figures symbolise his virtues.
Sculptor: James Pittendrigh MacGillivray
Unveiled: Designed in 1902 and placed in St Andrew Square in 1916, officially unveiled in 1917. Moved to its current location in Coates Crescent Gardens in 1995.

A dominant Victorian politician, Gladstone campaigned passionately on many issues, including widening the franchise and Irish home rule. He first entered Parliament as a Tory, but it was as a Liberal that he became Prime Minister, serving 4 times for a total of over 12 years.

A prosperous Liverpool merchant's son, he was educated at Eton and Oxford, his public speaking and oratory leading him to Presidency of its Debating Society. Entering parliament in 1832, he joined Peel's Conservative cabinet in 1843. Later a Liberal-Conservative he joined the Liberal Party, first becoming Prime Minister in 1868. He was Chancellor of the Exchequer three times.

Allegorical figures are symbolic: 'Eloquentia' arm outstretched - eloquence, fluency, persuasiveness, gift for public speaking; 'Historia' - his place in history and his knowledge of it; 'Faith' - his personal religious convictions; 'Fortitude' and 'Vitality' his courage and energy; 'Measure' his attention to detail.

Added in 1922, two boys, representing youth, present a wreath inscribed with Greek extracts from the Iliad: '*Speech that was sweeter than honey flowed from this tongue*' and '*His was a very eager heart and a bold spirit*'.

Red kites(Scots 'gleds') support the wreath, symbolic of Gledstane, Gladstone.

He was Member of Parliament for Midlothian (1880 - 1895).

Fierce rivals, Gladstone and Disraeli were both Prime Ministers. Gladstone was known for his integrity, referred to as 'The People's William' or the 'G.O.M'

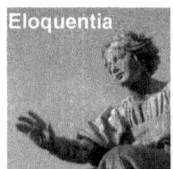
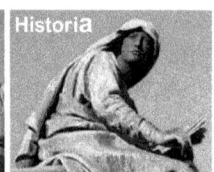

('Great Old Man'); though Disraeli described him as 'God's Only Mistake'. (Not far from Gladstone's monument, in the former Debenhams Store in Princes Street, is a stained-glass window dedicated in memory of Disraeli.)

Gladstone had a strained relationship with Queen Victoria (*5.1*). Accorded a State Funeral, Gladstone was buried in Westminster Abbey.

2.12 Robert Saunders Dundas, 2nd Viscount Melville, 1771 – 1851
Politician and Statesman

Robert Dundas was born in Edinburgh, the only son of Henry Dundas, 1st Viscount (*2.6*), and his wife Elizabeth. After education at the Royal High School he travelled in Europe before studying at Göttingen, Edinburgh and Cambridge Universities. In 1796 he married Anne Saunders, an heiress, taking her name to become Robert Saunders Dundas. They had four sons and two daughters

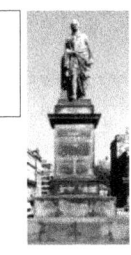

Description: Bronze on sandstone plinth inscribed: '*To commemorate the regard and esteem of his friends and fellow countrymen*'.
Sculptor: Sir John Steell   Unveiled: 1857

He worked as his father's private secretary, then Member of Parliament for Hastings, Rye and then Midlothian. In 1807 he became president of the Board of Control for India, where he worked to frustrate possible French aspirations on India.
Briefly Chief Secretary for Ireland he became First Lord of the Admiralty in 1812. He argued for maintaining the navy, supporting Wellington's concerns of inadequate naval protection for his convoys. He successfully fought to maintain the fleet, despite the British cabinet wanting to halve its size.
Interested in exploration, places in Canada (Melville Sound and Melville Island), and Australia were named after him. Melville Street in the New Town, on which his statue stands, was also named after him.
Like his father he was influential in Scotland: Keeper of the Signet for Scotland, Keeper of the Privy Seal for Scotland; Bank of Scotland governor; Chancellor of the University of St Andrews; Knight of the Order of the Thistle in 1821.

2.13 Heart of Midlothian Football Club
'Erected by the Heart of Midlothian Football Club to the memory of their players and members who fell in the Great War 1914 – 1919'

Description: Clock tower inscribed with names of Heart of Midlothian Football Club members who died in World War I. Names of those who died in World War II were added.
Designed by: H.S. Gamley   Unveiled: April 1922
Temporarily moved in early 21st century to allow tramway development; restored 2014 after the tracks were completed.

It honours Heart's World War I volunteers. At war's onset people asked: should professional football continue, British troops are dying? Hearts didn't hesitate, players & supporters enlisting in Sir George McCrae new volunteer battalion. Other clubs joined McCrae's, the '*footballer's battalion*'.
Hearts were leading the Scottish Football League, but putting national service before football it could not continue winning, the depleted side losing to Celtic.
A newspaper responded: '*There is only one football champion in Scotland, and its colours are maroon and khaki*'. Amongst the war dead: 7 Hearts 1st team players plus fans, many wounded. McCrae called for volunteers outside the Usher Hall, the square renamed McCrae Square in the early 21st century.
The monument is important in Heart's heart, wreaths laid annually to remember the team's sacrifice. Even when it was temporarily removed from Haymarket to make way for the tram development, supporters laid floral wreaths on Remembrance Day on the fencing where it had stood (upper photo). The monument was later returned to Haymarket (lower photo).

2.14 Woman and Child
To honour those who suffered under apartheid

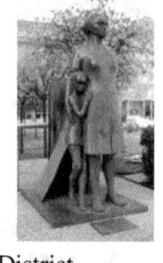

Description: Woman and child standing in front of a corrugated iron shelter, symbolic of township housing. Bronze
Sculptor: Anne Ross Davidson
Unveiled: 22nd July 1986 by Suganya Chetty, exiled member of the African National Congress, then living in Edinburgh

Inscribed '*Victory is certain*' it was commissioned by Edinburgh District Council, symbolising the city's opposition to South Africa's apartheid system. Edinburgh, like many UK cities, opposed the apartheid policies that separated people based on race. 'Non-whites' were suppressed and treated inferiorly. Only 'whites' had the vote, with best services reserved for whites. The native black South Africans were denied freedom, liberty and equality in their own country. Apartheid developed from informal racial separation of southern Africa's settler colonization, gradually entrenched in law, more rigorously from 1948 onwards. Laws, such as the Population Registration Act of 1950, classified people by race, and the Reservation of Separate Amenities Act that segregated facilities, formalised the system. The statue was erected whilst Nelson Mandela was still in prison and before the abolishing of apartheid in 1994.

2.15 Sir Arthur Conan Doyle, 1859-1930
Physician, Writer, creator of Sherlock Holmes

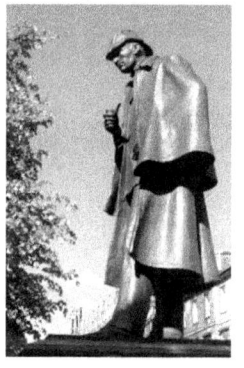

Description: Sir Arthur Conan Doyle commemorated by Sherlock Holmes holding his pipe, inscribed:
    '*Ceci n'est pas une pipe*' (this is not a pipe).
On the plinth, near Holmes' feet, are dog paw prints.
Sculptor: Gerald Ogilvie Laing, Cast in bronze at Kinkell Castle foundry, Sutherland   Unveiled: Unveiled 1991
Location: North side of Picardy Place. *Moved in 2017 for road and later for tram works. Returned on completion.*

A prolific novelist, Conan Doyle started writing whilst studying medicine, beginning with short stories. He continued whilst working as a doctor, initially struggling, as do many writers, to get published, and, when published, rewarded with only modest royalties. Literary success came with the Sherlock Holmes and Dr Watson detective stories, the first, in 1887, 'A Study in Scarlet'. It provided only a modest royalty, but the increasing demand for stories of the detective resulted in Conan Doyle becoming one of the best paid authors of the time.

The monument is of Sherlock Holmes, whose investigative skills were based on Edinburgh surgeon Dr Joseph Bell, one of his medical school lecturers. Dr Bell has a wall plaque on the house in Melville Crescent where he lived – it is near the statue of Robert Dundas (*2.12*). Dr Watson was based on another character from his medical school days, the surgeon Sir Patrick Heron-Watson.

Arthur Ignatius Conan Doyle was born in 11 Picardy Place, near the statue. His father's alcoholism dispersed the family around Edinburgh, but they re-united after 3 years in 1867. Wealthy uncles supported his education, and he studied medicine at Edinburgh University, good at sports: rugby, cricket, boxing, skiing and motor-racing. A field surgeon for a few months in 1900 during the Anglo-Boer War, he wrote a short work '*The War in South Africa: its Cause and Conflict*' justifying Britain's role in the war. This was followed in 1900 by '*The Great Boer War*' compiled from conversations with soldiers under his medical care. He was involved in the introduction of tin helmets for soldiers in the army and inflatable lifejackets in the navy.

He stood unsuccessfully for Parliament twice and was interested in the reform of divorce and criminal law. He promoted women's rights and inter-racial marriage. He also called for the construction of a tunnel under the Channel between England and France. His passion for justice helped ensure that two men were finally acquitted of crimes that they did not commit, helping to lead to the establishment of the Court of Criminal Appeal.

The inscription '*Ceci n'est pas une pipe*' (this is not a pipe) refers to René Magritte's painting of a pipe in 'The Treachery of Images' below which is the quote. True, it is not a pipe, but a picture. Detectives distinguish what is real.

Conan Doyle's interests in mystical subjects and continuing existence beyond earthly death saw him drawn to Spiritualism. He travelled, supporting it in Australia, New Zealand, continental Europe and the USA as well as Britain.

He died of a heart attack in the south of England where he was buried.

2.16 Manuscript of Monte Cassino
Commemorates the fierce 1944 battle at
Benedictine Abbey of Monte Cassino

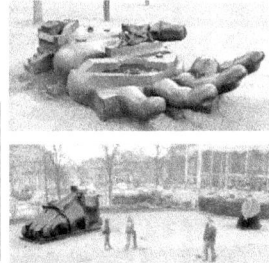

Description: Human fragments: hand, foot, ankle.
Sculptor: Sir Eduardo Paolozzi
Unveiled: 6th Sept 1991 by Sir Tom Farmer who helped fund it
Location: Picardy Place

It consists of body fragments, foot, ankle and hand (on it a ball, an engine and two grasshoppers) and discarded stones from the old Leith Central station, close to where the sculptor, Sir Edward Paolozzi, was born and lived as a child.

The Abbey's 1200 year-old Manuscript of Monte Cassino speaks of hospitality:
'*A manuscript of Monte Cassino addressed to Paul the Deacon. Letter from my hand; Go now with swift and easy flight; as you pass without delaying through the woods, hills and valleys. Seek out the welcoming house of Benedict, loved by God. There the weary always find rest; for guests there is an abundance of garden herbs, fish and bread. Among the brethren there is consecrated peace, lowliness of heart and uplifting harmony as they come together at every hour to offer praise to Christ in love and adoration.*'

The monument has two messages:
- Pilgrimage, the Abbey welcoming guests, symbolised by its elements: the foot which travels, the connecting ankle and the hand receiving hospitality.
- Destruction of war, symbolised by the fragmented body parts.

The monument recalls the ferocious battle at the Benedictine Abbey of Monte Cassino, on a hill outside Cassino, south-east of Rome. Believing it was used by the German army the Allies subjected it to a massive air raid in 1944 almost completely destroying it. Actually it was a war refuge for women and children, the Germans having agreed not to use it militarily whilst the monks were there.

After the Abbey's destruction the monks and civilians who had survived fled and the Abbey was occupied by German troops. Later a Polish army unit attacked and captured what by then had become a military fortress. The Polish unit is celebrated by the Wojtek statue in Princes Street gardens (*1.7*).

The Abbey was rebuilt after the war, financed by the Italian State. It had held important historical documents. Fortunately many were preserved at the initiative of two German officers who, during autumn 1943, suggested that the treasures should be taken to the Vatican and other safe sites. The officers persuaded the church and army to move the valuables using military transport.

The continuing message of this monument is shown by Christine De Luca, Edinburgh's Makar (Poet Laureate) for 2014-2017, writing poems inspired by Paolozzi's work and also by the University of Edinburgh's 'Transnationalizing Modern Languages' project call for short stories inspired by the monument.

2.17 Ken Buchanan MBE: 1945 – 2023
Boxing legend, 'the greatest boxer to emerge from the United Kingdom' [8]

Description: Buchanan in boxing pose, championship belt around waist, gloved hands. He attended the unveiling with many attending to see him and the new statue
Sculptor: Alan Herriot
Unveiled: 14th Aug 2022 by former Lord Provosts Frank Ross and Donald Wilson
Location: Little King Street, Picardy Place. With anticipation that it might be moved centrally to Picardy Place when road works there are complete.

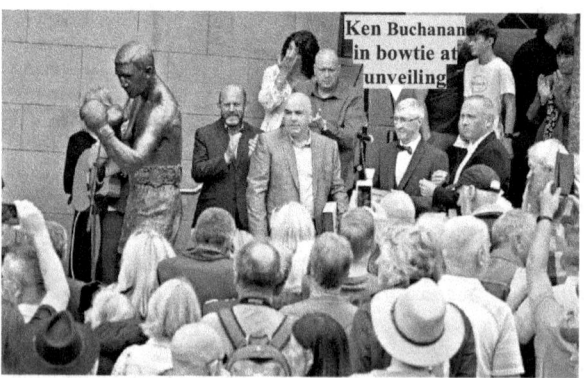
Ken Buchanan in bowtie at unveiling

After winning the British amateur ABA featherweight title in early 1965 Ken Buchanan turned professional, defeating Brian Tonks in London with a knockout blow. During the late 1960s his achievements grew, winning 23 consecutive bouts before becoming the British lightweight champion in 1968, when he challenged the incumbent title holder, winning with an 11th round knockout blow in London. The path to success (in any sphere in life) is not without setbacks and in January 1970 he was defeated after 15 rounds for the European lightweight title in Madrid. But undeterred he continued, with further wins that year, including beating his Madrid rival in a rematch, before in September 1971 he became world light weight champion. He beat, over the full 15-rounds, the existing champion in the heat of Puerto Rico. In 1971 he was declared undisputed world lightweight champion, holding both the World Boxing Association (WBA) and the World Boxing Council (WBC) titles.

His scorecard shows nearly 90% successes, 62 wins in 70 professional bouts around the world. He was inducted into the International Boxing Hall of Fame.

Ken was born in Edinburgh in 1945, his outstanding contributions recognized with an MBE and in 2016 with the Edinburgh Award (see **4.16**). Hundreds crowded the narrow Little King Street midday on a 2022 Sunday to witness, honour and see the living boxing legend with his unveiled statue and to listen to Kevin Gore singing '*Ken Buchanan, Edinburgh man*', a Scottish singer/writer whose work had been described as a 'knockout', appropriate for his role in honouring Ken. He died within a year on 1st April 2023, aged 77, remembered in a memorial service at St Giles Cathedral.

2.18 Regent Bridge
Commemorates Waterloo: 'Commenced in the ever-memorable year 1815'

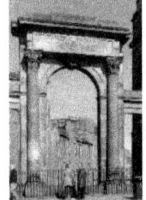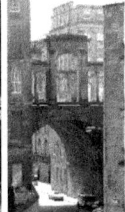

Description: Neoclassical stone bridge with celebratory arch (left) spans the Calton ravine (right). The ravine, the New Town's eastern edge, separated New Town and Calton Hill
Design: Archibald Elliot
Built by: Robert Stevenson, engineer and grandfather of Robert Louis Stevenson (*1.11*)
Date: Began 1815, 'ever memorable year', completed 1819

Regent Bridge's triumphant arches commemorate the 1815 Battle of Waterloo, ending, in that 'ever-memorable-year', decades of conflict referred to as the Napoleonic Wars and seeing the emergence of Britain's dominance of Europe. The street along the bridge was called Waterloo Place in honour of the battle. The bridge was officially opened by Prince Leopold of Saxe-Coburg on the 18th August 1819. 'Regent' refers to the Regency, ill-health preventing George III reigning, his son, later King George IV (*2.4*), ruling as Prince Regent.

After James Craig's (*2.8*) New Town, Edinburgh's continuing demand to expand required improved transport links, including east of Princes Street across the Calton ravine. Sir John Marjoribanks, Lord Provost, supported the bridge, the plan approved in 1814, with estimated cost of £20,000.

Regent Bridge is included as a monument as it commemorates the end of the Napoleonic Wars, emphasizing people's relief with peace restored in that 'ever-memorable-year'. Other monuments of that conflict are the nearby Wellington (*1.24*) statue, with the war casualties remembered by the National Monument (*3.4*) on Calton Hill, whose access the bridge facilitates

The statue of the Duke of Wellington (*1.24*) is nearby at the east end of Princes Street before Waterloo Place. Waterloo Place leads on to Regent Road. The casualties of the wars are also remembered by the National Monument (*3.4*) on Calton Hill, whose access the bridge facilitates.

Chapter 3: Calton Hill

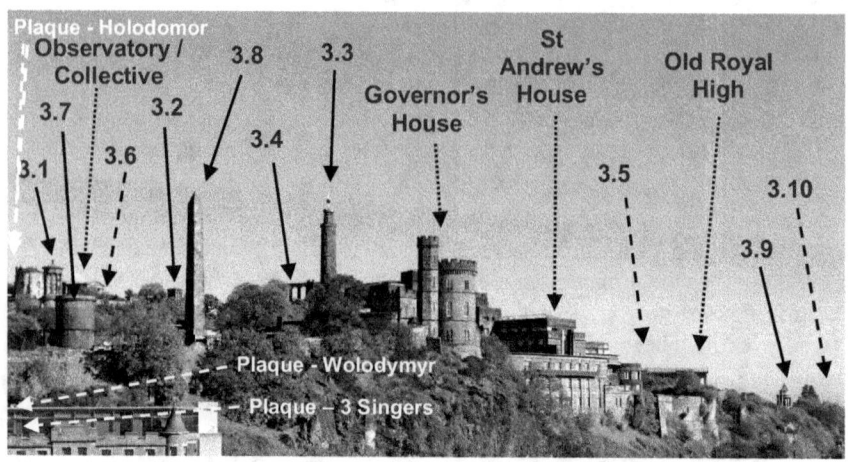

Map 3-1: Calton Hill monuments viewed from North Bridge
(See Map 3-2 on the next page for the abbreviations)

Calton Hill viewed from North Bridge, many of its monuments visible. The photo was taken shortly before 1pm, the ball (black) on Nelson's monument (*3.3*) raised, ready to be dropped at 1pm, so ships at Leith can check their clocks. At the same time the Castle's 1 o'clock gun is fired.

Dashed lines indicate approximate positions of monuments not visible. Dotted lines point to key buildings: Observatory (since its 2018 opening, home to the Collective Art Gallery); Governor's House; St Andrew's House (Scottish Government); and the Old Royal High.

Calton Hill, a public park, is one of the 'Seven Hills of Edinburgh'. A volcanic hill, its origins as a public park go back to 1724 when the Town Council of Edinburgh purchased the hill. Predating the New Town's development, it is one of the UK's oldest public parks. It remains a popular area for recreation as well as offering dramatic views over the city. The old Observatory is now a Collective Art Gallery.

Some key figures of the Scottish Enlightenment are remembered on the hill, including Dugald Stewart, John Playfair and David Hume. Hume campaigned for public areas for people to walk in; one of the hill's paths is named after him.

Many of its monuments are visible from the city, the National and Nelson Monument dominating the view to the east of Princes Street. The classical nature of the buildings on the hill helped justify Edinburgh's 'Athens of the North' nickname. Several were designed by William Henry Playfair to whom a statue was erected in 2016 in Chambers Street (*6.2*). Monuments on Calton Hill influenced by Athenian architecture are those to Dugald Stewart, Robert Burns and the National Monument. They are complemented by the design of the Old Royal High nearby on Regent Road.

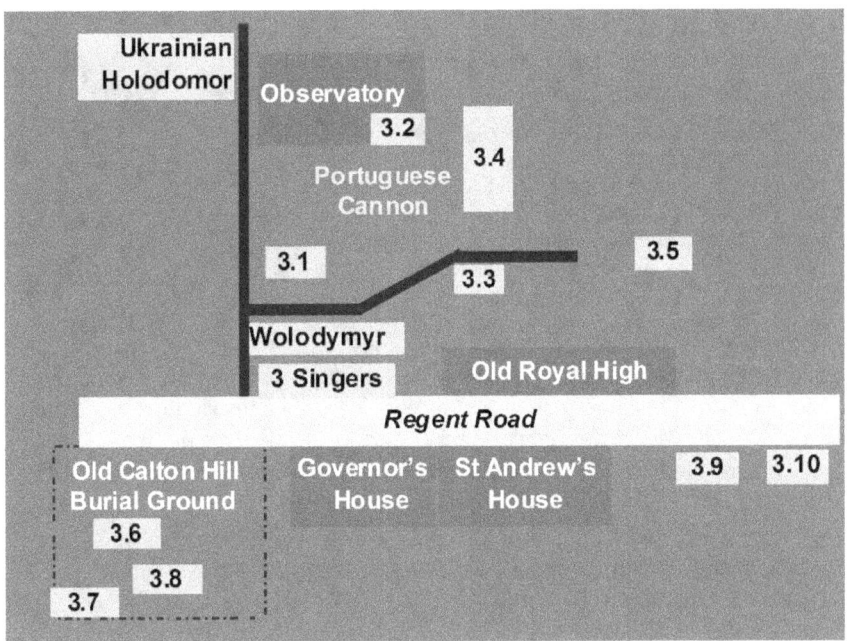

Map 3-2: Monuments on Calton Hill

3.1	3.2	3.3	3.4
Dugald Stewart	**John Playfair**	**Admiral Nelson**	**National Monument**

3.5	3.6
Cairn for Scottish Parliament Vigil	**Scottish-American Soldiers**

3.7	3.8	3.9	3.10
David Hume	**Friends of the People**	**Robert Burns**	**Stones of Scotland**

Plaques

St Wolodymyr of Ukraine	3 Singers 19th Century Scottish Singers	Ukrainian Holodomor

Notes:

1. **Portuguese Cannon:** Its position is shown on Map 3-2. Believed originally to be of Spanish origin, it was installed on Calton Hill in 1887 after being shown at the 1886 International Exhibition in the Meadows; see Chapter 6, **6.6.**

2. **Three plaques** are discussed at end of this chapter. Two are at the steps leading up to the hill from Regent Road, the third on the path that leads up the hill from the north.

In general memorials in graveyards are not included in this book, but three in the Old Calton Hill Burial Ground are included because of their significance: Scottish-American soldiers (**3.6**); the David Hume tower (**3.7**); Friends of the People (**3.8**).

The North Bridge is a good place from which to view many Calton Hill monuments, as shown in Map 3-1. Other vantage points are Holyrood Park, Edinburgh Castle, the Scott Monument and Princes Street.

The Dugald Stewart Monument (**3.1**) is often used in the foreground for city views.

3.1 Dugald Stewart, 1753 – 1828
Philosopher, teacher, writer, Scottish
Enlightenment leader, mathematician

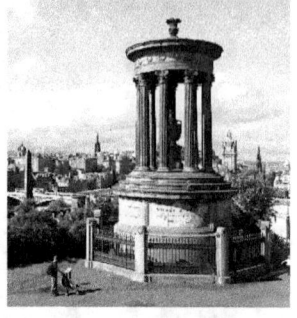

> Description: Circular temple of 9 fluted Corinthian
> columns surrounding an Urn; modelled on 'Tower of
> the Winds' built in Athens, 50BC
> Architect: William Henry Playfair
> Date: 1831. Commissioned by The Royal Society of
> Edinburgh

Dugald Stewart, Professor of Moral Philosophy at Edinburgh University, created
a centre of excellence that attracted students from around the UK, Europe and
America. Lord Cockburn, one of his students, described his lectures in glowing
terms [1]: *'To me Stewart's lectures were like the opening of the heavens. I felt
that I had a soul. His noble views, unfolded in glorious sentences, elevated me
into a higher world.'*

He taught ethics, political philosophy and the theory of government and
introduced the study of political economy. He published: the 3-volume
'Elements of the Philosophy of the Human Mind' (1792, 1814 and 1827);
'Outlines of Moral Philosophy' (1793); 'Philosophy of the Active and Moral
Powers of Man' (1828); biographies of Adam Smith, William Robertson and
Thomas Reid.

In the opening chapter of 'Elements of the Philosophy of the Human Mind'
Stewart writes of the *'frivolous and absurd discussions'* and *'vague use of
language'* to which can *'probably be ascribed the little progress, which has
hitherto been made in the PHILOSOPHY OF THE HUMAN MIND'*. It is *'a
science, so interesting in its nature, and so important in its applications, that it
could scarcely have failed, in these inquisitive and enlightened times, to have
excited a very general attention'*. He goes on to introduce the word *'Mind'* as
something of whose existence *'we are not immediately conscious'* but *'we are
conscious of sensation, thought and volition; operations, which imply the
existence of something which feels, thinks and wills'*.

He is credited with comparing Edinburgh to Athens, *'Athens of the North'*.

Dugald Stewart was born in Edinburgh, commencing his studies at the
University of Edinburgh aged 13. In his late teens he briefly studied under
Thomas Reid at the University of Glasgow, from whom he developed his theory
of morality. This study was cut short when aged 19, on behalf of his ill father, he
gave lectures in mathematics at Edinburgh
University. He was soon professor of
mathematics, appointed about 10 years
later to the chair of Moral Philosophy. He
retired in 1822 and was succeeded by
John Wilson (statue *1.19*). In the early 21st
century the University of Edinburgh
named a new building in his honour.

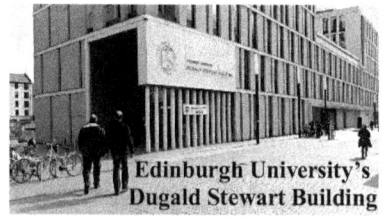

Edinburgh University's
Dugald Stewart Building

3.2   John Playfair, 1748 – 1819
Mathematician, philosopher, geologist, Enlightenment

Inscription	
Inscription Joanni Playfair Amicorum Pietas Desideriis Icta Fidelibus Quo Ipso Loco Templum Uraniae Suae Olim Dicaverat Hoc monumentum Posuit MDCCCXXVI	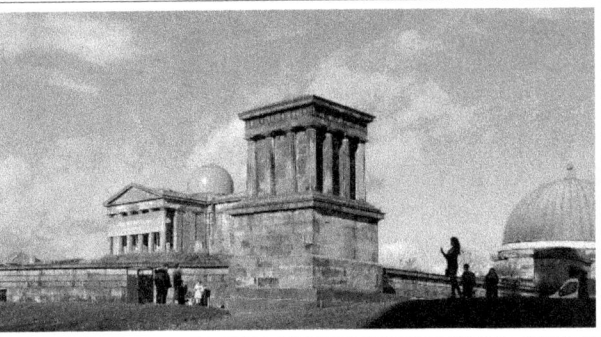

Translation of Inscription	Description: Square Greek Doric
Translation of Inscription 'To John Playfair / His friends' piety / Spurred on by constant longings / In the place where he himself / had once dedicated a temple to his Urania / Placed this monument 1826'	Description: Square Greek Doric monument at south east corner of the Observatory. The site opened as a 'Collective' art gallery in 2018 Architect: William Henry Playfair, John Playfair's nephew. Date: 1826

John Playfair was a leader in the Scottish Enlightenment. He advocated the establishment of the City Observatory, becoming the first president of the Astronomical Institute of Edinburgh. It is fitting that his monument stands at a corner of the walls of the Observatory, seen behind the corner-piece. He was a Professor of Mathematics and Natural Philosophy at Edinburgh University. The Observatory now houses the Collective Art Gallery; in the photo it is just possible to see a banner advertising its opening in November 2018.

Playfair also developed and publicised the geological ideas of his friend James Hutton (*6.8*), publishing, in 1802, '*Illustrations of the Huttonian Theory of the Earth*'. This helped disseminate and explain Hutton's ideas; Hutton had died in 1797. The ideas revolutionised geological thinking: explaining, for example, that a river cuts its own path through the landscape, and that geological events affect the features of the Earth. Playfair was to spend the last years of his life exploring geological features of Europe and drafting a 2nd edition of the '*Illustrations*'. Unfortunately, he died before its completion, but, through his publications, communicated Hutton's theories, helping create the modern science of geology.

Playfair published essays in the Edinburgh Review and in the Philosophical Transactions of the Royal Society (including, in 1779, 'On the Arithmetic of Impossible Quantities') and in the Transactions of the Royal Society of Edinburgh (including 'On the Causes which Affect the Accuracy of Barometric Measurements'). Between 1812 and 1816 he published the two-volume book 'Outlines of Natural Philosophy'.

Born near Dundee, the son of a Kirk minister, John studied at St Andrews University. He was to become a Kirk minister prior to his university career. He moved to Edinburgh where he became involved in its literary and scientific societies. In 1785, he succeeded Dugald Stewart (*3.1*) as Professor of Mathematics at Edinburgh University when Stewart became Professor of Moral Philosophy. In 1805 Playfair became Professor of Moral Philosophy.

John adopted his nephew William when John's brother, James, died suddenly in 1793. William Henry Playfair was to become a leading Edinburgh architect (statue in Chambers Street, *6.2*). John died in Fife, in 1819.

3.3 Admiral Horatio Nelson, 1758 – 1805
Military hero, Victor of Trafalgar at which he died

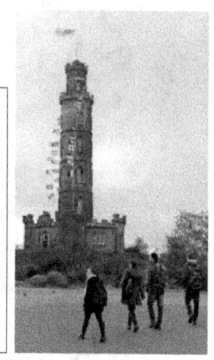

Description: Stone tower, shaped as an upturned telescope, topped with a time ball dropped at 1pm daily. 32 Metres high, 147 steps lead to a public viewing gallery. It is at the highest point on Calton Hill, 171 metres above sea level.
Design: Tower - Robert Burn; Time ball - Maudslay, Sons & Field
Commissioned: On 25th Nov 1805 Edinburgh' people agreed to fund a monument to Nelson. Funded by public subscription
Date: Completed 1816; time ball added in 1853. Restored in 2009, including the time ball

Horatio Nelson is one of Britain's greatest military heroes, ranked with Wellington (*1.24*). In a 2002 BBC '100 Greatest Britons' programme he was voted the 9th greatest Briton of all time. His influence at his death was such that in the month following his death Edinburgh decided to erect a monument to him; this was erected before his monument in London's Trafalgar Square.

He was born in Norfolk in 1758, the village rector's son. Through an uncle's influence he joined the Navy, gaining rapid promotion from his ordinary seaman enlistment, achieving his own command aged just 20. After the American War of Independence he suffered unemployment, but returned to naval service in the late 18th and early 19th centuries European wars.

He was an inspirational leader and superb strategic planner, willing to adopt unconventional tactics that achieved decisive naval victories, particularly during the Napoleonic Wars. A man of personal valour, he led from the front despite being wounded during battle. He suffered the loss of an arm during the attempt to conquer Santa Cruz de Tenerife, the loss of one eye in Corsica and, finally, killed whilst leading the Battle of Trafalgar, Britain's greatest naval victory. Trafalgar was decisive, determining whether the French under Bonaparte would invade Britain. Five of the 27 British ships at the battle were captained by Scots.

He received many honours, an honorary Doctor of Civil Law from Oxford and Freeman of several English cities. His many titles were read out at his funeral:

> *'The Most Noble Lord Horatio Nelson, Viscount and Baron Nelson, of the Nile and of Burnham Thorpe in the County of Norfolk, Baron Nelson of the Nile and of Hilborough in the said County, Knight of the Most Honourable Order of the Bath, Vice Admiral of the White Squadron of the Fleet, Commander in Chief of his Majesty's Ships and Vessels in the Mediterranean, Duke of Bronté in the Kingdom of Sicily, Knight Grand Cross of the Sicilian Order of St Ferdinand and of Merit, Member of the Ottoman Order of the Crescent, Knight Grand Commander of the Order of St Joachim.'*

A plaque at the tower entrance appeals for the young to follow his example:

'To the memory of Vice-Admiral Horatio Lord Viscount Nelson,
and of the great victory of Trafalgar. Too dearly purchased with his blood.
The grateful citizens of Edinburgh have erected this monument:
Not to express their unavailing sorrow for his death;
Nor yet to celebrate the matchless glories of his life;
But, by his noble example,
to teach their sons to emulate what they admire, and, like him,
when duty requires it, to die for their country.'

Charles Piazza Smyth, Astronomer Royal for Scotland, added the time ball as a time signal for ships at the port of Leith. Erected in 1853, it weighs 762kg. Procedure: raised halfway at 12h55 (warning), fully at 12h58, drops at 13h00. The Castle's 1 o'clock gun followed in 1861. The 2019 bi-centenary of Smyth's birth was marked by an exhibition of his work in the monument's museum.

The design of the monument included housing for sailors, but this was not used. The wife of a Petty Officer opened a restaurant in the 1820s, now a museum.

Nelson's influence continues. His legacy was called upon by Poet Laureate Alfred Tennyson to oppose the defence funding cuts proposed by Prime Minister Gladstone (*2.11*) in the 1860's. Winston Churchill took inspiration from Nelson in his leadership of the country during World War II.

The Royal Navy's White Ensign flags with his message *'England expects that every man will do his duty'* are flown from the monument on 21st October, Trafalgar Day – see photo above.

3.4   National Monument
To commemorate Scots who died in the Napoleonic Wars

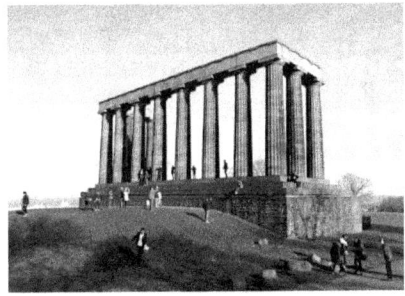

<u>Description</u>: Inspired by the Parthenon in Athens, but never completed, only 12 columns constructed
<u>Architect</u>: Charles Robert Cockerell and William Henry Playfair
<u>Dates</u>: Work started 1826, stopped 1829

In 1816, after the Battle of Waterloo ending of the Napoleonic Wars, there was a call for a national monument to commemorate the fallen. Calton Hill was chosen as the site. Funds were to be raised by public appeal. The foundation stone was laid in 1822 and funds raised enabled work to start in 1826. Based on the Parthenon in Athens, the design was by Charles Robert Cockerell and William Henry Playfair; the plan included a Hall of Heroes of famous Scots.

The inscription sums up the intended theme: *'A Memorial of the Past and Incentive to the Future Heroism of the Men of Scotland.'*

However, the funds raised were insufficient, the work was never completed. Only the 12 columns intended to be the front of the building were built. This lack of completion led to various derogatory nicknames: '*Edinburgh's folly*'; '*Edinburgh's Disgrace*'; '*The Pride and Poverty of Scotland*'. During the early 20th century there were proposals for 'completing' its completion as: monument to Queen Victoria; commemoration of the bicentenary of the 1707 Act of Union; memorial to those who died in World War I. None came to pass. Edinburgh's citizens and tourists have accepted the monument as it is, with many climbing onto the wall between the pillars to have their photographs taken. Its unfinished state has merit, arguably to have built over more of the hill to complete it would have been a disgrace. Furthermore, Don Ledingham in his poem 'The Unfinished Monument' accompanying Gordon Hunter's photograph of the monument writes of it: '*Yet perfect in Your imperfection*' going on to note that 'none of us .. have any greater claim to be complete' (see Hunter & Ledingham in bibliography). A monument that recognizes that we are not complete!

The stone for the monument, as for many 19th century Edinburgh buildings and monuments, came from Craigleith Quarry, now a retail park, but for over 300 years the source of building material. Each column weighed 10 to 15 ton, costing £1000. The Carboniferous Period stone is 330 million years old.

The Napoleonic Wars ended in 1815 with Wellington's victory at Waterloo. They followed the French Revolutionary Wars after the late 18th century French Revolution. The wars involved 11million combatants from across Europe (1million British) with about 2million casualties (300,000 British).

These wars and the French Revolution changed the political map in Europe. Germany and Italy emerged as unified national states from their historical city-states and principalities. Britain emerged as the strongest European power with world-wide naval supremacy. Constitutional reform gradually spread across Europe, limiting the power of monarchs. The political treaties that followed, in particular the Congress of Vienna in 1814-15, led to a period of peace in Europe lasting nearly 100 years, to be shattered by the outbreak of World War I.

3.5   Cairn for the vigil for the Scottish Parliament
Commemorating the Vigil for return of the Scottish Parliament

Description: Stone cairn with beacon. Constructed from many different stones, some bearing inscribed plaques commemorating movements for democracy.
Designed by: keepers of the Vigil for a Scottish Parliament
Erected by: Democracy for Scotland, 10th April 1998

Erected by campaigners for the return of the Scottish Parliament, it symbolises the struggle for democracy. Incorporated plaques recall other struggles. Inscribed:

'*This cairn was built by the keepers of the Vigil for a Scottish Parliament. The Vigil was kept at the foot of this road. It began on the night of the 10th April 1992 as news broke of the fourth Conservative General Election victory. It ended 1980 days later. The previous day, 11th September 1997, Scotland voted 'YES, YES' for her own Parliament.*'

Re-enforcing the cairn's message of the democratic equality of all, it includes a stone from the Mauchline home of Scotland's National poet, Burns. The verse recognises each person's inherent value: '*The man's the gowd for a that*'.

THIS STANE WIS TAEN FRAE

THE MAUCHLIN HAME O ROBERT BURNS AND JEAN ARMOUR DURIN THE RENOVATION IN 1966 THE BICENTENARY O THE POETS DAITH

"THE RANK IS BUT THE GUINEA'S STAMP THE MAN'S THE GOWD FOR A THAT."

Stones on the cairn recall other struggles:

'*Destiny Marches, 1993, Lochmabin.*' *This stone from Bruce's Castle represents an earlier struggle for self-determination by the people of Scotland.*

'*This stone from Auschwitz is in memory of Jane Haining, Scottish missionary and all others who died in the death camp.*'

'*Paving stone from Paris used for defending democracy. Donated to the people of Scotland by supporters in Paris to commemorate the Auld Alliance.*'

Belief in Scotland and its future (MacDiarmid): '*For we hae faith in Scotland's hidden poo'ers, The present's theirs, but a' the past and future's oors*'.

3.6 to 3.8: In Old Calton Hill Burial ground

The Burial ground contains monuments of many famous citizens, three of whom are included here, exceptions to excluding cemetery monuments: one is not a burial site, whilst there are wider significances to the Scottish-American Soldiers Monument and that to David Hume.

3.6 Scottish-American Soldiers, 1861-1865
Emancipation; To Scots who fought and died in the American Civil War

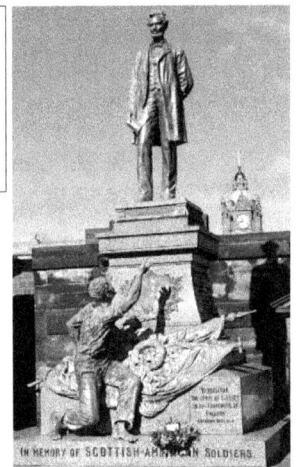

Description: Abraham Lincoln holds the 'Proclamation of Emancipation' in his right hand. A freed slave extends an arm in gratitude.
Sculptor: Sculpture by George Edwin Bissell of USA; stone work by Stewart McGlashan & Son of Edinburgh
Unveiled: August 1893

The monument was erected by citizens of the USA to six Scots who fought and died in the American Civil War. It is the only monument to the American Civil War in Scotland and includes the first statue of a U.S. President erected outside the USA. It is inscribed with words written by Abraham Lincoln: '*To preserve the jewel of liberty in the framework of freedom*'.

It followed a request to the U.S. Consul from Mrs McEwan, widow of Sergeant Major McEwan, one of the six, desperate for her war pension. Mrs Bruce, the Consul's wife, met her. Wanting to pay tribute at his grave she learnt he had only an unidentified pauper's grave. The Consul then requested Edinburgh City Council for a burial site and to erect a monument. The Council agreed to an Old Calton Burial ground site. Funding was raised in USA.

Six Scots who died fighting on the Union side in the American Civil War are named on the granite plinth: John McEwan, William Duff, Robert Steedman, James Wilkie, Robert Ferguson and Alexander Smith.

It is also a monument to the campaign to abolish slavery. The American Civil War was fought between southern and northern States. A core issue in the presidential election of November 1860 was abolishing slavery. The Republicans, led by Abraham Lincoln, wished to ban slavery, opposed by the Southern States reliant on slave labour for the farms. The Republicans won the presidential election, Lincoln elected as the first Republican president. But before his inauguration in March 1861 the country was breaking apart, with seven southern states forming the Confederacy, the Confederate States of America. Diplomacy and compromise failed. Hostilities began in April 1861, a bitter civil war between northern (Union) and southern (Confederate) states that lasted till 1865. Over 600,000 Confederate and Union soldiers were killed. The deadliest war in American history, the death toll was estimated as 10% of all Northern males aged 20 to 45, and 30% of all Southern males aged 18 to 40.

The war left a divided hurt country. Much of the infrastructure of the south was destroyed. Slavery was abolished. The task of healing the country commenced in what is known as 'The Reconstruction' that was to take over 12 years.

3.7   David Hume, 1711 – 1776
Leader of Scottish Enlightenment

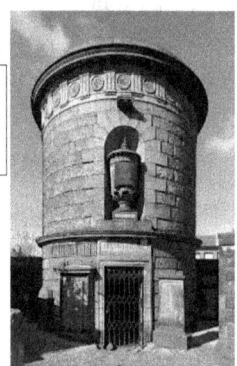

Description: Large neo-classical cylindrical tower, open roof.
Architect: Robert Adam   Date: 1778
See also: 4.15, summary of Hume's life and philosophy

On the edge of the Old Calton burial ground, having the appearance, when viewed from the Old Town, of a tower along the wall, is the dominating circular mausoleum for the philosopher David Hume. David Hume is remembered here for several reasons. Firstly, in recognition of his campaigns for open spaces in which the public could walk – with Calton Hill's opening as a public park a good example; the David Hume walk on Calton Hill recognizes his contribution. Secondly, the irony of the Christian message on Hume's mausoleum. And thirdly it is included because of its iconic design.

Hume requested in his will that he be buried in a Romanesque mausoleum on Calton Hill, overlooking Edinburgh, visible from the Old Town. It was designed by Hume's friend, the architect Robert Adam. The monument thus symbolises two Scottish Enlightenment leaders whose complementary contributions in philosophy (Hume) and urban design (Adam) secured *'Scotland's place at the very forefront of European taste and thought'* [2].

Robert Adam's design was inspired by his studies of Italian architecture. The classical design had echoes in later buildings on Calton Hill. The original design included the urn, though it is thought that the urn in place was not of Adam's design. An open cylinder without roof, the design symbolises Hume's philosophical ideas and universality.

Hume was critical of organized religion for which he faced strong public hostility. In accordance with his views he directed that his tomb should bear no inscription other than his name and dates of birth and death. However, this was not to be and there is an irony in that his resting place should have a Christian message. This arose because his niece was later interned in this grave site, the Christian message inscribed to reflect her beliefs:

> *'Behold I come quickly. Thanks be to God which giveth us*
> *the victory through our Lord Jesus Christ.'*

The mausoleum was originally dramatically visible on the undeveloped craggy slopes of Calton Hill before the building of the prison and Governor's House (the Governor's house remains, see Map 3-1). It is a striking and appropriate reminder of the Enlightenment, mutually supported by philosophy, thought, reason and architectural genius. It is still visible from some Old Town views.

A 19th century epitaph described the tomb [3]:

> *'Within this circular Idea,*   *The Impressions and Ideas rest*
> *Called vulgarly a Tomb,*   *That constituted Hume.'*

3.8 The Martyrs' Memorial, The Friends of the People
To the Political Martyrs who strove for Parliamentary Reform

Description: 90 ft obelisk with names of the political martyrs: Thomas Muir; Thomas Fyshe Palmer; William Skirving; Maurice Margarot; Joseph Gerrald.
Designer: Thomas Hamilton
Unveiled: Foundation stone laid on 21st August 1844 by Joseph Hume, MP. In 1837 he proposed the monument and campaigned for public subscriptions. The publisher William Tait wrote to the Lord Provost requesting that land be made available on Calton Hill for the memorial.

The obelisk was erected in memory of the 'Political Martyrs' who strove for Parliamentary reform in Scotland, campaigning for universal franchise. They were encouraged by the French Revolution and other freedom movements but opposed by the established powers including Dundas (*2.6*).

At the turn of the 19th century few in Scotland had the vote. But it was a time of political unrest with the clamour for universal representation fuelled by the French Revolution and the American War of Independence. The five martyrs listed were leaders of the campaign for extending the franchise, but their efforts aroused the hostility of the authorities of the day who had them tried. Lord

Braxfield, the 'hanging judge' (remembered by the 'Jolly Judge' pub in James Court on the Lawnmarket of the Royal Mile), banished them to Australia.

Nearly forty years after their trials the Scottish Reform Act of 1832 extended the franchise, but only to a limited extent, increasing the electorate from about 5,000 to 65,000. Later in that decade, in 1838, the martyrs were pardoned.

Universal franchise was only achieved in the 20th century. Firstly, the February 1918 'Representation of the People Act' enfranchised men over 21, but women only if over 30 and meeting other conditions. Ten years later the 1928 Act gave equal voting rights to women and men. Half a century later the 1969 Act reduced the age to 18. Currently there is debate about lowering the age to 16.

The obelisk records Muir and Skirving speaking at their trials:

> *'I have devoted myself to the cause of THE PEOPLE. It is a good cause – it shall ultimately prevail – it shall finally triumph.'*
> Thomas Muir, 30th August 1793.

> *'I know that what has been done these two days will be RE-JUDGED.'* William Skirving, 7th January 1794.

Thomas Muir (1765 – 1799), born near Glasgow, had intended to enter the church but studied law, being admitted to the Faculty of Advocates in 1787. He was a church elder, a man of principle, an 18th century reform leader. Tried in August 1793 before a jury composed of anti-reformists, he was banished to Australia for 14 years. He escaped in 1796, travelling to France where he died.

William Skirving (1745 – 1796) was born in Edinburgh and educated at Edinburgh University, intending to enter the church, but became a farmer. Active in the 'Edinburgh Society of Friends of the People' he was appointed general secretary of its first convention in December 1792. He was tried and sentenced to 14-years transportation to Australia where he died of dysentery.

Thomas Palmer (1747 – 1802), born in England, educated at Eton and Cambridge, became a minister in the Unitarian church in Scotland. Arrested in 1793 charged with sedition for calling for universal suffrage, he was banished for 7 years. He died of dysentery on his way back to Britain.

Joseph Gerrald (1763 – 1796), born in the West Indies, the son of an Irish planter, was educated in England. He spent some time in the USA, serving as an advocate and publishing essays on universal suffrage. Returning to England in 1788 he joined the political reform movement. He argued for universal suffrage and, with English and Scottish delegates, attended the 1793 Edinburgh convention. Arrested, he was tried for sedition in March 1794 and sentenced to 14-years banishment, leaving London in May 1795, arriving in Australia in poor health later that year, dying of tuberculosis.

Maurice Margarot (1745 – 1815), a founding member of the London Corresponding Society, a radical society demanding parliamentary reform, travelled to Edinburgh with Joseph Gerrald to attend the 1793 Edinburgh convention organised by the Friends of the People. This led to his arrest in December 1793 and banishment to Australia. He was the only one of the five to return to Britain, but he died in poverty.

3.9   **Robert Burns,** 1759 – 1796
Scotland's National Poet

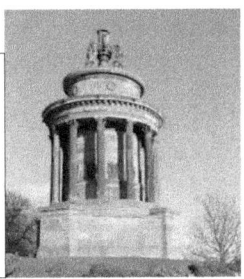

Description: Circular Greek Corinthian style, based on
Choragic monument of Lysicrates. Ashlar sandstone.
Architect: Thomas Hamilton. Initially contained John
Flaxman's statue of Burns. But it was moved for protection
and now in the Scottish National Portrait Gallery (see *2.10*)
Foundation stone laid: 1831
See also: Chapter 5, *5.2* for Burn's Leith statue

On Regent Road is one of Edinburgh's two monuments to Robert Burns, more
details of whom are in Chapter 5 (*5.2*) when discussing his Leith statue.

Proposals were made, after Burns' death to erect an Edinburgh monument.
These arose, not in Scotland, but in Bombay, with firm ideas by 1812, then
followed up by a group of Bard admirers at the Free Mason's Tavern in London,
under the chairmanship of the Duke of Atholl. They commissioned John
Flaxman to produce a life-size marble statue, which he did with the poet holding
a bunch of daisies and reciting his poem '*To a mountain daisy*'.

The statue cost only half the funds and Thomas Hamilton was asked to design a
monument to house it. Hamilton had designed Alloway's 1820 Burns monument
(and Calton Hill's Royal High School). His design, like that in Alloway, is based
on the Athenian Lysicrates monument that celebrated dramatic performances. In
tribute to the poet it is topped with a bronze tripod, fashioned on the award given
to the best orator in 334BC. The tripod is mounted on winged lions (dolphins in
Alloway) below which laurel wreathes honour Burns. Lyres, ancient Greek
harps, surround the central base, around which are 12 fluted Corinthian columns.

The monument was designed to house Flaxman's marble statue of Burns.
However, the statue was removed in 1839 to avoid smoke damage from the gas
works below. Initially it was moved to the Edinburgh University library. It was
moved to the National Gallery of Scotland and then to the Scottish National
Portrait Gallery where it now graces the entrance hall.

Burns grew up in rural Ayrshire, the ploughman poet. His love of nature
influenced his writing, its theme in many of his poems. To reflect this, flowers
were planted around the monument. '*My Luve is like a red, red rose*' is a well-
known Burns poem. In '*The Bonnie Moor-hen*' he wrote of the heather
blooming, the meadows mawn, but the plumage of the moorhen outshining the
flowers' pride. The poem warns the moorhen to beware of the hunting young
men. Burns wrote of snowdrops and primroses adorning the woodlands, of
harebells (bluebells) and the '*stately*' foxglove.

The Kilmarnock Edition ('*Poems Chiefly in the Scottish Dialect*') of Burns
poetry was published in July 1786 and Burns was invited by Professor Dugald
Stewart (*3.1*), also from Ayrshire, to produce a second enlarged publication.
Burns arrived in Edinburgh to critical acclaim, staying initially with a friend in
what is now Deacon Brodie's Tavern, marked by a plaque at the Lady Stairs
Close entrance on the Lawnmarket. Burns was welcomed into high society and

on one evening briefly met the young Walter Scott (*1.21*); Burns had asked about a verse below a painting and it was the 15-year-old Scott who alone amongst the assembled dignities knew the artist's name.

Burns' 2nd edition, resulting from his visit to Edinburgh, was published in 1787. His visit is also remembered for his liaison with Nancy, Mrs Agnes Maclehose, nicknamed Casandra. On parting Burns wrote and sent her perhaps his best loved poem: '*Ae Fond Kiss and then we sever; ae fareweel and then forever!*'.

A link between Ludwig van Beethoven and Burns has been described by Dr Zachs in the presentation 'Beethoven, Burns and the Folksong [4].

3.10 The Stones of Scotland
Commemorates the Scottish Parliament's rebirth

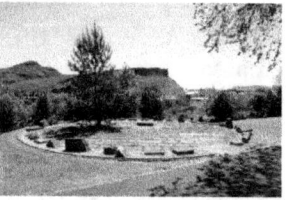

Description: Poetry and a ring of 32 stones from the regions of Scotland
Designed by: George Wyllie
Date: Started 2000, completed 2002

The 'Stones of Scotland' celebrated the restoration of the Scottish Parliament, ushering in a new era in Scottish life. Inspired by Hugh MacDiarmid's poem 'Scotland', George Wyllie developed a memorial embracing all Scotland with a ring of stones from all its regions, and pulsating with moving poetry. The monument overlooks the Scottish Parliament.

'*It requires great love of it deeply to read the configuration of a land.*' With these words Hugh MacDiarmid (see 'Poets', *6.12*) opened his poem 'Scotland', speaking of the deep love needed to understand it. The poem is inscribed in a plaque in front of the ring of 32 stones surrounding a Scots pine.

It requires great love of it deeply to read
The configuration of a land,
Gradually grow conscious of fine shadings,
Of great meanings in slight symbols,
Hear at last the great voice that speaks softly,
See the swell and fall upon the flank
Of a statue carved out in a whole country's marble,
Be like Spring, like a hand in a window
Moving New and Old things carefully to and fro,
Moving a fraction of flower here,
Placing an inch of air there,
And without breaking anything.

So I have gathered unto myself
All the loose ends of Scotland,
And by naming them and accepting them,
Loving them and identifying myself with them,
Attempt to express the whole.

Hugh MacDiarmid (1892–1978)

Beyond the 'stones' (centre-right in the photograph) is the Scottish Parliament. The Royal Palace of Holyrood is just visible through the trees to the left. Behind are Arthur's Seat and Salisbury Crags.

A stone with a footprint is inscribed:
    '*whose the tread that fits this mark?*'.

With those words Tessa Ransford concluded her poem '*Incantation*' written for the memorial. It talks of us stepping forward into a new era, with
    '*a parliament without a throne
    a country each of us can own*'.

Tessa Ransford (1938 – 2015), literary leader, founded the Scottish Poetry Library.

Three plaques

Three plaques conclude this chapter: Saint Wolodymyr of Ukraine (on rock-side to right ascending steps from Regent Road up Calton Hill; three Scottish singers (on Regent Road to east of start of steps); Ukrainian Holodomor (start of path up Calton Hill from north).

Saint Wolodymyr of Ukraine, 956 – 1015
1000 Years of Christianity in Ukraine,1988

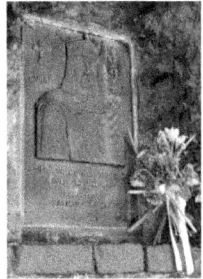

Description: Plaque with image of the Saint
Erected by: Ukrainians living in Scotland   Date: 1988

St Wolodymyr, Vladimir the Great, was Grand Duke of Kieff and ruler of All Russia, the first major Russian ruler to convert to Christianity. He was baptised in 988, before marrying Anna, the sister of Emperor Basil II of Constantinople. His mother, Princess Olga, had been baptised about 30 years earlier, taking the Christian name Helen. He ordered a mass baptism in Kiev in the Dnieper River in 988.

Three 19th century Scottish Singers

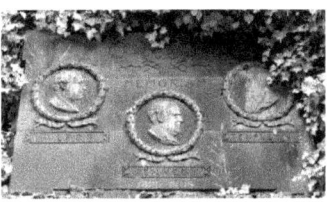

John Wilson (1800 – 1849); John Templeton (1802 – 1886); David Kennedy (1825 – 1886).

John Wilson, Edinburgh born, was aged 10 apprenticed to a printer, working on the Waverley Novels. Taking up music, he joined Duddingston church choir, then becoming precentor at Roxburgh Place and St Mary's church. His tenor voice was much admired. He taught music and sang in concerts and operas in Edinburgh, London and in the USA. Publications include: 'The songs of Scotland' and 'A selection of Psalm tunes'.

Description: Plaque with portraits
Sculptor: William Grant Stevenson
Date: In 1887 Edinburgh Burns Club raised funds for this monument

John Templeton was born in Kilmarnock into a musical family. He became precentor to the Rose Street Secession church in 1822 and then studied music in London. A tenor, he is known for his operatic work, singing in England, Paris, Scotland and the USA.

David Kennedy was born in Perth, his father a weaver and precentor of the Perth United Secession Church. David was apprenticed as a painter and, aged 20, became precentor of the South Kirk in Perth, after which he continued to practice as a painter in Edinburgh, London and Perth. He then became a precentor in Edinburgh, beginning weekly concerts in 1859. Concert tours followed, initially around Scotland and then to London and then across the Atlantic to Canada and the USA. Further tours followed, singing in the UK, South Africa, India, Australia, New Zealand, Canada and the USA.

Ukrainian Holodomor, 1932-33 forced famine

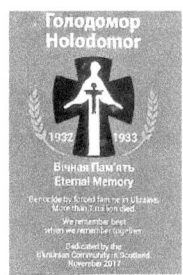

Holodomor is the Ukrainian for 'death by hunger, by starvation'. A severe harvest failure in 1932-33 was exacerbated by harsh food rationing, millions dying (estimates of over 7 million across the Soviet Union). The farm failure has been blamed on Stalin's soviet farm reorganisation policy of collectivisation. Ukraine was particularly badly affected, with the forced removal of peasants from their land which was handed over to state owned enterprises that suffered from poor leadership and management.

The plaque was erected in 2017 by the Ukrainian community in Scotland.

Chapter 4: The Royal Mile,
from Historic Castle to Royal Palace

Volcanic and glacial activity millennia ago shaped Edinburgh's geology. Glaciers gouged out soft sedimentary rock, exposing hard igneous volcanic rock. In Edinburgh's centre they left a crag-tail formation, the crag now called Castle Rock and behind, sloping down eastward, the gouging left a ridge, now called the Royal Mile, with deep valleys to its north and south. The valley to the north became Princes Street gardens (Chapter 1); to the south the valley became the Grassmarket and Cowgate. Before bridges were built north and south across the valleys the city developed down the ridge, seeking protection of fortifications built on Castle Rock. These became Edinburgh Castle whose oldest remaining building is the 12th century chapel built by King David 1 to honour his mother, St Margaret of Scotland, who died in the castle in 1093. But evidence of earlier 3000 year-old Bronze Age habitation has been found.

The city was enclosed: the Nor Loch protected from the north, the Flodden Wall from the south. From the Netherbow Port at the eastern end of the High Street, near where the 'End of the World' pub now stands, the Wall extended south down what is now St Mary's Street and along the southern flank of the city.

External threats and the destruction of the city by the English in the 16th century wars of the Rough Wooing, kept Edinburgh's growth concentrated on the ridge, protected by the Castle. Tall tenements accommodated the growing population, the medieval skyscrapers. Stevenson (*1.11*) wrote that "*houses sprang up, story after story, neighbour mounting upon neighbour's shoulder until the population slept fourteen or fifteen deep in a vertical direction. The tallest of these lands, as they are locally termed, have long since burnt out, but to this day it is not uncommon to see eight or ten windows at a flight.*" [1]

The origin of the name Royal Mile, the popular name for the road from Castle to Palace, is uncertain. Used in W.M. Gilbert's 1901 account of 'Edinburgh in the Nineteenth Century', it echoes back to 'Via Regis', the way of the king, laid out by King David I in the early 12th century. The Royal Mile starts with Castlehill, from the Castle Esplanade; it is followed by, successively, the Lawnmarket, the High Street, the Canongate and finally Abbey Strand.

The Lawnmarket derives its name from its medieval cloth and linen markets. Its shops today are largely aimed at tourists who throng the Royal Mile. Along the Lawnmarket are the late 16th century Riddle's Court, recently restored as the Patrick Geddes Centre (*4.11*), James Court, the Writers Museum and Makars' Court. The photo depicts the gilt-copper hawk, symbol of Gledstane, the 17th century owner of what is now Gladstone's Land restored and owned by the National Trust for Scotland – gled a Scots word for bird of prey.

The High Street continues down the ridge, with Parliament Square and St Giles Cathedral on the south and Edinburgh City Chambers on the north. The 1824 Great Fire of Edinburgh (*4.21*) destroyed the original buildings on the south side from St Giles to the Tron. The Tron Kirk dates from the mid-17th century, ceasing to function as a church in 1952. It was badly damaged in the 1824 fire, its steeple destroyed. A few decades previously it had been remodelled, smaller, to make way for the South Bridge. During the 18th century bridges were built to span the valleys north and south of the ridge. South Bridge spans the southern valley but is barely visible as a bridge, concealed by tall buildings. It leads from the North Bridge (see Chapter 1), together both known as 'The Bridges', crossing the High Street about midway along its length. Down the ridge is John Knox's house, beyond which brass studs in the road mark the former Netherbow Port, the gateway of the Flodden Wall, the eastern end of Edinburgh, the 'End of the World', recalled by the pub there.

Beyond the former Netherbow Port the Royal Mile continues along the Canongate, originally a separate burgh, not part of Edinburgh. It took its name from the road used by the Christian canons of Holyrood Abbey. Notable buildings along it include Moray House, Huntley House and the Canongate Tolbooth (both now museums), the Canongate Kirk and the Scottish Parliament.

Abbey Strand is the short section between Parliament and the Palace of Holyrood. Within the Palace's forecourt is a statue of King Edward VII (*4.26*).

The close living conditions in the crowded ridge proved a fertile environment for the Enlightenment, a period of rich challenging developments in thought, philosophy and ideas. In the pubs and clubs of the crowded closes thinkers and literary figures congregated, sharing writings, debating and discussing, aided by liquid refreshment. Amongst these was the 'Oyster Club' a weekly dining club established by Adam Smith (*4.22*), the chemist Joseph Black and James Hutton (*6.8*) and attended by other intellectuals including John Playfair (*3.2*), Adam Ferguson and David Hume (*4.15*). The social classes mixed, the free exchange of ideas nurturing philosophical and literary discourse. It is fitting that some of the leading thinkers now have statues on the Royal Mile, recently erected.

The peace and prosperity following the crushing of the Jacobite rebellion in 1745 were to change the city from its crowded constricted environment. The increasing pressure to expand into more genteel surroundings led to the New Town. The Old Town declined as the wealthy moved to the New Town, leaving slums, briefly discussed in section (*4.24*, Joseph McIver). Recently, the Old Town has been reclaimed as an attractive place, a restoration emanating from a town planning ethos pioneered by Sir Patrick Geddes (*4.11*).

The Royal Mile, from Castle to Palace, is filled with history, monuments, memorials and memories. Many buildings are monuments in their own right, monuments to those who built them and to those who lived and worked in them. The Royal Mile has two Mercat Crosses, one near St Giles and the other, the Canongate Mercat Cross, at the Canongate Kirk. Neither is technically a monument, so not described in this book. Whilst of interest, John Steell's statue of Alexander the Great and his horse Bucephalus in the courtyard of the City Chambers is a work of art and hence is excluded from this book.

Plaques are excluded, but some are worth a mention. A plaque on the left-hand entrance to the City Chambers commemorates Mary Queen of Scots' last night in Edinburgh 15th June 1567, staying in the Provost's, Sir Simon Preston, house. As the plaque recounts, she was then *conveyed to Holyrood and thereafter to*

Loch Leven Castle as a State Prisoner'.

In Anchor Close a plaque recalls Smellie's Printing House where works of Burns (*3.9*, *5.2*) and the 1st edition of the Encyclopaedia Britannica were printed. The city's intellectual fervour and output led to a publishing boom, the 6 printing houses in 1763, nearly tripling to 16 twenty years later. At the entrance to Carrubers Close a plaque recalls the site where Allan Ramsay (*1.5*) opened a theatre, soon afterwards to be closed by the magistrates.

The site of the last public execution is marked by a plaque on the south-east corner intersection of the Lawnmarket and George IVth Bridge. By the mid-19th century public executions had become less common, the city aspiring to be more civilised. George Bryce, an uneducated man from Ratho to the west of the city, became fond of a fellow servant in the mansion where both worked. Other servants didn't approve, telling the girl to break off the relationship, which she did. George, angered, and believing Jane, another servant, to be responsible, attacked her and cut her throat with a razor. George was soon caught, pleading not guilty by reason of insanity, many testifying to his unsound state of mind. However, the jury found him guilty of murder; he was sentenced to be hung, with the proviso that the execution be as merciful as possible because of his mental frailties. Edinburgh had no professional hangman, hiring hangmen from other cities when required. An executioner from York was hired, but either because of incompetence or drink, failed to carry out the execution efficiently. George took 40 minutes to die, angering the crowd who would have turned on the hangman were it not for the strong police force. The furious City Council decided that future executions would take place within the Calton prison.

The Heart of Midlothian (**B** on Map 4-2 that introduces Part 4.2) marks the doorway of the grim Old Tolbooth jail. It was said that freed prisoners spat on the ground as they left the prison. To this day visitors can be seen spitting on it, most unaware of the origin of the tradition, some believing it to be a sign of good luck. Others associate the heart-shape with the Edinburgh football 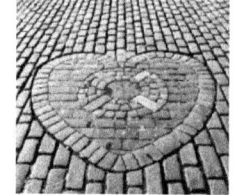 club of that name (see *2.13*). Originally built in 1561 as a customs house for merchants, the Old Tolbooth became the town hall but by the mid-17th century it had become a prison. The building was demolished in 1817.

The turbulent religious quarrels of the 16th to 18th centuries are remembered by a plaque in Jackson's Close describing Jenny Geddes flinging her stool at the head of the minister of St Giles Cathedral as he tried on 23rd July 1637 to introduce Anglican liturgical worship (**F** on Map 4-2). She is reputed to have shouted *'Dost thou say mass at my lug'* as she flung the chair – lug is Scottish for 'ear'.

Sir Chris Hoy (Chapter 1, *1.18*) won two Gold medals at the 2012 Olympics and consequently had two post boxes painted gold in his honour. One is in Hanover Street near its corner with Princes Street (*1.18*). The other is in Hunter's Square, off the High Street and its intersection with South Bridge (**G** on Map 4-2).

Plaques in the Canongate include one to George Chalmers, master plumber, who left money for *'founding a New Infirmary or Sick and Hurt Hospital'*. The legacy resulted in the Chalmers Hospital in Lauriston Place, opening in the mid-19th century, still operational today.

The Canongate was the site for the Playhouse or Canongate Theatre opened in 1747 offering a variety of entertainment. It staged 'Douglas', a tragic Scots play by the Reverend John Home. Disapproval of theatrical performances by the Kirk of Scotland led to closure in 1786. A plaque at the entrance to Old Playhouse Close marks the site.

Nearby on the road is a Maltese cross where in the middle ages the Cross of St John marked the boundary between that part of Edinburgh outwith the city walls and the Canongate and the property of the Order of the Knights of St John.

Further down the Canongate, on the north side on the walls of the Canongate Tolbooth, now the 'People's Story Museum', a tablet honours the memory of the men of the old burgh of Canongate who died in The Great War, 1914 – 1918, listing those who died. The panel bears the historic coat of arms of the Canongate with its white hart and golden cross and the motto '*Sic itur ad astra*' ('thus you shall go to the stars', a quote from Virgil's Aeneid).

Further down the Canongate, on the northern side, are the Scottish Veterans Residences, Scotland's oldest ex-Service charity, founded in 1910 by two soldiers in response to squalid living conditions of some Edinburgh veterans. Premises were acquired in the Canongate thanks to the generosity of Mrs WG McLaren whose sons had died in service. On its 2010 centenary a bas relief sculpture was erected on a garden

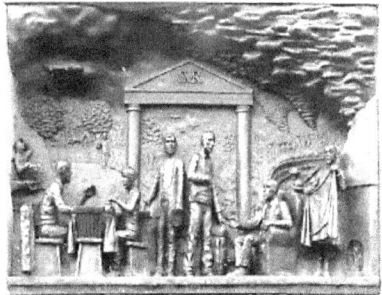

wall along the Canongate (**H** on Map 4-2). It was donated by Angus Pelham Burn, a grandson of one of the founders of the charity.

Part 4.1 – Monuments on Castle Rock

There are many monuments in the Castle and its Esplanade, only a few of which are included here. Not described is the Scottish National War Memorial, commemorating those who lost their lives in the First and Second World Wars and subsequent military campaigns. Also excluded are plaques and memorials on walls, including those on the south side of the Esplanade and monuments within the Castle walls.

Included are the free-standing monuments on the Esplanade's northern edge, the Earl Haig monument now within the Castle, the monument honouring those accused of witchcraft and the statues to Robert the Bruce and William Wallace at the Castle Entrance. The positions are shown on Map 4-1 overleaf.

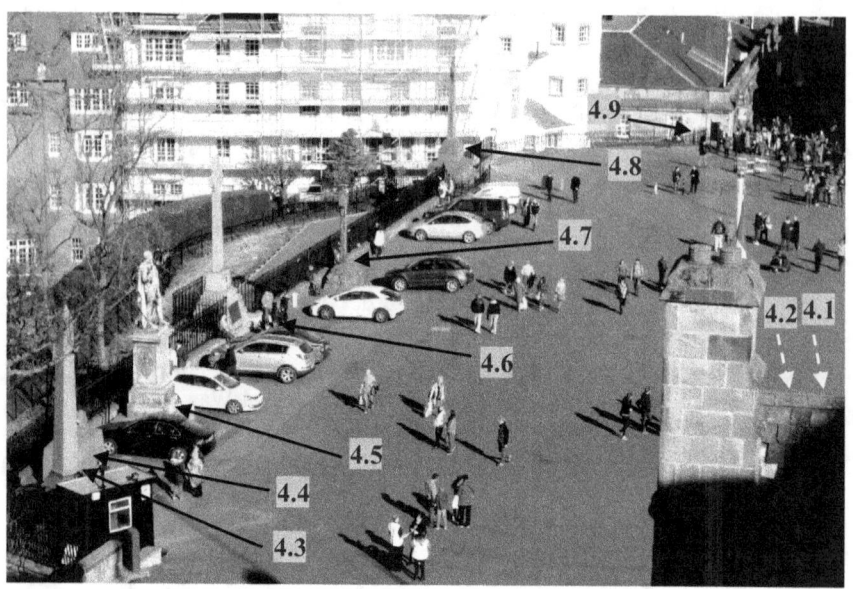

Map 4-1: Monuments on Esplanade's north looking down from the Castle.

4.1	4.2	4.3
Robert the Bruce	**William Wallace**	**Afghan Needle, 72nd Highlanders**

4.4	4.5	4.6	4.7
Ensign Ewart	**Duke of York**	**Scottish Horse**	**Colonel Mackenzie**

4.8	4.9	4.10 Earl Haig
India Cross, 78th Highlanders	**Witches fountain**	**Within Castle**

- Robert the Bruce (*4.1*) and Wallace (*4.2*) are on the castle entrance, not visible in photo of Map 4-1.

- The statue of Earl Haig (*4.10*) was moved from the Esplanade in 2009 to make space available on the esplanade for structural supports for the Tattoo stands. In March 2011 the statue was unveiled in a new location in front of the regimental museum within the Castle walls – position not shown on the photo of Map 4-1.

4.1 King Robert the Bruce, 1274 – 1329
4.2 William Wallace, c1270 – 1305

13th century Scottish leaders for Scottish independence

4.1 King Robert the Bruce

Robert was of noble birth, descended from kings of Scotland, taking the title Earl of Carrick (South Ayrshire). Since the 15th century the title has been given to the heir to the throne. He initially supported Wallace's revolt against Edward 1st of England, but by the start of the 14th century he had submitted to Edward 1st. After his father's death in 1304 he inherited his family's claim to the throne, killing rival John Comyn (for which he was excommunicated by the Pope, but absolved by the Bishop of Glasgow).

In 1306, seizing the throne, Robert was crowned King of Scots at Scone. Initial defeats by Edward's army saw Robert fleeing to the Hebrides and Ireland. Returning in 1307 he defeated an English army at Loudoun Hill (Ayrshire), a victory commemorated by a stone on the hill. Gradually over the next few years he consolidated his power by defeating his Scots enemies. By 1314 he controlled much of Scotland.

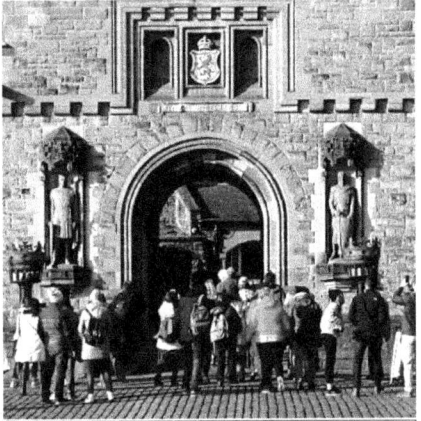

Robert the Bruce   William Wallace
Description: Bronze statues, standing in armour on either side of the entrance to Edinburgh Castle in covered wall niches
Sculptors:
   Bruce   - Thomas John Clapperton;
   Wallace - Alexander Carrick
Origin: To commemorate the 600th anniversary of Robert the Bruce's death.
Bequest: Captain Reid's 19th century bequest to erect monuments to the two heroes of Scottish independence
Date: May 1929, Lord Provost Edinburgh

His celebrated June 1314 victory over Edward II's army at Bannockburn cemented his position as king, but without widespread recognition, Edward still claiming sovereignty over Scotland. In 1320 the nobles submitted the Declaration of Arbroath (see *1.13*, Royal Scots) to Pope John XXII. It asserted Robert as rightful King of the Scots. The Pope's 1324 response recognised his kingship of the independent Scotland. Three years later Edward III renounced all claims to the Scottish throne; the Treaty of Edinburgh-Northampton concluded peace between England and Scotland. The Declaration's 700th anniversary in 2020 gave opportunities to re-explore it and its continuing meaning.

Robert died in June 1329, asking his friend Sir James Douglas to carry his heart to the Holy Land, recognizing he would be unable to fulfil his oath to go there on pilgrimage (see Douglas in *2.10*, Portrait Gallery). His body was buried in Dunfermline Abbey, his removed heart taken by Douglas on crusade to the Holy Land. Douglas was killed in heavy fighting, but his body and Bruce's heart were returned to Scotland, the heart interned in Melrose Abbey.

4.2   William Wallace

William Wallace, son of Sir Malcolm Wallace, had a peaceful early life in Ayrshire, showing physical and intellectual abilities. But his adulthood was not to be peaceful, seeds sown when Edward I, to become his bitter enemy, was crowned King of England when William was 2 years old. Years later, when he was 17, Edward I required the nobles to pledge allegiance; William's father did not, fleeing with his eldest son. William went with his mother to Dundee.

William's anger at the English increased, fuelled by exile from Ayrshire and his father's death by the English. When he killed the son of the Englishman in charge of Dundee castle he was declared an outlaw, sentenced to death. He fled to Ayrshire where he lived in hiding, engaging in intermittent skirmishes. He ambushed an English convoy at Loudon Hill, defeating the English and plundering their goods. William's reputation grew. In 1297 he jointly led the Scots at the Battle of Stirling Bridge, defeating a much stronger English army through clever tactics. He was knighted and proclaimed Guardian of Scotland.

But the following year William's forces were to suffer defeat by the English at Falkirk. Wallace survived, but, resigning the Guardianship, fled, probably attempting to get support from France. By 1304 he was back in Scotland evading the English till August 1305 when he was handed over to the English by a Scottish knight. He was taken to London where Edward I had William, defiant to the end, executed for treason.

4.3   The Afghan Needle to the 72nd Highlanders
Commemorates the Anglo-Afghan war of 1878-1879 and those killed in it

Description: Pink Peterhead granite obelisk
Built by: MacDonald, Field and Co;   Date: 1882

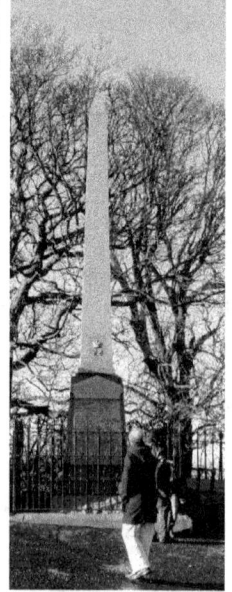

Known as the Afghan Needle, it commemorates those who died in the 19th century Afghanistan campaign. The regiment won four battle honours in the campaign. It played a decisive role in the final battle, having marched 320 miles from Kabul before defeating Afghan forces at Kandahar.

The war was caused by the Afghans refusal to allow a British embassy to open in Kabul, despite opening a Russian embassy.

The regiment saw action early in the campaign leading to the short-lived establishment of a British embassy in Kabul. A fierce campaign, it cost many lives from fighting and disease, the names on a plaque on the obelisk's base. Lance Corporal Sellar was awarded the VC for valour fighting in the hills outside Kabul.

72 On the obelisk refers to the regiment, the 72nd.

The regiment was formed in 1778, raised with a corps of 1,130 men by the 'Earl of Seaforth' in gratitude for the restoration of his title previously forfeited because of the family's involvement in the 1715 Jacobite Rebellion. But a few months later, whilst in Edinburgh preparing to leave for the East Indies, the regiment mutinied, demanding better conditions. They marched to the top of Arthur's seat and were fed by sympathetic locals till their demands were met.

Initially called the 78th Highland Regiment of Foot, it became the 72nd (Highland) Regiment of Foot in 1786 following army re-organisation. It took the name of the Duke of Albany's Own Highlanders in the 1820's from Prince Frederick (Duke of York and Albany, see *4.5*), incorporating his coronet in its badge. It amalgamated with the 78th Highlanders in 1881 as the 1st Battalion Seaforth Highlanders. 19th Century service included the Channel Islands, Ireland, South Africa, Gibraltar, Canada, India and Afghanistan.

4.4   Ensign Charles Ewart, 1769 – 1846
Captured the Eagle of the 45th French regiment at Waterloo

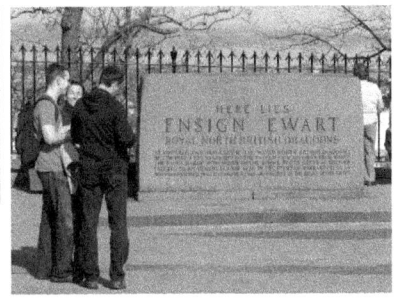

Description: Swedish granite tombstone
Sculptor: William Kininmonth
Erected by: The officers, non-commissioned officers and men past and present of the Royal Scots Greys
Date: April 1938

Charles Ewart is remembered for capturing the French standard at the Battle of Waterloo. With his regiment he had charged forward to break up the French columns. During the close-quarter fighting Sergeant Ewart found himself near the standard-bearer of the French '45th Regiment of the Line' and he seized the standard with its Eagle.

The capture of the Eagle brought Ewart fame and he was awarded a commission as an Ensign (Lieutenant). The regiment adapted the eagle as part of its cap badge. The Eagle is in the regimental museum at Edinburgh Castle.

Born near Kilmarnock in Ayrshire, Charles Ewart enlisted in the armed services aged 20, serving in the French Revolutionary wars during which he was briefly taken prisoner. Promoted to Sergeant he was a tall strong soldier, serving in the Royal North British Dragoons, more commonly known as the Scots Greys.

After the wars he moved to England, dying in Salford in 1843 where he was initially buried. In the 1930's his body was moved to Edinburgh and reburied on the esplanade of the Castle marked by the monument.

On the north side of the Lawnmarket in the upper part of the Royal Mile is the Ensign Ewart pub. The regiment's campaign in the Anglo-Boer War is commemorated by the mounted horse in west Princes Street gardens (*1.4*).

4.5 Frederick, Duke of York and Albany, 1763-1827
Commander in Chief of the British Army

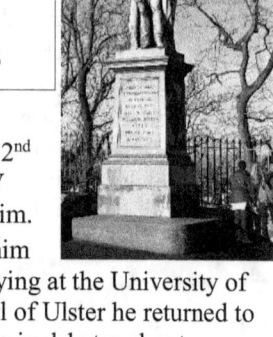

Description: The Order of the Garter on his left leg, the duke wears Knight Grand Cross of the Bath insignia. His Field Marshall's baton is that of the Commander in Chief of the British Army. (Bronze)
Sculptor: John Greenshields;   Date: 1836

Prince Frederick, 2nd son of George III and Queen Charlotte, had the title 'Duke of York and Albany' as 2nd in line to throne. (His elder brother became George IV (*2.4*)). Frederick Street in New Town is named after him.

His father selected a military career for him, making him a Colonel at 17. He lived in Hanover for 6 years, studying at the University of Göttingen. Created Duke of York and Albany and Earl of Ulster he returned to Britain, taking his seat in the House of Lords, speaking in debates about preserving government during the king's mental illness. Promoted to full General in 1793 he commanded a British force in Flanders, winning some engagements, but suffering defeats. Promoted to Field Marshall, he took part in the Anglo-Russian invasion of Holland in 1799, but he was forced to withdraw from an unsuccessful military campaign

It has been suggested that this led to him being mocked in the rhyme '*The Grand Old Duke of York*'; the Duke marching ten thousand men to the top of the hill and marching them down again. However, other dukes and kings have been associated with the rhyme including Richard, Duke of York, defeated in the 15th century Wars of the Roses between York (white rose) and Lancaster (red rose).

His experience in these campaigns highlighted to Frederick the many weaknesses of the British army. He used his position as Commander-in-Chief of the British Army to carry out a programme of reform. He helped create the Royal Military Academy at Sandhurst to professionally train officers. These reforms helped create a stronger more effective British Army. Through these reforms it was said that he did more for the British Army than anyone previously. For this he was credited of building an army capable of being successful in the Napoleonic Wars.

He continued administrative work for the Army, but excessive gambling left him in debt. Dying in 1827 he was buried in St George's Chapel at Windsor Castle.

4.6 Scottish Horse
Commemorates those dying in Anglo-Boer war, 1899-1902

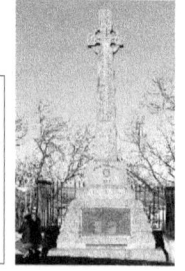

Description: Celtic cross in Peterhead pink granite decorated with detailed scrollwork and a sword. A shield with lion rampant has the motto 'Nemo me Impune Lacessit' (no one provokes me with impunity), the St Andrews Cross and the date, 1900, the year the regiment was raised. A bronze plaque lists those who died.
Built by: Stewart McGlashan and Son.   Date: 1905

The pink granite Celtic Cross was erected to honour the officers and men of the Scottish Horse who died during the Anglo-Boer War. It lists those who died in action and those who died from accident or disease.

The Scottish Horse, comprising two regiments, was raised in South Africa for service in the Anglo-Boer war where it saw distinguished service. It was disbanded in 1902 after the end of the Anglo-Boer, but later that year was reconstituted by the Duke of Atholl, serving in World War I and World War II. The regiment now forms part of the Queen's Own Yeomanry and the Duke of Connaught's Squadron Army Air Corp (AAC), a helicopter support squadron made up of volunteers.

4.7 Colonel Kenneth Mackenzie, 1811 – 1873
Soldier and leader

Description: Dark stone engraved cross on rocky plinth
Sculptor: Sir John Steell
Date: 1875. in affectionate remembrance by his friends

Kenneth Douglas Mackenzie was born in Dundee in 1811, dying on duty in Dartmoor in 1873. He served in the 92nd Highlanders, the Gordon Highlanders. He was the regimental quartermaster for many years, ensuring that the regiment was well provisioned with supplies.

The inscription honours a leader greatly admired: '*In memory of Colonel Kenneth Douglas Mackenzie, C.B. who served for forty two years in the 92nd Highlanders and on the Staff of the Army in all parts of the world. He saw much service in the field and deserved well of his country, both in war and in peace. Active, frank and loyal, he won the confidence of his superiors, the respect of those under him and the love of all who knew him.*'

He served in many parts of the world including Crimea, India and China. His lifelong motto was: '*Godliness with contentment is great gain.*'

4.8 The India Cross to the 78th Highlanders
Commemorates the 78th Highlanders who died during the Indian Mutiny of 1857-1858

A Celtic cross, it commemorates those who died in the Indian mutiny of 1857 to 1858. It is inscribed:
'*Sacred to the memory of the officers, non-commissioned officers and private soldiers of the 78th Highland Regiment who fell in the suppression of the mutiny of the native army of India in the years 1857 and 1858.*
This memorial is erected as a tribute of respect by their surviving brother officers and comrades and by many officers who formerly belonged to the regiment.'

The regiment recaptured the town of Cawnpore and the subsequent relief of the British garrison at Lucknow following the Indian Mutiny. Their gallantry earned 8 men of the regiment the Victoria Cross, also awarded to the regiment itself.

The 'mutiny', alternatively called the 'War of Independence' in India, had many causes, including the lack of respect shown by the East India Company to the Indian people. The East India Company, originally formed as a trading company, ruled India on behalf of the British government. The campaign was brutal on both sides, leading to shock in Britain. It showed that a change in administering India was required. Britain replaced the East India Company's rule by direct British rule under a Governor General who was given the title Viceroy of India. Later, in 1877, Queen Victoria (*1.16, 5.1*) was given the title of Empress of India.

The regiment was raised in the late 18th century by Francis Mackenzie, chief of the Clan Mackenzie, for service against the French. The regiment was to see service in many parts of the world including the Napoleonic Wars, Canada, India and South Africa. In 1881 the regiment amalgamated with the 72nd Highlanders as the 2nd Battalion Seaforth Highlanders.

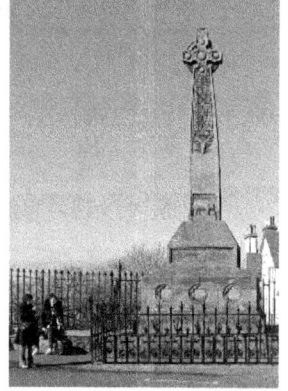

The regiment's elephant badge was granted after the 1803 Indian Battle of Assaye. 30 Years later they brought an elephant back to Edinburgh. Staying at the Castle, the elephant led parades, drank beer and slept in the stables.

Description: 27ft high sandstone Celtic Cross with stag's head and Indian elephant
Designed by: Robert Rowand Anderson
Built by: S. Hunter (carvings) and Messrs Sutherland
Date: April 1862

4.9   The Witches Fountain

Commemorates and reminds us of the women accused of witchcraft and brutally killed on Castlehill

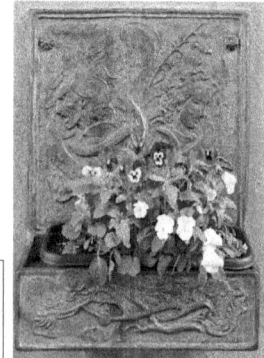

To honour the 300 women tied to the stake, strangled and burnt on Castlehill between 1492 and 1722.

The design highlights good and evil, remembering the innocent women wrongly condemned.

Description: Engraved drinking fountain with flower pot
Designed by: John Duncan, 1894, who was commissioned by Patrick Geddes (*4.11*). Erected 1912

The serene head of Hygeia, goddess of health, contrasts with the wicked head. The serpent, symbol of Aesculapius, god of medicine, has dual symbolism of good and evil, as does the foxglove. The Evil Eye is counteracted by the Hands of Healing.

4.10 Field Marshall Douglas Haig, 1st Earl Haig, 1861 – 1928
Military Commander World War I

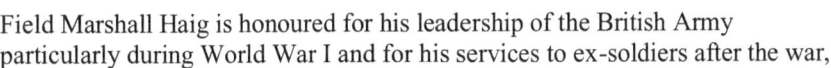

Description: Earl Haig in military uniform on horse. Bronze on stone pedestal
Sculptor: George Edward Wade
Date: 1923 on the Castle Esplanade. Transferred to the Hospital Square within Edinburgh Castle in 2011

The statue is inscribed:

'This statue was presented to the City of Edinburgh by Sir Dhumjibhoy Bomanji of Bombay in admiration of the services rendered to the British Empire by the Field Marshall.'

Field Marshall Haig is honoured for his leadership of the British Army particularly during World War I and for his services to ex-soldiers after the war,

Douglas Haig was born in Hope Street, off Charlotte Square, Edinburgh. His father, head of Haig and Haig whisky distillery, was an alcoholic. Douglas attended Clifton College. Both his parents died before he was 18. With his brother he toured the USA before studying at Oxford where he enjoyed the social life and excelled as a horse rider. Military training at Sandhurst followed, Haig finishing first in the order of merit.

Commissioned as a lieutenant in 1885 he served in India, where he was known as a disciplinarian. His excellent administrative skills were recognized, as was his meticulous analysis of training exercises. Various other posts followed and then further training at the army Staff College where the tactical training that he was taught probably influenced his later leadership in World War I battles.

Haig then distinguished himself by his service in the Sudan and later in the Anglo-Boer War in South Africa where he escorted the Boer leader General Jan Christiaan Smuts to the peace negotiations. (General Smuts went on to lead South Africa's war effort in both World War I and World War II, allied to Britain against Germany. This led to Smuts' unique position as the only person to sign the peace treaties after both the 1st and 2nd World Wars.)

Mentioned in dispatches, Haig was appointed a Commander of the Order of the Bath and promoted to lieutenant colonel. Returning to Britain he spent a year in Edinburgh before serving again in India.

Haig was promoted to major general in 1904. He married Dorothy Maud Vivian in 1905 whilst on home leave from India and they had 4 children. He returned to Britain in 1906 as Director of Military Training and helped reform the British

Army, shown to be necessary by the experiences of the Anglo-Boer War. He continued to serve at the War Office before returning to India for a few years.

When World War I started Haig had been back in Britain for nearly 3 years. Some predicted a short war, but Haig envisaged a lengthy bitter campaign, with Britain and Germany fighting for their very existence. This led him to argue that a large army was required to withstand against the German forces.

His World War I service began in August 1914, leading an army Corp to support the French. By the end of 1915 Haig was Commander in Chief of the British Expeditionary Force in Europe. He was appointed Field Marshal on 1st January 1917. World War I was long and hard, with enormous casualties – evidenced to this day in war memorials across Britain. Significant battles included the Battle of the Somme (July to November 1916) in which over a million were wounded or killed and the final Hundred Days Offensive in 1918 which led to the German surrender. The total number of casualties, military and civilian, is estimated at over 40 million, with an estimated 15 to 19 million of those killed.

After the war Haig was initially praised for his leadership, in honour of which he was created 1st Earl Haig in 1919. Later, historians were to be critical of the huge loss of life in the war, blaming this on Haig.

Horrified by the plight of many former soldiers, unemployed, homeless and facing poverty, Haig campaigned after the war for state aid for demobilised soldiers. Retiring in 1920 he devoted the rest of his life to the welfare of ex-servicemen. All, whatever their rank, should be eligible to join The Royal British Legion, founded in 1921. He helped set up the Haig Fund and Haig Homes to support and house ex-servicemen. Learning of French widows making and selling silk poppies to support their ex-serviceman, he and his wife, Lady Haig, built on the idea, developing it and started poppy-making factories. The poppy, inspired by Lt Colonel John McCrae's poem 'In Flanders Field', remains the powerful symbol of remembrance of the continuing sacrifice by members of the armed forces. Recognizing this, and the fund raising of the annual poppy appeals, the Floral Clock in 2018 (*1.6*) honoured Poppy Scotland as it remembered the centenary of the end of World War I.

During retirement Haig enjoyed golf, captaining the Royal and Ancient Golf Club in St Andrews for whose University he served as Lord Rector and later Chancellor.

He died of a heart attack in 1928, aged 66, honoured in a funeral that started in Westminster Abbey, London, after which his body was escorted to Edinburgh where it lay in state in St Giles Cathedral for 3 days. He was then buried at Dryburgh Abbey in the Scottish Borders with a simple standard Commonwealth War Graves Commission headstone.

Early in the 21st century, the Haig monument was moved, from the Castle Esplanade to a site in front of the Castle Hospital. This enabled improvements in erecting scaffolding for the seating, on the Esplanade, of the Military Tattoo and other events.

Part 4.2 - Along the Royal Mile, from Castle to Palace

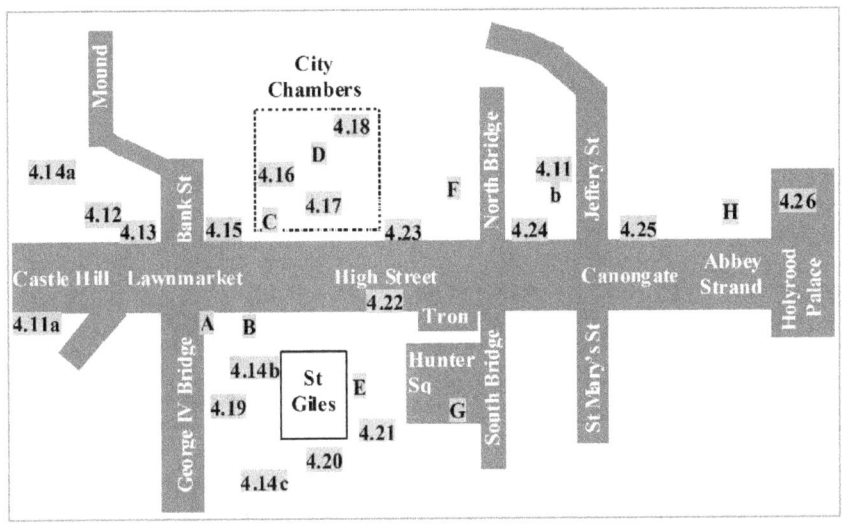

Map 4-2: Monuments of the Royal Mile.

4.11	4.12	4.13	4.14
Sir Patrick Geddes	Susannah Alice Stephen	Makars' Court	John Knox

4.15	4.16	4.17	4.18
David Hume	Edinburgh Award	Stone of Remembrance	General Maczek

4.19	4.20	4.21	4.22
Buccleuch & Queensberry	Charles II	James Braidwood	Adam Smith

4.23	4.24	4.25	4.26
Dr Elsie Inglis	Joseph McIver	Robert Fergusson	Edward VII

Notes:
- Very approximate positions of the monuments around St Giles are shown
- Sir Patrick Geddes:
  4.11a   plaques of Geddes Heritage Trail in Royal Mile, shown on Castlehill;
  4.11b   bust on beehive, Trunks Close in Sandeman house
- John Knox
  4.14a   Statue in the forecourt of the Assembly Hall on the Mound
  4.14b   Statuette on the outside wall of St Giles Cathedral, to left of entrance
  4.14c   A pavement slab marking the grave of John Knox is in the car park to the south of St Giles Cathedral, to the west of the statue of Charles II.

Some Royal Mile wall plaques and noticeable landmarks
(for descriptions see the introductory pages of this chapter)

A	B	C	D
Wall plaque Last Public Execution	Heart of Midlothian	Wall plaque Mary Queen of Scots	Alexander & Bucephalus

E	F	G	H
Edinburgh Mercat Cross	Wall plaque Jenny Geddes (in Jackson Close)	Gold Post Box Sir Chris Hoy (in Hunter Square)	Centenary Scottish Veterans Residence

4.11 Sir Patrick Geddes, 1854 – 1932
Thinker, visionary, polymath,
Father of modern town planning

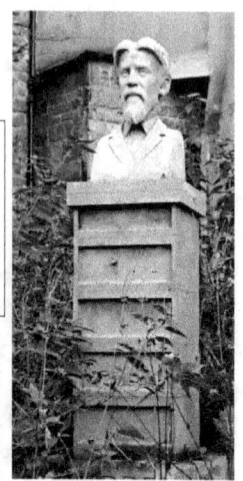

Description: Bust of Geddes on beehive. Bees on hive & bust.
Sculptor: Kenny Hunter
Unveiled: Sept 2012
Location: Sandeman House Garden, Trunks Close, High Street
Visible from north window of Scottish Story Telling Centre.
Entrance to Close is west of John Knox house

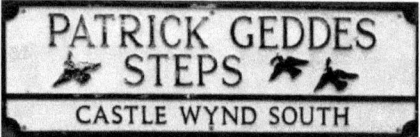

PATRICK GEDDES
STEPS
CASTLE WYND SOUTH

Three doves on steps named in his honour

Patrick Geddes, encouraged by his parents, gained an appreciation of nature from his youth in Perthshire. He developed a holistic view of people living in harmony within and interacting with their environment, symbolised by three doves: Sympathy – people and environment; Synthesis – bringing all together; Synergy – working together, combining energy.

His philosophy was also described by the synergy of Heart (vision, ideas), Head/Mind (analytical, learning) and Hands (practical, manual).

He had an enquiring mind, exploring ideas. He emphasized the importance of continuing learning, the university-of-life, as important as formal education:
'by living we learn',

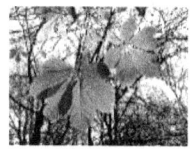 Urban environments require green spaces, light. This guided his approach to urban regeneration, removing decaying building to let in the light into structures worth saving – conservative surgery. It also led he and his daughter Norah to create gardens in the opened places for children to explore and enjoy, some still cared for today. The hive and bees on his memorial illustrate the importance he placed on nature. He saw in nature the basis of life:
'by leaves we live'.

Cities need green spaces for well-being. To create gardens he sought gap-spaces released by the constructive surgery of old decaying buildings. Several gardens developed by Geddes, his wife and daughter Norah continue to green the city, for example the West Port Garden, supported by volunteers

A polymath, Geddes advocated combining people's diverse skills and talents. Specialisation blinds people: he warned against seizing only *'upon one petal of the six-lobed flower of life'* [2], tearing it apart from the whole flower, denying the whole. Taking a holistic view, corporately and individually in sympathy with our environment, synthesising all together, working together, combining energy, each benefiting from the resultant synergy. The need to think holistically, globally, does not deny detailed focussed action:
'think global, act local'.

The technological developments and industrialisation of the late 19th century saw people flocking to cities, increasing urban populations and changing its environment. In Edinburgh's Old Town he found slum conditions, blighted by poor housing, the wealthy having moved to the New Town. Believing in urban renewal that harmonised the urban landscape with peoples' needs, he and his wife Anna Morton purchased slum tenements in James Court. Rather than tearing them down, they embarked upon a process of 'conservative surgery' restoring the best houses and weeding out the worst. Narrow closes were widened, bringing in light and air. Fellow occupants of the tenement were encouraged to clean and improve their properties.

Urban planning, he argued, should consider the inherent values of the urban space, and its relationships with the people living in it. These are as important as the technicalities of design. Gardens and green spaces are vital parts of urban spaces. Its geography, climate, economic life and social institutions should contribute to its design. His pioneering town planning concepts are recognized in his title: *'Father of modern town planning'*.

To encourage people to understand the urban environment Geddes developed the Outlook Tower on Castle Hill. Its origin was the popular 'Short's Observatory' that had been established on Castle Hill by the pioneer Maria Theresa Short with a camera obscura in the topmost room. Maria Short had died in 1869 and Patrick Geddes purchased the building in 1892, building on Short's ideas with a museum, renaming it the Outlook Tower. Through this Geddes sought to demonstrate urban planning, utilising the camera obscura to enable the public to view their local environment. It is still a museum and outlook tower.

His influence on urban planning spread beyond Edinburgh, throughout the UK and further afield with the American town planner Lewis Mumford regarding Geddes as a *'global thinker in practice'*. He was asked to draw up plans for Jerusalem and for Tel Aviv. Asked to improve urban planning in India, he sought to improve the urban environment to harmonize the people's traditions and social and religious practices. Town planning should preserve human life and energy, rather than focus on superficial beautification.

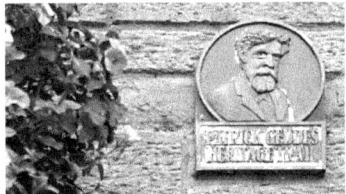

Patrick Geddes Heritage Trail plaque, Old Town
The Patrick Geddes Heritage Trail through the Old Town celebrates his urban renewal work. There is also a Patrick Geddes Garden Tour of the Old Town.

Riddles Court, where he founded university teaching facilities and accommodation, has been converted into 'The Patrick Geddes Centre for Learning and Conservation' recognizing Geddes's ethos: *'Vivendo Discimus'* (*By Living We Learn*).

Patrick Geddes was born in Aberdeenshire, a soldier's son, the family then moving to Perthshire where he grew up. He often found academic study unsatisfactory, for example leaving Edinburgh University after a week. He studied botany and zoology from private tutors, and, without completing a degree, became a demonstrator in the Physiology department at University College London. He travelled to Mexico to collect biological specimens, but an eye infection forced his return. Based at the Royal Botanic Gardens he became an assistant in practical botany at Edinburgh University. Later he was to benefit from the income from a part-time Chair of Botany at University College Dundee. The Geddes Institute for Urban Research at the University of Dundee is named in his honour. He was given the Chair of Sociology at the University of Bombay. Geddes was keen to revive academic links between Scotland and France, recalling its long historical alliances. He lived in Montpellier, France, for 10 years, establishing a Scots college, the Patrick Geddes Collège des Ecossais. It was restored in 2004 to mark the 150th anniversary of his birth.

He was knighted in 1832, dying later that year.

4.12 Susannah Alice Stephen, 1960 – 1997
Landscape Architect

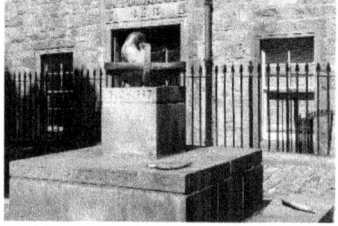

Description: Parakeet with in its beak a garden trug (basket for flowers and vegetables) mounted on Morayshire sandstone ziggurat plinth. Bronze leaves indicate her garden landscape interest.
Sculptor: Frances Pelly   Date: Sept 2000
Location: James Court

The plinth is inscribed with her name, years of birth and death, and a verse:
Keep your face towards the sun and the shadows will fall behind you

Susannah Alice (Zannah) Stephen was a landscape artist and keen explorer who helped establish the Scottish Society of Garden Designers. She was influenced by Patrick Geddes (*4.11*) whose approach guided her interest in incorporating green spaces into urban town planning.

Her friends erected her memorial in James Court, a site with links to her interests and family: Geddes had lived in James Court; the family link to the site was serendipitous, discovered during the application for planning approval process. Behind and to the north of the monument is the rear entrance to the Free Church of Scotland which has a portrait of one of her forbears, Alexander Moncrieff. He was one of the leaders of the 1733 first major secession from the Church of Scotland, arguing for purity of church doctrine.

She was born in Renfrewshire in 1960, graduating with a modern languages degree from St Andrews. A year's backpacking followed initial work in Glasgow and London, after which she studied Landscape Architecture at Edinburgh University. This led her to set up business as a Landscape Architect. She died in a diving accident in the Galapagos Islands in 1997.

4.13 Makars' Court: Inscribed pavement slabs
National literary monument celebrating writers

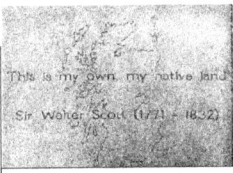

Description: Quote on pavement slab. Design: Carter McGlynn, Landscape Architects Date: PEN's International Conference (Poets, Essayists, Novelist) was held in Edinburgh in 1997, its president unveiling the first slab (14th century poet John Barbour). A further 11 were unveiled in 1998 by Iain Crichton Smith (see *6.12*, Twelve Poets). More continue to be added.

"This is my own, my native land."
Sir Walter Scott

Makar is a poet or author, skilled in the craft of writing. Outside the Writers' Museum, this literary monument consists of stone slabs inscribed with quotes from Scottish authors, celebrating their work and acknowledging Edinburgh as a UNESCO City of Literature. To be included, authors must have been born, lived or worked in Scotland, their work of literary merit and have died.

The Writers Museum itself focuses on three writers, Burns (*3.9*), Scott (*1.21*) and Stevenson (*1.11*). Each is depicted on its northern wall in a panel designed and sculpted by Kathleen Gibson and Tim Chalk.

John Barbour's '*Fredome is a noble thing*' is the oldest quote. It is from his 1375 poem '*The Brus*' (Robert the Bruce) about the wars of independence and the 1314 Battle of Bannockburn. John Barbour's statue is on the National Portrait Gallery (*2.10*). Lachlan Mor MacMhuirich in 1411 was also to write of war, encouraging the '*Children of Conn to remember hardihood in battle*' (translation of '*A Chlanna Cuinn cuimhnichibh, Cruas an àm na h-iorghaile*'). The MacMhuirichs were, for over 700 years, professional poets to the Lord of the Isles and other prominent highland clans. In the poem 'Incitement to Battle' Lachlan inspires the army of the Lord of Isles to victory against the Earl of Mar.

But not all the quotes encourage war: '*Weird hou men maun aye be makin war insteid o things they need*' (Tom Scott in the 1975 poem '*Brand the Builder*'). Sir David Lyndsay argued for the need of literature, writing in 1554 '*Lat us haif the bukis necessare to common weill*' (*Let us have the books necessary for our common good*). His statue is on the exterior of the National Portrait Gallery (*2.10*). The 15th century poet and schoolmaster Robert Henryson encouraged us to live a simple life: '*Blissed be sempill lyfe withoutin dreid*'.

George Buchanan in the 16th century wrote of the sovereignty of the people: '*Populo enim jus est ut imperium cui velit deferat*' (*For it is right that the people confer power on whom they please*) – for statue and further information see also *2.10*, National Portrait Gallery. Robert Burns in 1785 recognised that all are equal: '*that man to man the world o'er shall brithers be for a'that*'. Naomi Mitchison (Twelve Poets, *6.12*) echoes this theme in '*Early in Orcadia*': '*Go back far enough and all humankind are cousins*'.

(Anna) Nan Shepherd in '*The Quarry Wood*' encourages us to give ourselves permission to live life fully: '*It's a grand thing to get leave to live*'. Helen Cruickshank reminds us of the resilience of the human spirit: '*the spirit endures for ever*'. James King Annand calls us to be joyful: '*Sing it aince for pleasure,* sing it twice for joy'.

Robert McLellan in 1947 in 'The Carlin Moth' wrote of the unique power of humans: 'The pouer to big a braw warld in his brain marks man the only craitur that can greit'. Yet Neil Gunn in the 'The Green Isle of the Great Deep' in 1944 advised caution: 'Knowledge is high in the head ... but the salmon of wisdom swims deep'.

Quotes tell of love for Scotland, as that by Sir Walter Scott in the picture above and Nigel Tranter in the late 20th century writing: 'You intend to bide here? To be sure. Can you think of anywhere better?' Fionn MacColla (pen-name of Thomas Macdonald) wrote in 1932 of being a Scot in 'The Albannach': 'the land of the people of my blood – my fathers of the thousands of years, over the face of the world my roots in the soil of Alba' (the final part of this phrase, underlined, is inscribed on a slab). James Boswell recalls in his London Journal of 1762 his feelings of pleasure as he left for London after a visit to Edinburgh: 'I rattled down the High Street in high elevation of spirits'. Robert Garioch wrote of fun in Edinburgh ('Embro to the ploy', 1977): 'in simmer whan aa sorts forgether in Embro to the ploy'.

What we now think of as 'New' will become 'Old'. An inscription proclaims this: 'And yet – yet, this New Road will some day be the Old Road, too', Neil Munro writing in 'The New Road', 1914. 'The New Road' is a historical novel set in 1733, the title referring to General Wade's military roads constructed in the Highlands to control the country after the Jacobite uprising of 1715. (Amongst Munro's other works is a poem, 'Lament for the Lads', a verse from it inscribed on the Celtic Cross of the Scottish War Poets Corner – see below.)

We are encouraged to improve the world we leave behind. John Buchan in 1937 wrote: 'We can only repay our debt to the past by putting the future in debt to us'. John Muir, famous conservationist, wrote: 'I care to live only to entice people to look at Nature's loveliness'.

How do we guide ourselves through life? George Campbell Hay on a slab inscribed in April 2017suggests in Scots and in Gaelic we listen to our hearts and heads: in Scots "The hert's the compass tae the place that ye wad gae whan land ye lea"; in Gaelic "Cha chuir ceann is cridh' air iomrall thu, Bi iomlan is bi beò" (head and heart will not lead you astray, be complete and alive).

Language and the art of writing uses words, weaving words wonderfully. (Is this what 'www' really means?) W.S. Graham (see *6.12* 'Twelve Poets') explored the use of words and challenges us in the pavement slab inscribed in 2018: 'What is the language using us for'.

Each time I visit I am struck by different quotes. To conclude with the words of Dorothy Dunnett: 'Where are the links of the chain joining us to the past?' Do monuments serve as links?

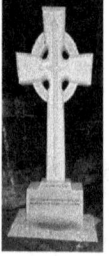

The Makars' Court's remit was extended in late 2018 when a granite Celtic Cross was unveiled to remember

Scottish War Poets Corner
Description: granite Celtic Cross. Within the cross is a sword, its tip shaped as a pen nib.
Unveiled: 23rd Nov 2018 by Lord Provost

Scotland's War Poets. On its base at the front is inscribed words from Neil Munro's 'Lament for the Lads': '*Sweet be their sleep now wherever they're lying, far though they be from the hills of their home*', chosen by a public poll organized by the Scottish Poetry Library. Neil Munro was a war correspondent during World War 1, his son killed in action in 1915. On the rear, across the cross, is inscribed: "*their words touched us more than conflict could hurt us*".

Edinburgh instituted its Makar in 2002, part of its bid to be first UNESCO City of Literature, achieved in 2004. The first was Stewart Conn (2002-2005) then Valerie Gillies (2005-2008), Ron Butlin (2008-2014), Christine De Luca (2014-2017), Alan Spence (2018-2021), the current being Hannah Lavery.
(The Edinburgh Makar should not be confused with the Scots Makar, created in 2004 by the Scottish Parliament. Scots Makars: Edwin Morgan, (2004), Liz Lochhead (2011-16); Jackie Kay (2016-21); Kathleen Jamie (2021-2026). See Edinburgh Park Poets – *6.12*.)

4.14 John Knox, c1513 – 1572
Leader of the Scottish Reformation

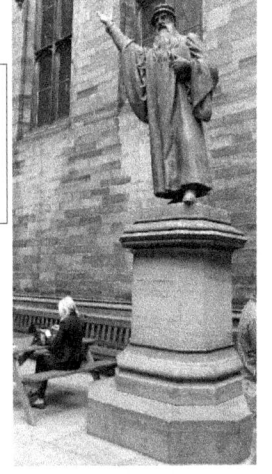

Description: John Knox standing, preaching.
Inscribed: 'Erected by Scotsmen who are mindful of the benefits conferred by John Knox on their native land'
Sculptor: John Hutchison   Date: 1896
Location: New College, top of the Mound

John Knox was the powerful passionate Scottish religious reform leader, fiercely opposing the Roman Catholic Church and establishing the dominance of the protestant Church of Scotland.

He was born near Haddington in East Lothian, the son of a merchant. Early records of his life are vague, but he is described as a priest in 1540 and 1543, the later in St Andrews. He tutored the sons of two lairds in East Lothian. It is not clear when he became Protestant, but he would have been aware of the movement's growth in continental Europe. He knew of George Wishart who fled Scotland in 1538 after accusations of heresy. On Wishart's return Knox became his bodyguard and was involved in the clash with Cardinal Beaton who had Wishart burnt at the stake. (See *2.10*, Beaton's statue on Portrait Gallery.) Wishart's followers then killed Beaton in his St Andrews Castle. A year later Knox came to St Andrews Castle, invited to be pastor, preaching Protestantism, the Bible as the sole authority and justification by faith. He denounced the Pope as the Antichrist and rejected the service of Mass. However a French naval force, following a request from the Scottish court, besieged the castle. The garrison surrendered; Knox was taken prisoner and as a galley slave forced to row the ship back to France.

Released after 19 months, he initially moved to England where Protestantism was tolerated, serving as a priest in Berwick-upon-Tweed and then Newcastle.

John N. Amoore

In Durham he met and married Margery Bowes. Knox made influential contacts and was offered a bishopric but refused. He was ordered to serve in London.

Knox did not tolerate religious practices he considered idolatrous, for example kneeling during communion. A compromise was reached based on a statement that the act of kneeling does not imply adoration.

> Description: John Knox (right). One of many statues at the west door of St Giles Cathedral. Installed during late 19th century restoration of the cathedral.
> On left of Knox is Gavin Douglas, Provost of St Giles in early 16th century.
> Sculptor: John Rhind   Date: 1884
> There is also a statue of Knox inside St Giles.

When Mary Tudor became Queen and Roman Catholicism was re-established in England Knox, on advice from his friends, fled to Europe, firstly to Geneva. There he met and admired Calvin. He briefly ministered to English exiles in Frankfurt and, after a short visit to Scotland, returned with his wife to Geneva to be a church minister. He worked tirelessly, preaching 3 two-hour sermons a week. He denounced the rule of Queens in his pamphlet: '*The first blast of the trumpet against the monstrous regiment of women*'.

Knox returned to Scotland in 1559. He was installed as minister at St Giles, preaching a historic sermon that fermented the reformation movement. Continuing hostilities between Protestants and Catholics culminated in the Scottish Parliament approving a protestant Scots Confession, abolishing the jurisdiction of the Pope and forbidding the celebration of Mass. Knox and his friends were given the task of organising the new Kirk based on principles described in 'The Book of Discipline'. It called for congregations to choose their own pastor, with bishops replaced by superintendents. However it was not approved by Parliament due to financial concerns.

When Mary Queen of Scots ascended the throne and insisted on attending Mass hostilities between her and Knox broke out. Knox denounced Catholic practices from the pulpit at St Giles. He was instrumental in her abdication and went on to preach at James VI's coronation.

Legend suggests that he briefly lived in what is now known as John Knox House on the north side of the High Street. He died surrounded by his friends and some of the leading Scottish nobles, his young wife (whom he had married 8 years previously) reading from Paul's 1st letter to the Corinthians.

Knox was buried in St Giles kirk-yard. It is now the car park, his burial place marked by a ground plaque to the west of the statue of Charles II. It has been suggested that later work on the car park unearthed many graves, with the bones reburied in Greyfriars Kirk where the bones of John Knox may now be buried in an unmarked area.

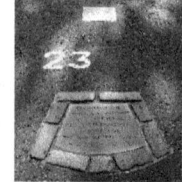

4.15 David Hume, 1711 – 1776
Philosopher, historian, leading figure of Scottish Enlightenment

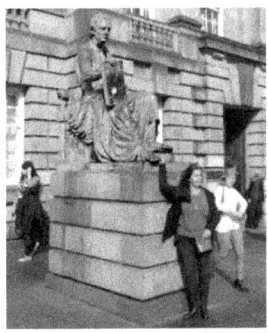

Description: Hume on chair with blank book. Bronze
Sculptor: Alexander Stoddart
Commissioned by: Saltire Society
Unveiled: 30 Nov 1997, St Andrews Day, by Sir
Stewart Sutherland, Principal & Vice Chancellor of
Edinburgh University.   See also: Chapter 3, *3.7*

Philosopher, economist, historian Hume was a leader of the Enlightenment, critically dissecting established beliefs. He wrote: I *'long entertained a suspicion, with regard to the decisions of philosophers upon all subjects, and found myself a greater inclination to dispute, than assent to their conclusions'.*

He is regarded as the most acute thinker in 18th century Britain, influencing succeeding generations through his critical approach requiring evidence rather than simply accepting assumed ideas. Albert Einstein credits Hume's approach for helping him develop his theories of relativity. However, during Hume's lifetime many of his radical ideas were not well received, harming his career.

He believed that passion, not reason, governs human behaviour. People only know that which they experience, and the relationships between experiences. Humans have no intrinsic knowledge of self. Rather, they experience a bundle of sensations. Knowledge of self, who we are, is simply this bundle of sensations.

The intellectually powerful *'A Treatise of Human Nature: being an attempt to introduce the experimental Method of Reasoning into Moral Subjects'* and *'Essays Moral, Political and Literary'* remain important philosophical works. He sought 'experimental' evidence to base philosophical reasoning. His critical analysis, particularly of established religion, proved controversial causing his failure to gain a chair at Edinburgh University. But he found support in Paris where he was honoured and respected.

His historical masterpiece, the 6-volume 'History of England' provided fame and fortune in Britain during his lifetime. He wrote this whilst librarian to the Faculty of Advocates in Edinburgh, now the National Library of Scotland.

Seated, David Hume wears a toga, robes of a Greek philosopher. He holds in his right hand a blank unmarked book, symbolising his belief that the Bible has no place in rational thought. His left foot symbolically stamps on the tablet denoting the Ten Commandments. On the back is the head of Helio-Medusa from which snakes and light emanate. Helio represents the Enlightenment, Medusa, critical thought, withering established beliefs to stone.

An irony is the practice of rubbing Hume's big toe to bring good luck, particularly for students before exams. What would the rationalist make of this? David Hume was born David Home in Edinburgh's Old Town, in a tenement on the north side of the Lawnmarket in 1711. His father died when he was only 2 years old and his mother raised him. He changed his surname in 1734. He studied at Edinburgh University, becoming absorbed in philosophy. He had little regard for the professors of the day. For ten years he devoted himself to self-study, reading and writing, to the detriment of his health and he had to be persuaded to lead a more active life.

Hume, who never married, had several homes in Edinburgh, the last of them in the New Town in a street off St Andrew Square where he moved in 1771. At that early stage in the New Town's development the street had yet to be named. It is said that friends jokingly arranged that 'St David's Street' be painted on the outside of Hume's house –the name stuck. A fond cook, he entertained Adam Smith (*4.22*), with vegetables from Smith's garden.

Diagnosed with bowel cancer, Hume bravely approached death, noting, as recounted by Adam Smith (*4.22*):

> *'I have done every thing of consequence which I ever meant to do.*
> *I therefore have all reason to die contented'*.

He was buried in the Old Calton burial ground – see Chapter 3, *3.7*.

4.16 Edinburgh Award
Recognising outstanding contributions to Edinburgh

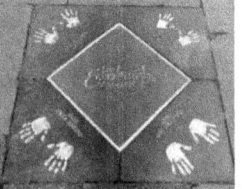

Description: Handprints on a flagstone in the City Chambers quadrangle
Date: Established 2007, annual awards

Edinburgh Council established this award to honour those who make positive impact, gaining for the city national and international recognition. Recipients:

2007: Ian Rankin, author, creator of Rebus

2008: J.K. Rowling, author, creator of Harry Potter

2009: Sir Chris Hoy, cyclist; see also the Post Boxes painted gold in his honour, *1.18* and Chapter 4, Map **4-2**.

2010: George Kerr, President of the British Judo Association

2011: Professor Peter Higgs, scientist, Nobel Prize for his work on sub-atomic particles, predicting a "new" particle now known as the 'Higgs boson'.

2012: Dame Elizabeth Blackadder, artist, first woman to be honoured as the Queen's Painter and Limner in Scotland

2013: Richard Demarco, artist and promoter of the visual and performing arts

2014   Thomas Gilzean, charity fund raiser and war veteran, often seen in the Royal Mile fundraising from his wheelchair

2015: Sir Tom Farmer, entrepreneur and philanthropist, the first Scot to be awarded the 'Andrew Carnegie Medal' for philanthropy

2016: Ken Buchanan, Undisputed World Lightweight Boxing Champion. 1971

2017: Professor Sir Timothy O'Shea. Principal and Vice-Chancellor of the University of Edinburgh, for enhancing the University and City. He had placed "Scotland's Capital on the world stage as a beacon of knowledge, research and further education"

2018: Doddie Weir, Scottish Rugby player with 61 caps; champion of motor neurone disease research and his charitable work for tackling the disease

2019 Ann Budge, business leader, owns and transformed 'Hearts' football club

2020 Alexander McCall Smith recognizing writing success, and legal & academic careers. Became well known through '*The No. 1 Ladies Detective Agency*' set in Botswana.

2021 Fergus Linehan, Director, Edinburgh International Festival. "His innovative and ambitious approach has brought the EIF to a whole new audience."

2022 Professor Sir Geoffrey Palmer, Chancellor of Heriot- Watt University and pioneering scientist and human rights activist, knighted in 2014.

2023 Nicola Benedetti, CBE, Renowned musician and Director of the Edinburgh International Festival. Receiving her award in Dec 2023 Nicola spoke of the award as a gift: *Each gift holds the potential for responsibility to others, that you choose to serve and grasp, or not. Each gift is a reminder of our place in a lineage of contributors to bettering life for ourselves and for others.*'

Contributors to the arts feature strongly: authors received first two awards and subsequent years have honoured other artists and art promoters.. Philanthropists have been honoured, Thomas Gilzean in 2014; Sir Tom Farmer's in 2015; Doddie Weir's in 2018.

4.17 Stone of Remembrance, Edinburgh War Memorial

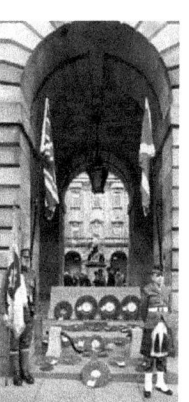

Description: Granite block inscribed on the front:
'*Their name liveth for evermore*';
on rear: '*1914-1918*' and '*1939-1945*'.
Funded by: Public subscription to remember those from Edinburgh who died in World War I
Unveiled: Armistice Day, 11th Nov 1927, by Prince Henry, son of King George V

The Stone of Remembrance is under the arches of the City Chambers in the High Street. It is the site of Scotland's national remembrance ceremony, on Remembrance Sunday, the Sunday closest to the 11th November, with wreathes laid.

Originally installed to remember those who died in the Great War, World War I. Sadly the hope that it was the war to end all wars was not to be and the dates of the 2nd World War were added.

Behind the Stone of Remembrance is the sculpture by Sir John Steell of Alexander the Great taming Bucephalus, symbolising the power of the mind over brute force. Sculptured in 1832, cast in bronze in 1883, it was moved to this site in 1916 from its original St Andrew Square site.

4.18   General Staniskaw Maczek, 1892-1994
Distinguished Polish General

The '*Independent*'s' obituary described General Maczek as [3]: "*the born troop commander more than a staff officer. Forceful, humorous, intelligent, imaginative, crafty even, and immensely brave. He hardly ever stayed in his Armoured Control Vehicle but usually went forward in his command tank directing the battle from the forward line as in former centuries. At night, like his men, he slept underneath his tank.*

Although a strict disciplinarian he was adored by officers and men. He was generous, far-sighted and any pettiness was alien to him. With all his ardour to beat the Germans, revenge was not in his mind, only the restoration of his beloved Polish Fatherland. Indescribable was his despair when he and his men learnt that Poland had been virtually abandoned at Yalta. Nevertheless, they remained indomitable in their loyalty to the Allied cause, but demanded to pursue the enemy into his heartland until final victory.

Description: General Maczek in military uniform, seated on a bench, outstretched arm welcoming us to join him. On bench his name and dates.
Sculptor: Bronislaw Krzysztof (Polish sculptor)
Funded by: Public subscription
Unveiled: 3 Nov 2018; unveiling wreathes shown
Location: City Chambers

General Maczek was a tank commander, a veteran of both World Wars. His World War II service began valiantly defending Poland against German Panzer divisions, frustrating their progress, his unit un-defeated in combat. With the fall of Poland he moved to France, promoted to brigadier-general and developing a Polish unit. He then led his troops to the UK where he formed the 1st Armoured Polish Division, initially tasked with defending the coast from Edinburgh to Aberdeen. In 1944 the division moved to the continent, in decisive victories spearheading the Allied forces against Germany. His unit went on to free the Netherlands city of Breda from German occupation, without incurring civilian losses in the town. After the war, in gratitude, he was made an honorary Dutch citizen. Promoted to Major-General, after the war he commanded all Polish forces in the UK until demobilisation in 1947.

Poland fell under communist control after the war, leaving Maczek, stripped of Polish citizenship, settling in Edinburgh. With no war pension he worked as a bartender till the 1960's. Fortunately the Dutch heard of his financial plight and from about 1950 paid him a General's war pension, secretly because of post-war sensitivities. The Dutch were also to help meet financial costs of treating his severely ill daughter about a decade later.

Finally, he was to receive recognition from Poland, the government of 1989 issuing him an apology and in 1994 he was presented with the Order of the White Eagle, Poland's highest state decoration. He was to die later that year. In accordance with his wishes he was buried in Breda, Netherlands, among his soldiers in the Polish military cemetery.

It was at the General's funeral that Lord Fraser of Carmyllie, representing the UK Government, learnt of the man and his achievements. In 2013 Lord Fraser launched the public appeal for funds to create a memorial to the General, taken on by his wife and daughter, reaching their target of £85,000 in 2018.

4.19 Walter Francis Montagu Douglas Scott, 1806 – 1884
5th Duke Buccleuch, 7th Duke Queensberry

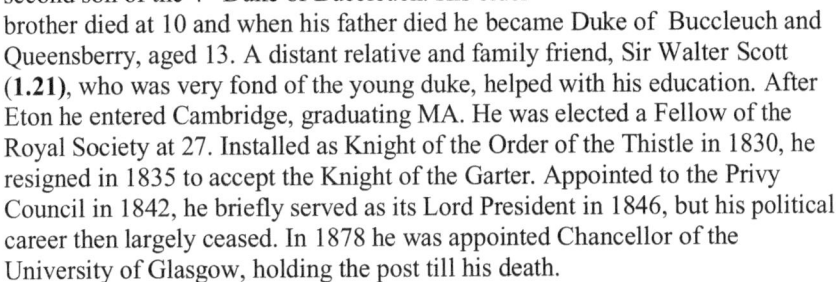

Description: 10 ft high bronze statue of Duke in Order of the Garter robes, on 32 ft pedestal. Two rows of 6-panels depict family scenes
Sculptor: Duke   - Sir Joseph Edgar Boehm;
              Panels - various artists
Architect: Sir Robert R Anderson
Commemorates: The Duke's building of Granton harbour, depicted in one of the panels.
Monument cost £6,700, paid by 1200 subscribers
Unveiled: February 1888 by the Earl of Stair

Walter Scott was born at Dalkeith House, Edinburgh, second son of the 4th Duke of Buccleuch. His elder brother died at 10 and when his father died he became Duke of Buccleuch and Queensberry, aged 13. A distant relative and family friend, Sir Walter Scott (**1.21**), who was very fond of the young duke, helped with his education. After Eton he entered Cambridge, graduating MA. He was elected a Fellow of the Royal Society at 27. Installed as Knight of the Order of the Thistle in 1830, he resigned in 1835 to accept the Knight of the Garter. Appointed to the Privy Council in 1842, he briefly served as its Lord President in 1846, but his political career then largely ceased. In 1878 he was appointed Chancellor of the University of Glasgow, holding the post till his death.

A prominent Scottish landowner, it was said that he could travel from his Dumfries estate across the central belt to the Lothians without leaving his land. He was responsible for building Edinburgh's Granton harbour on one of his estates, Caroline Park, at a cost of over £500,000, its planning depicted in one of the panels. He hosted King George IV at Dalkeith House during the 1822 royal visit (commemorated by the King's statue – Chapter 2, *2.4*) and later was honoured by Queen Victoria (*5.1*) with a visit.

The Buccleuch dukedom was created in 1663 for the eldest illegitimate son of King Charles II whose statue (*4.20*) is nearby. The 3rd Duke inherited the Queensberry dukedom in 1810.

On the monument's plinth six upper panels, by Thomas Stuart Burnett, depict aspects of the duke's life: Coat of Arms; Duke as Colonel at head of regiment; Installation as Chancellor of Glasgow University; 1878 Anniversary dinner of the duke's tenants; Planning Granton harbour (shown on next page, left); Receiving Queen Victoria at Dalkeith on her 1842 visit to Scotland.

Six lower panels, by Clark Stanton, depict family history scenes: Death of ancestor in battle at Northumberland, 1402; Appeal in 1596 by Sir Walter, 1st Lord Scott of Buccleuch, to Queen Elizabeth I to release a man from Carlisle Castle; Rising of clan to recover spoil taken by English in raid; Burning of Branxholm by the English in a 1532 raid; Attempted rescue of James V from the Earl of Angus, 1526; Burning of Catslack Tower by the English in 1548, Lady Buccleuch and her household perishing (detail in photo on next page, right).

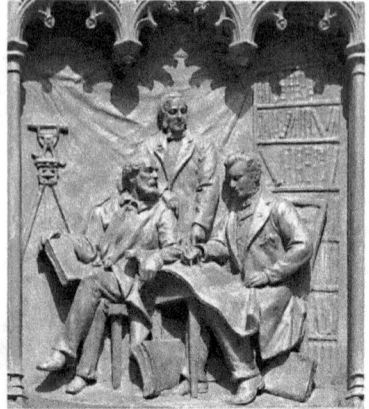

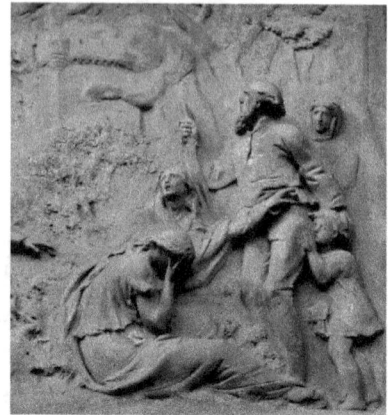

Scientific instrument and shelves of books show the scholarly Duke planning Granton Harbour.	Detail from panel depicting burning of Catslack Tower, Yarrow, 1548. The family's grief as flames engulf the tower is palpable. A child cowers for protection.

Between the upper and lower panels six rampant bucks hold shields with the arms of families allied by marriage to the Buccleuch's (sculptors David Watson and William Grant Stevenson).

Six allegorical figures between the upper panels represent virtues of the Duke [4]:

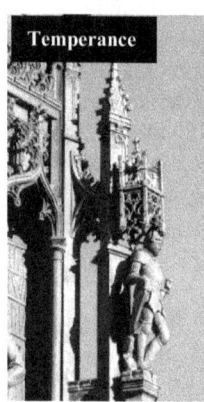

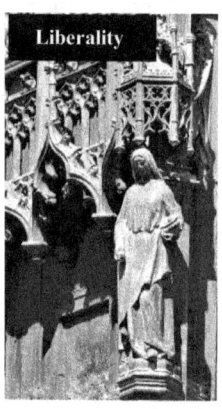

Temperance (knight in armour – shown left); Prudence (woman holding purse to her chest); Charity (figure holding object); Truth (blind woman holding object); Fortitude (man with shield, object in right hand); Liberality (woman offering bread from bowl – shown left). Each stands under an ornate canopy.

Urban art suffers decay, weathering and vandalism. 'Liberality', depicted to the left, went missing during midwinter 2017-2018, but with no knowledge as to its whereabouts.

At the top of the pedestal, immediately below the statue of the Duke, men and women on horseback ride with hounds, the figures sculptured with great detail.

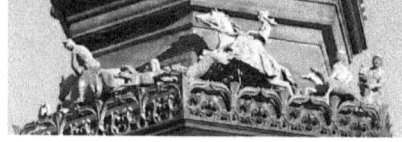

Walter Scott died in Bowhill, Selkirkshire, aged 77 and was buried in the Buccleuch Memorial Chapel in St. Mary's Episcopal Church in Dalkeith, at the entrance of Dalkeith Country Park in which is Dalkeith House, his birth place.

4.20 King Charles II, 1630 – 1685
Restoration of the monarchy; King of England, Scotland and Ireland

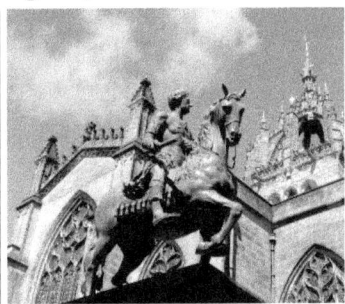

Description: King in Imperial uniform on horse.
Lead supported by inner oak and mild steel frame
Sculptor: Grinling Gibbons. Gibbons, the King's
master carver, best known for fine wood carvings.
His fame led him lead a large London workshop.
Funded by: Council, £2,580
Restored: April 2011: cracks in lead fixed;
framework restored; covered with protective wax.
Part of the '12 Monument Restoration Project'.
Date: 1685, Edinburgh's oldest outdoor statue

When Charles was 18 his father, Charles I, was executed during the English Civil War, Oliver Cromwell then ruling as Lord Protector. On his father's death Charles was proclaimed King Charles II of Scotland where he was crowned two years later. He ruled as King of Scotland till later that year when Cromwell defeated his army at the Battle of Worcester. Charles then fled into exile in continental Europe. Cromwell then ruled as Lord Protector of England, Scotland and Ireland with almost dictatorial powers. After Cromwell died there was political turmoil with calls for the restoration of the monarchy to stabilise the country. Charles was crowned King of England, Scotland and Ireland in 1661. The site of Charles II's statue had been considered as for Cromwell [5], but with the restoration of the monarchy the statue of Charles II was erected instead.

Charles was born in London in 1630, the son of Charles I and Henrietta Maria, the sister of the French king Louis XIII. He was baptised by the Anglican Bishop of London. The Kingdom was religiously divided, England, Scotland and Ireland, respectively Anglican, Presbyterian and Roman Catholic. Religious discord was to dominate his life. His teenage years coincided with the English Civil War and after some initial involvement in the campaign he was sent to France where his mother was living and where his cousin, the 8 year-old Louis XIV, was king. From there he moved to The Hague where he had a brief affair with Lucy Walter with whom he had a son, James Croft, later to become Duke of Monmouth and Duke of Buccleuch, one of whose heirs is honoured by a statue (*4.19*) nearby at the west end of St Giles.

After the restoration of the monarchy Charles II was forced to agree to Protestantism in England and Scotland, with the Anglican Church recognized as the established Church of England and the Church of Scotland established in Scotland. But his wife was Catholic. His attempts to introduce religious freedom for Catholics and others were thwarted by the English Parliament. Symptomatic of the religious discord that was to dominate much of his life Charles married his wife Catherine in two weddings, a secret Catholic and a public Anglican.

He reigned during the Great Plague and the Great Fire of London. Early in his reign, through his marriage to the Portuguese Catherine of Braganza, Charles negotiated for independence for Portugal from Spain. England gained Bombay, influencing the later incorporation of India into the British Empire with consequent trading privileges. Later Charles was to grant the British East India Company rights and jurisdiction over the acquired areas of India. He arranged for French support in wars with Holland for which he agreed to become a Catholic. Conflict with the Dutch met with some successes including the capture of New Amsterdam in North America; it was renamed as New York in honour of Charles's brother, James, Duke of York. But later the Dutch in a surprise attack destroyed much of the English fleet docked in the River Thames, taking the flagship, 'Royal Charles', back to the Netherlands.

Bitter religious rivalries were ignited by hostility to James, his brother and heir, a Catholic. Attempts were made to introduce the Exclusion Bill, preventing a Catholic becoming monarch, into law, but Charles dissolved Parliament to prevent its enactment. A plot to murder King and James was foiled, ringleaders executed. Charles II ruled without parliament from 1681 till his death in 1685.

Charles and Catherine had no children, but he bore at least 12 from his many mistresses, rewards of dukedoms for many. Charles converted to Catholicism on his death bed and was succeeded by his brother, James (VII and II).

4.21 James Braidwood, 1800 – 1861
Father of the British Fire Service, Founder of the first city fire service, he pioneered a scientific evidence-based approach to fire fighting

Description: Bronze, Braidwood standing in Fire Officer uniform on marble cylindrical pedestal inscribed with his name and years of birth & death. A rear plaque pays tribute to his pioneering scientific approach to fire-fighting, to his courage and that of fire fighters world-wide.
Sculptor: Kenneth Mackay
Motivated by: Dr Frank Rushbrook CBE, one-time Edinburgh Firemaster, who helped fund the statue
Unveiled: September 2008, by Sir Timothy O'Shea, Principal of Edinburgh University

Braidwood was born in Edinburgh and educated at the Royal High School. His father was a builder and James was apprenticed in the company, learning about building construction, including how fires spread through them. Edinburgh's New Town (Chapter 2) was attracting people, leaving a crowded dirty Old Town in slum conditions, many of its buildings derelict.

Their poor condition left many susceptible to fires which the fire-fighting services of the insurance companies could not tackle effectively. Braidwood argued for a municipal fire service, working with city leaders and the insurance companies. In 1824, the 'Edinburgh Fire Establishment', the world's first municipal fire service, was created.

Within weeks the fledgling service was tested: a series of fires, the 'Great Fire of Edinburgh', engulfed parts of the Old Town. The fires started in a 7-story printing house on Old Assembly Close, rapidly spreading to neighbouring buildings. Within hours much of the south side of the central High Street was ablaze. The newly recruited fire fighters, still in early days of training, struggled to control the fire, but some success was achieved, starting to get the fire under control. However, strong winds fanned flames from smouldering embers, ignited the nearby Tron Kirk. The fire spread, an 11-storey Parliament Square building was soon ablaze as was much of the south of the Old Town. The destruction was enormous, 13 died and hundreds hurt. Many buildings were destroyed, damage estimated at the time as £200,000. Most of the south side of the High Street between St Giles and the Tron Kirk had to be rebuilt.

The devastation provided compelling and urgent argument for the fire service and its development. Braidwood, commander, built up a reliable effective brigade, pioneering the application of scientific principles to fire-fighting. Expert tradesmen, slaters, carpenters, masons and plumbers and ex-seamen were recruited to the fire brigade, each contributing from their skills to the development of methods of fighting fires. James published a methodology of fire-fighting and the organisation of fire brigades in 1830. These methods were to be adopted throughout Britain.

James's achievements and success led to him being invited to establish and lead London's first municipal fire brigade. He was appointed in 1833 as the first head of the newly formed 'London Fire Engine Establishment'. He pioneered training schemes for fire officers. He was also concerned more widely for his fire fighters, arranging for the London City Mission to visit them and their families.

Despite his leadership role and responsibilities, he remained active in front-line fire service, personally fighting fires. Aged 61, in the summer of 1861, he was in the forefront leading fire fighters tackling fires that had broken out in warehouses on the south bank of the Thames. Whilst fighting this fire he was killed when a wall collapsed on him.

He was held in high esteem, evident from the huge crowds who attended his funeral. A plaque in the form of a burning building was erected near the London site in 1862. Inscribed in a laurel wreath are the words: '*To the memory of James Braidwood, superintendent of the London Fire Brigade, who was killed near this spot in the execution of his duty at the great fire on 22nd June 1861*'. A plaque on the former Lauriston Place fire station in Edinburgh also honoured him.

4.22 Adam Smith, 1723 – 1790
Philosopher, pioneer of political economy, Scottish Enlightenment, author

Adam Smith was born in Kirkcaldy, Fife. After good local schooling he studied moral philosophy at Glasgow University, developing a passion for liberty, reason and free speech. A scholarship took him to Oxford. He found the teaching inferior, but benefitted from self-study in its large library.

His teaching career began with public lectures in Edinburgh sponsored by its Philosophical Society. He became friends with David Hume (*4.15*) sharing ideas, the two leading the Scottish Enlightenment.

Within a few years Smith moved to Glasgow University enjoying a productive period, publishing '*The Theory of Moral Sentiments*' (1759), the first of his two classics. Based on his University lectures, the book explored how people learn to form moral judgements. He argued that, as we observe how others react and perceive us, we develop our own sense of identity. He discussed the importance of empathy between peoples, recognizing mutual feelings. He proposed free markets, self-regulated by competition, supply and demand and promotion of self-interest. He introduced the concept of 'an invisible hand' guiding supply and demand in which the labour of self-centred individuals supports the common good. The book established his reputation as an author and thinker, students flocking to attend his lectures.

Description: 3m bronze, 3m pedestal, Glasgow academic robes partly obscure his hand (symbolic of Invisible Hand). Agricultural tools behind, left behind by the march of industry – symbolised by beehive. He looks towards Canongate (home and grave) and Leith (trade).
Sculptor: Alexander Stoddart; plinth David Lindsay
Commissioned by: The Adam Smith Institute
Unveiled: 4th July 2008, by Nobel Laureate Vernon Smith. Date symbolic of his belief in free trade

He left Glasgow to travel in Europe tutoring the young Duke of Buccleuch, meeting leading European intellectuals. He saw how war destroyed much of France's wealth.

His second classic '*An Inquiry into the Nature and Causes of the Wealth of Nations*', abbreviated to '*The Wealth of Nations*', was published in 1776. Still influential it laid the foundations for the science of political economy. He explored the nature and causes of wealth and how rational self-interest in a positive competitive environment leads to prosperity. This approach contrasted with the accepted wisdom that the 'Wealth of Nations' depended on and could be measured by vaults of precious metals, particularly gold and silver. Smith disagreed, asserting that productive labour is the basic source of a nation's wealth. He argued that free trade between communities and countries benefitted all and supported the creation of wealth. He warned against unnecessary state intervention. This ushered in concepts such as the Gross National Product, contrasting with emphasis on gold-reserves. He advocated a new approach to social order based on mutual self-interest and individual freedom. The book extended the concept of the 'invisible hand' promoting the public good which the individual unwittingly delivers whilst pursuing his own interest.

Smith was concerned with wealth distribution in the 'Wealth of Nations' arguing that '*No society can surely be flourishing and happy, of which the far greater part of the members are poor and miserable*'. Panmure House, where he made his home, is now Heriot Watt's Edinburgh Business School, appropriately 'The Home of Economic and Social Debate', linking these concepts.

In Panmure the sociable Smith entertained friends, including David Hume, the physicist Joseph Black and geologist James Hutton. Smith was a founding member of the Royal Society of Edinburgh. He was buried in Canongate churchyard.

4.23 Dr Elsie Maud Inglis, 1864 – 1917
Medical Pioneer, Suffragette, Founder of the Scottish Women's Hospitals

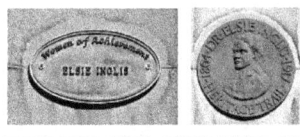

Description: Plaques, "Women of Achievement" [6]
and "Heritage Trail", on north side of High Street
Location: 219 High Street where Dr Inglis
established her midwifery resource centre
Other memorials to Dr Inglis:
- Within St Giles Cathedral in north-west chapel, a
  tablet by Pilkington Jackson
- Stone on her Walker Street house in New Town,
  recalling her medical practice there. Inscribed:
  'Elise Maud Inglis, Founder Scottish Women's
  Hospitals. France Serbia, Russia 1914-1918. Practised
  medicine here 1898-1914.'
- Elise Inglis Glade; Holyrood Park, near the former
  Elsie Inglis maternity hospital.
Monument: Being sculpted, installation pending

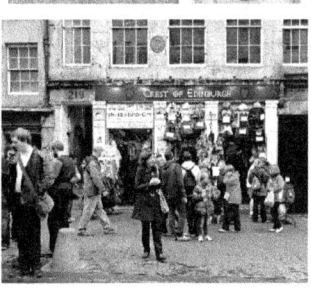

Medical pioneer who advanced the role of women as doctors and healthcare for
women. Dr Inglis also developed and ran field hospitals in World War I for
which Serbia awarded her the 'Order of the White Eagle' in 1916, the first
woman to receive this honour. Her dissatisfaction with medical care for women
led to her involvement with the Scottish Women's Suffragette movement.

Elsie was born in India, her father working for the Indian civil service. Her
visionary parents considered education of daughters as important as sons. She
decided to study medicine, enrolling in the new 'Edinburgh School of Medicine
for Women', completing her training in Glasgow. Appalled by the generally
poor standard of care for women patients she joined London's 'New Hospital for
Women'. From there she accepted a post at a leading Dublin maternity hospital

Dr Inglis returned to Edinburgh in 1894, setting up a medical practice with a
former fellow student. She opened a maternity hospital, 'The Hospice', for poor
women and a midwifery resource centre, located at 219 High Street. A caring
doctor, she paid for some patients to recuperate by the sea, often waiving fees.

The hospice was the forerunner of the 'Elsie Inglis Memorial Maternal Hospital'
founded in 1925 as a memorial to Dr Inglis. Elsie's, as it was affectionately
known, closed in 1988, but is still fondly remembered.

With the outbreak of World War I she developed women-staffed relief hospitals.
When she offered the Royal Army Medical Corps a staffed medical unit the War
office told her to '*go home and sit still*'! Dr Inglis was not one to accept this
(inaction). Fortunately, the French Government accepted her offer and the
Scottish Women's Hospital set up a medical unit in Serbia. A fellow Edinburgh
medical graduate, Lady Kathleen Isabel Emslie, wrote of serving in Serbia
treating the French, whilst nearby a British regiment had to endure the lack of
hospital facilities. Dr Inglis's leadership and inspiration improved cleanliness
and hygiene, reducing epidemics. Captured in 1915 she was sent back to Britain.
Determined to continue active contribution, she raised funds for a Scottish
Women's Hospital team in Odessa, Russia which she joined in 1916.

Cancer forced her return to Britain in 1917 where she died on 26th November, the day after her return, in the Station Hotel in Newcastle. Her funeral at St Giles Cathedral three days later was '*the occasion of an impressive public tribute*' (The Scotsman newspaper). Winston Churchill reflected that Dr Inglis and her nurses '*will shine in history*'.

On the centenary of her death in November 2017 wreaths were laid at her grave in the city's Dean cemetery (including from Serbia – '*We will never forget you*'). A memorial service was held in St Giles cathedral, her home church, the place of her funeral at which the Princess Royal laid a wreath at her monument there.

4.24   Joseph McIver, Paisley Close
Poor state of High Street housing;
14-year old boy rescued from rubble of a
collapsed High Street tenement

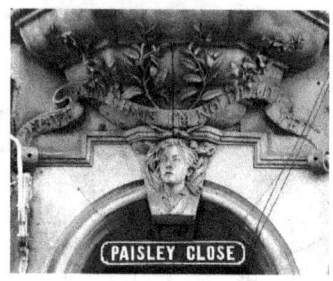

Description: Bust of boy, inscribed: '*Heave Awa' Chaps I'm No Dead Yet*'	
Sculptor: John Rhind	Date: 1862

The continuing increasingly fragile state of the High Street housing that had earlier caused the Great Fire of 1824 (see Braidwood, *4.21*) are remembered by the bust of a boy at the entrance to what is now Paisley Close. It recalls the collapse, on 24th Nov 1861, of 250-year old tenement-housing above Bailie Close at 99 and 103 High Street. The 7-storey tenement housed 77 occupants, of whom 35 died. As the rubble was being cleared a voice cried out: 'Heave Awa' Chaps I'm No Dead Yet'. It was that of 14-year old Joseph McIver, who was trapped in the rubble. His words are inscribed above the bust.

The collapse and the tragic loss of life focussed attention on the High Street's poor housing. This led to much agonizing, forcing the Edinburgh authorities to improve the living conditions of those remaining within 'old' Edinburgh. The tenement had been of a timber construction with a facade of stone that gave a false impression of sturdy security, but hiding the decayed interior of the building. Exacerbating the fragility of the building were dangerous alterations.

Those who could afford to had moved from the High Street to the New Town, leaving slum conditions in the Old Town, its population rising from about 80,000 in 1800 to nearly 170,000 by 1861. Families were crammed into tenements that had seen no maintenance for generations, leaving them in poor condition, grim and filthy. The state of the housing was described in the Builders Journal of 1861: '*We devoutly believe that no smell in Europe or Asia can equal in depth and intensity, in concentration and power, the diabolical combination of sulphurated hydrogen we came upon one evening .. in a place called Todrick's Wynd*'[7]. The Scotsman went onto report that the nearby Bailie Fyfe's Close that collapsed would have been no different.

Charles Dickens frequently visited Edinburgh and is reported to have spoken of seeing '*more poverty and sickness in the course of an hour's stroll through the*

Old Town' than people would believe in a life [7].

The '*calamitous and heartrending*' collapse led to recognition of the appalling state of the Old Town housing. In response: building control regulations were developed; Dr Henry Duncan Littlejohn was appointed the city's first Medical Officer of Health; the City Improvement Act of 1867 was passed by Lord Provost William Chambers (*6.1*). A plaque on St Mary's Street, near its south-east corner with the Canongate, notes that its building was the first rebuilt as a result of the Improvement Act. The Act also led to significant changes in the Old Town, including in the Cowgate which had once been a fashionable part of town, but by then had become neglected and deprived.

Dr Littlejohn (later knighted Sir Henry) held the post of Medical Officer of Health for 46 years till retirement aged 81. His pioneering report on the poor sanitary conditions demonstrated that poor living conditions contributed to poor public health and susceptibility to disease.

Paisley Close and its tenement were built to replace the collapsed building.

4.25 Robert Fergusson 1750–1774
Pioneering Poet, 'Scotia's poet'.

An urban poet, he described Edinburgh life in its exciting enlightenment. Prolific, he died in poverty aged only 24. He had a major influence on Burns who, in *'Lines Under the Portrait of Fergusson'*, wrote:
> *'O thou, my elder brother in misfortune,*
> *By far my elder brother in the muses,*
> *With tears I pity thy unhappy fate!*
> *Why is the bard unpitied by the world,*
> *Yet has so keen a relish of his pleasures.'*

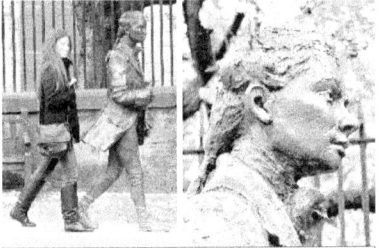

Description: Fergusson, clasps book, striding. Plaque has life details in Braille. Inscribed on paving are first lines of 'Auld Reekie', his name and birth & death dates. Life size bronze
Sculptor: David Annand
Erected: Friends of Robert Fergusson
Unveiled: 17th Oct 2004, 230th anniversary of his death
Also: Plaque, St Giles Cathedral

Robert Fergusson was born in the former 'Cap and Feather' Close off the Royal Mile (demolished to build the North Bridge). His parents had moved from Aberdeenshire to Edinburgh a few years before his birth, his father working as a copyist. Robert, the youngest of three surviving children, studied at the Royal High School and then at Dundee High School before St Andrews University.

His time at St Andrews was cut short by his father's death and he returned to Edinburgh to care for his mother, working at the Commissary Records Office as a copyist. It gave time to write, both in Scottish English and in native Scots.

Edinburgh was vibrant, a bohemian lifestyle in clubs encouraging and developing intellectual discourse. Robert became active in club life, in particular the Cape Club in Craig's Close. Each member had a nickname, his was 'Sir Precentor'. A plaque in Cockburn Street near the foot of the former Craig's Close, now demolished, recalls the club and his membership.

Although dying young he had a major impact on Scottish literature, influencing many. Whilst at St Andrews he had begun drafting poems and, it is believed, a play on William Wallace (*4.2*). He wrote about some of its staff, including one on his maths professor '*Elegy on the Death of Mr David Gray*', each verse ending with a humorous note. Through the Edinburgh club scene he met an Italian singer, Tenducci, who asked Robert to write verse in Scots for an opera he was presenting. This was an important breakthrough for the young Robert and his writings were published with the material of the opera.

He contributed poetry to the 'Weekly Magazine', initially writing in English but latterly in both Scots and English. His work proved popular and Walter Ruddiman, proprietor of the 'Weekly' published a collection of his works in 1773. This sold about 500 copies generating a profit. Some of his poetry was satirical, others pastoral. In 1773 he published 'Auld Reekie', a poem about a day in the life of Edinburgh, depicting its grandeur, fun, poverty and depravity. The first line of the poem is engraved on a paving slab in the Makars' Court: '*Auld Reekie, wale o ilka town*'. It talks of the dawn kissing the '*air-cock o' St Giles*' with servant lassies who '*early being their lies and clashes*'. One of them has been scolded by her mistress and would rather '*wi her joe in turnpike stair .. snuff the stinking air*' than '*be subjected to her tongue, when justly censur'd in the wrong*'. It goes on to refer to the practice of emptying chamber pots into the street, referring to the contents as '*Edina's Roses*':

'*They kindly shower Edina's Roses,*
To quicken and regale our noses'

Sadly, he was not in good health, perhaps not helped by the club lifestyle. A heavy fall down an Edinburgh flight of stairs left him with a serious head injury, and he was confined, against his will, to the Darien House 'hospital' (near today's Bedlam Theatre). There, within two weeks, he died, aged just 24 years. Two days later he was buried in an unmarked grave in the Canongate Kirk yard.

It is a mark of the respect for Fergusson that two Scottish literary giants sharing his first name Robert determined that his grave should be recognised. When in 1786 Burns (*3.9, 5.2*) came to Edinburgh, seeing no gravestone, he was incensed and sought permission and paid for a gravestone. Burns wrote a poem, '*Inscription on the tomb of Fergusson the Poet*', the first verse of which is inscribed on the headstone at his Canongate grave:

'*No sculptur'd Marble here nor pompous lay*
No stoned Urn nor animated Bust
This simple Stone directs Pale Scotia's way
To pour her Sorrows o'er her Poets Dust'.

Later Stevenson (*1.11*) planned to renovate the tombstone, adding an inscription: '*This stone, originally erected by Robert Burns, has been repaired at the charges of Robert Louis Stevenson and is by him re-dedicated to the memory of Robert Fergusson as the gift of one Edinburgh lad to another*'. Stevenson died before doing so, but the Saltire Society commemorated the three Roberts by inscribing the above words.

In the 20th century Robert Garioch wrote 'At Robert Fergusson's Grave' of respectful mourners at the grave where '*Robert Burns knelt and kissed the mool*' (soft humus-rich grave soil).

Fergusson died in Edinburgh's brutal bedlam. The harsh conditions led the young Doctor Andrew Duncan (1744-1828) to develop improved hospital treatment for mental health; the doctor is remembered by the Andrew Duncan Clinic of Royal Edinburgh psychiatric hospital.

For the statue's unveiling on Sunday 17th October 2004 Stewart Conn, Edinburgh Makar (see *4.13*), composed a poem the last lines being [8]:

> "*So let us – in fancied ritual – celebrate*
> *his genius by washing down our oysters*
> *with remaining noggins; raised in roisterous*
> *praise of Auld Reekie's peerless laureate.*"

4.26 King Edward VII, 1841 – 1910
King of the United Kingdom and the British Dominions, Emperor of India

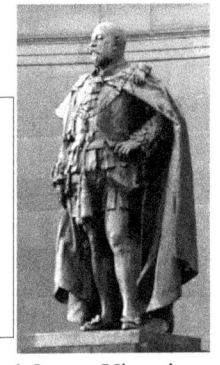

Description: Edward VII robed with Order of the Thistle, St Andrew Cross medallion on chain. 9-ft High bronze, stone pedestal. Part of 'National Memorial to King Edward VII', a colonnaded sandstone hemicycle designed by architect Sir G. Washington Browne, in Holyrood Palace forecourt.
Sculptor: Henry Snell Gamley
Unveiled: King George V, his heir, 10th Oct 1922
See also: Victoria Park, Leith, *5.13* for his 'Peacemaker' role

Born Albert Edward, the eldest son of Prince Albert (*2.1*) and Queen Victoria (*1.16, 5.1*), he was from birth trained to be king. However, many of his long years as heir apparent were spent in a playboy life-style, eating, drinking, and gambling and with many love affairs, despite his marriage to Princess Alexandra of Denmark in 1863. They had six children, five surviving to adulthood.

Edward succeeded Queen Victoria to the throne in January 1901, reigning till his death in May 1910. Acute appendicitis struck him two days before his planned coronation. His willingness to accept new radical surgery helped make appendix surgery routine. His operation was successful, he was reported to be sitting up in bed smoking the following day.

Once he ascended the throne he put the wild life-style behind him, devoting himself to serving the country. But the excesses of his early life were to take its toll and, after several heart attacks, he died in May 1910.

Thanks to wise advice the monarchy's financial state was good. He refurbished the royal palaces. He donated his parent's Isle of Wight house, Osborne Palace, to the nation; it is now in the care of Historic England, open to visitors. He reintroduced the state opening of Parliament and other traditional ceremonies.

He was succeeded by his second son, King George V. his eldest son, Prince Albert Victor, had earlier died of pneumonia. Albert Victor, five years before his death, opened the 1886 International Exhibition in Edinburgh (*6.6*).

Chapter 5: Leith

The history of Leith reflects its coastal location on the Firth of Forth, on the banks of the Water of Leith. Trade was the basis for much of its development and its harbour remains an important part of its economy. Two parts of Leith grew separately on either side of the Water of Leith till the first substantial bridge was built across the river in 1493 by the Abbot Bellenden. The town on the south was the larger; it was where the ships landed their cargo along 'The Shore', still the road's name today. The towns' developments can be traced back to the granting, by King David I, of the then existing harbour on the north to the Abbot of Holyrood through the 1128 Foundation Charter for Holyrood Abbey. Later the King gave the lands on the south to Peter who took the name of the lands he was given, becoming Peter de Lestarig – the origin of Restalrig.

The two towns developed through trade and commerce, particularly that on the south which remained under the Barony of Restalrig. The northern town, wealthier, stayed associated with Holyrood Abbey, the source of its wealth. The loss of the port of Berwick upon Tweed to England in 1296 had benefitted Leith, now the principal port of Scotland. However, developing trade routes to North America in the 18th century saw Glasgow become Scotland's principal port.

Leith has witnessed important Scottish historical events. Its port and proximity to Edinburgh led it to be fought over by English, Scots and French. In 1544, as part of the 'Rough Wooing', Henry VIII's forces sacked Leith as he attempted, unsuccessfully, to ensure that his son, later to be Edward VI, married the infant Mary Queen of Scots. The objective of the marriage: to create an England – Scotland alliance, thereby weakening the Scottish link with France. It followed Henry VIII's 1542 attack on Scotland triggered by King James V's (*6.18*) refusal to break with Rome which Henry VIII, his uncle, had requested.

Shortly after this James V died, his infant daughter, Mary Queen of Scots, becoming monarch. Mary of Guise, Regent for her daughter Mary moved the Scottish Court to Leith in 1560. There she and her French troops were besieged by Scottish Protestant troops, Mary of Guise fleeing to Edinburgh Castle, dying there that June. The siege ended with the Treaty of Leith, also known as the Treaty of Edinburgh, the French departing. The following year Mary Queen of Scots landed at Leith on her return from France. Mary abdicated in 1567.

Later troops of James VI of Scotland were based in Leith, now fighting against his mother's supporters in Edinburgh Castle in what is known as the 'Wars between Leith and Edinburgh'. It pitched supporters of Mary Queen of Scots as the rightful monarch against supporters of her son, James VI, fighting for a Protestant Scotland.

Testament to Leith's importance was Vice-Admiral Sir William Monson's request in the 1630s that it should be Scotland's capital. He wrote to King Charles I [1]: "*Instead of Edinburgh .. I wish his Majesty did fortify .. Leith, and make there to settle the seat of justice, with all the other privileges Edinburgh enjoys.*" His arguments were based on Leith's status as a port.

In 1649, an earthen defensive barrier was built from Leith to Calton Hill to protect against an attack by Oliver Cromwell's English forces. Initially the Scots under General Leslie held out, but with the Scottish defeat at the Battle of Dunbar, both Leith and Edinburgh surrendered to Cromwell. Cromwell went on to rule Scotland as dictator. Plans to fortify Leith alarmed Edinburgh and instead Cromwell's General Monck built the defensive Citadel in Leith, only a small part surviving as most was destroyed after the restoration of the monarchy a few years later. The line of the earlier earthen defensive barrier became Leith Walk.

Leith gained formal independence from Edinburgh through the Burgh Acts of 1833 with its own Town Council. Shortly before this, in 1822, King George IV was to land at Leith to begin his royal visit (*2.4*). Two decades later Queen Victoria (*5.1*) was to pass through Leith from the deep-water port at Granton for her royal visit. Leith's independence was to end with the 1920 merger of Leith and Edinburgh, but the spirit of Leith as a separate town persists amongst many 'Leithers'. The Leith motto of 'Persevere' sums up its strong spirit.

Leith covers much of north Edinburgh from Pilrig church on Leith Walk in the south, from Trinity in the west to most of Restalrig in the East. The 2011 census gave its population as 25,000 out of an Edinburgh population of nearly 480,000.

Leith hosts the Scottish Government's administrative headquarters, The 'Scottish Executive'.

5.1   Queen Victoria, 1819 – 1901
Long reigning (63 years) British Monarch
Queen, 1837-1901; Empress of India, 1877-1901

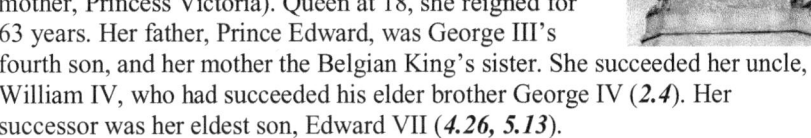

Description: Queen Victoria with coronet, on panelled plinth
Sculptor: John Stevenson Rhind (statue & bas-relief panels)
Unveiled: 12th Oct 1907 by Lord Roseberry. The bronze panels were added in 1913   Location: Foot of Leith Walk

Born in 1819, she was named Alexandrina Victoria (after Emperor Alexander I of Russia, a god-parent, and her mother, Princess Victoria). Queen at 18, she reigned for 63 years. Her father, Prince Edward, was George III's fourth son, and her mother the Belgian King's sister. She succeeded her uncle, William IV, who had succeeded his elder brother George IV (*2.4*). Her successor was her eldest son, Edward VII (*4.26, 5.13*).

Victoria married Prince Albert of Saxe-Coburg (*2.1*) in 1840. They had 9 children several of whom were to marry into royal families across Europe, hence her nickname the 'grandmother of Europe'. These relationships helped ensure peace in Europe, but Victoria's reign was not without conflict. Wars included the Crimean and Anglo-Boer wars. A battalion who fought in the Anglo-Boer war is remembered by one of the monument's panels – see next page.

She established in 1856 the UK's highest award for bravery, the Victoria Cross, to honour bravery in the Crimean War, with 111 VCs awarded. 78 Were awarded during the Second Anglo-Boer War, to date over 1300 awarded.

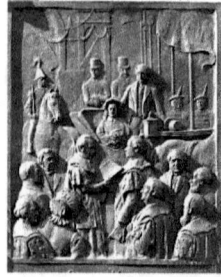

Queen Victoria
Entering Leith Sept 3, 1842

5th Volunteer Battalion,
'The Royal Scots.'
South Africa 1900 – 1902.
A memorial to
Patriotism and Loyalty.

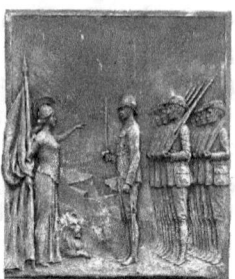

Queen Victoria was born after the Napoleonic Wars left Britain the dominant European power. Her 63 year-reign saw Britain prosper with an expansion in its world-wide British Empire. Known as the Victorian age, it was a period in which Britain underwent technological and cultural expansions, which, together with scientific advances and inventions, transformed society and life-styles.

The Victoria era is associated with conservative restrictive morality, echoed in her childhood which she described as 'rather melancholy' under her protective mother who limited her association with other children. Her father had died when she was less than a year old. The norms of the day didn't help; Victoria, even when Queen, was forced to live with her mother whilst unmarried. Marriage to Albert brought with it a new freedom and the couple were devoted. Victoria was distraught after Albert's early death in 1861; she went into deep mourning, often seen wearing black – she was to be a widow for 40 years.

Other memorials to Queen Victoria are the statue on the Mound (*1.16*) and Castle Street's 'The Queen's Nursing Institute', a charity set up in 1887 with a £70,000 grant by Queen Victoria to provide 'training, support, maintenance and supply of nurses'. The statue on its roof is allegorical.

5.2   Robert Burns, 1759 – 1796   *Scotland's National poet*

A reviewer of 'The Kilmarnock Edition', Burn's first published work, wrote in the Edinburgh Magazine [2] that the reader of the poems '*will perceive with what uncommon penetration and sagacity this heaven taught ploughman, from his humble unlettered station, has looked upon men and manners*'. His insight into human life still inspires readers.

Robert Burns, the Ayrshire 'ploughman poet', was a prolific poet, composing on many themes including love, country life and the human spirit. His poetry remains fresh and alive, verses well known, for example '*O wad some Pow'r the giftie gie us to see oursels as ithers see us*' (from 'To a Louse, 1786'). Towards the end of his life he sought out Scots folk verse, collecting and preserving it.

Burns was born on 25th January 1759 in the Ayrshire village of Alloway, the eldest of seven children. His father was a poor tenant farmer who built the cottage where Robert was born (now the Burns Cottage Museum in the care of the National Trust for Scotland). The family moved to a farm south-east of Alloway when Robert was 7. The hard manual labour of his childhood was to leave him with a premature stoop.

<u>Description</u>: Bronze statue, Burns on red sandstone plinth, each of its 4 sides depicting scenes from one of his poems. They are, clockwise from the south-facing front panel (shown below):

- The Cottar's Saturday Night: '*The priest-like father reads the sacred page – From scenes like these old Scotia's grandeur springs*';
- Hallow'een: '*In order, on the clean hearth-stane, the luggies three are ranged*';
- Death and Dr Hornbrook: '*I there wi' something did forgather, that pat me in an eerie swither*';
- The Smiddy: '*When Vulcan gies his bellows breath an plowmen gather wi' their graith*'.

<u>Sculptor</u>: David Watson Stevenson, statue & panels
<u>Commissioned by</u>: Leith Burns Club
<u>Unveiled</u>: Oct 1898. North and south panels date from 1898, the others added in 1901
<u>Location</u>: Junction of Bernard & Constitution Streets
<u>See also</u>:   Chapter 3, *3.9,* monument on Calton Hill;
         Chapter 4, *4.13*, quote from poem at Makars' Court.

There was not much formal education in those days, but his father was keen that he be educated, teaching his son, employing a local teacher and ensuring summer education during lulls in the farm work.

The young Burns had a love for verse and was equally quick to appreciate the

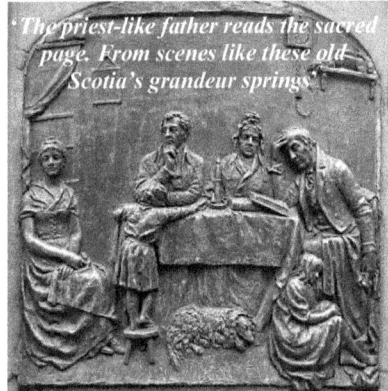

women he met. An early encounter was at harvest time when aged 15 he met Nelly Kilpatrick, penning a poem to her. A year later during the summer education break from farming Peggy Thompson caught his attention, writing two poems to her.

His father's hard work as a farmer never paid off and, when Robert was 18, the family moved to a farm near Tarbolton. There Robert joined a country dancing school and with his brother Gilbert formed the Tarbolton Bachelor's Club.

After his father died the family moved to a farm near Mauchline where Robert met 'The Belles of Mauchline' a group of girls amongst whom was Jean Armour. Robert was to marry Jean and they had nine children, only three of whom survived infancy. Robert had several love affairs, including that to Mary Campbell prior to marrying Jean Armour. He dedicated poems to Mary including 'The Highland Lassie O'. Lack of funds prevented tentative plans for Robert and Mary to emigrate to Jamaica, attracted by possible bookkeeper work on a slave plantation as a way out of financial difficulties.

Instead he was encouraged to publish his poems. 'Poems, Chiefly in the Scottish dialect', also known as the 'Kilmarnock Volume', was published in July 1786, selling for 3 shillings. An immediate success, the 612 volumes printed sold in a little over a month. His popularity spread, leading to an invitation to Edinburgh with the prospect of a second volume. He was received enthusiastically in the capital and the second volume eventually published.

His love affairs continued in Edinburgh, notably Mrs Agnes Maclehose, better known by her nickname Clarinda used in their correspondence, Burns using the name Sylvander. This was to inspire Burns to compose 'Ae Fond Kiss' which he sent her after their last meeting, regarded as Burns most popular love song.

However, he returned to Jean Amour in Ayrshire, continuing to write poems and lyrics. But his health was failing, and he died in Dumfries aged just 37.

In his short life his literary output was such as to ensure his legacy as Scotland's National Poet. His birthday is celebrated around the world at 'Burns night' with recitations of his poetry, folk singing and dancing. His poetry and lyrics remain relevant and vibrant, confirmed by his selection, in a 2009 contest run by the Scottish Television company, as the greatest Scot.

'*Should auld acquaintance be forgot*' opens his popular 1788 poem 'Auld Lang Syne' (literally 'Old long ago', 'for old times sake', remembering love and friendship in times past); particularly apt for this book on memories explored through monuments.

5.3   Leith Links, "The home of golf", 1744
The 250th anniversary of the first golf tournament played to official rules

In the 17th and 18th centuries Leith was a popular area for golf. 'The Gentleman Golfers of Edinburgh' organized, in 1744 at Leith Links, a golf tournament. Played with rules (*5.4*) to allow the award of a trophy, it was the first tournament played to official rules. The 13 rules still form the basis for the modern game. Thus Leith Links is sometimes referred to as the home of golf. The competition was commemorated in 1994 by a cairn and a 250th anniversary match was held.

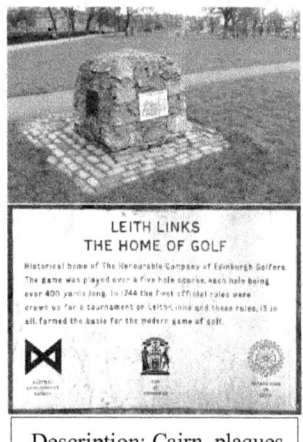

Golf was not without controversy, particularly Sunday play. For example, the South Leith Kirk session set a 20 shilling (£1) fine and confession of sins for Sunday play. The last Kirk prosecution was perhaps against an innkeeper for serving food to Sunday golfers.

Description: Cairn, plaques.
Erected: 1994
Location: Leith Links
See also: *5.4*

Leith Links also claims to be the venue for the first international golf match. In 1681 the then Duke of York and his partner John Patersone played against two Englishmen, the Duke and John winning. John, a champion golfer, earned a living as a cobbler and golf ball maker. He purchased a house on the Canongate with his winnings; a plaque on the house, known as 'Golfers Land', describes the match. The Duke's clubs were carried by Andrew Jackson, making Andrew the first recorded caddy. The Duke was to become King James VII / II (VII of Scotland, II of England), succeeding his brother, Charles II (*4.20*).

5.4   John Rattray, 1744
Signed off the approval of the first official rules of golf

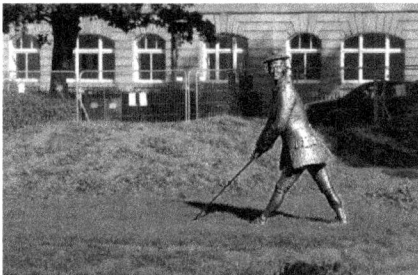

Description: 2-m high figure of Rattray on Leith Links, the setting landscaped to follow that of the playing conditions in the 18th century.
Date: 11 September 2019
Design: Sculptor: David Annand; landscaping: landscape architect William J Cairns.
Commissioned: Leith Rules Golf Society

Edinburgh Council offered a silver trophy for the 1744 golf tournament (see *5.3*) conditional on it being played to defined rules. John Rattray led a team drafting a set of 13 rules, signing them. The competition went ahead, Rattray winning. The rules were widely circulated, providing the basis for fair play at golf.

In 2011 Edinburgh Council was approached by the Leith Rules Golf Society for permission to erect a statue to John Rattray to commemorate his 1744 drafting and signing of these first formal rules of golf, honouring this and the role of Leith Links in golf's development. The Council agreed, followed in 2014 by approval by the Scottish Parliament, Parliamentary approval required because of laws restricting construction on parks in Edinburgh.

Articles & Laws in Playing at Golf, 1744

1. You must Tee your Ball within a Club's length of the Hole.
2. Your Tee must be upon the Ground.
3. You are not to change the Ball which you strike off the Tee.
4. You are not to remove Stones, Bones or any Break Club, for the sake of playing your Ball, Except upon the Fair Green & that only within a Club's length of your Ball.
5. If your Ball comes among watter or any wattery filth, you are at liberty to take out your Ball and bringing it behind the hazard and Teeing it, you may play it with any Club and allow your Adversary a Stroke for so getting out your Ball.
6. If your Balls be found any where touching one another, You are to lift the first Ball, till you play the last.
7. At Holling, you are to play your Ball honestly for the Hole, and not to play upon your Adversary's Ball, not lying in your way to the Hole.
8. If you shou'd lose your Ball, by it's being taken up, or any other way, you are to go back to the Spot, where you struck last, & drop another Ball, And allow your adversary a Stroke for the misfortune.
9. No man at Holling his Ball, is to be allowed, to mark his way to the Hole with his Club, or anything else.
10. If a Ball be stopp'd by any Person, Horse, Dog or anything else, The Ball so stop'd must be play'd where it lyes.
11. If you draw your Club in order to Strike, and proceed so far in the Stroke as to be bringing down your Club; If then, your Club should break, in any way, it is to be Accounted a Stroke.

A larger than life bronze statue, by David Annand, was installed on Leith Links in a landscaped setting designed by landscape architect William J Cairns. Landscaping began in late 2018, including planting of Marram grass, with the Leith Rules Golf Society near the fundraising target.

At the time of the tournament Scotland was in political turmoil, the '45 Jacobite uprising unfolding. John Rattray, a surgeon, tended the Jacobite army wounded. He was seized after the 1746 Jacobite defeat at Culloden with all those with Bonnie Prince Charlie's army. He was reputedly spared execution by the personal plea of Lord Forbes, a golfing partner.

5.5   Musicians
Honouring Boz Burrell

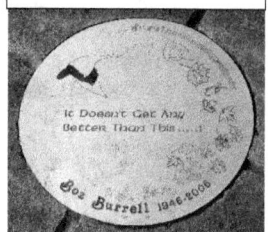

Description: Slate seat shaped as base clef; in centre a disc commemorates Raymond 'Boz' Burrell
In front are two discs, one inscribed, *Derek 'Dell Boy' Allen 1933-2001*; the other, '*Tam White 1942-2010 Scottish Blues legend*' with a hat in the centre and a musical score arc around part of its circumference
Sculptor: James Parker   Unveiled: about 2010
Location: Shore, Leith

Description: Disc commemorating 'Boz' Burrell (1946-2006) inscribed: '*It doesn't get any better than this...!*'

The focus of this memorial is Raymond Boz Burrell, musician, vocalist and guitarist. Aged 21 he joined the group 'King Crimson' as a vocalist, touring with them for two years. With 'Bad Company' he enjoyed considerable success: platinum status albums; UK Top Twenty hits; popularity in North America. The group split after about 10 years, but briefly came together in 1998 for a reunion tour and the release of a new compilation.

During the 1990s Burrell worked with Scottish blues singer, Tam White, remembered by a disc in front of the memorial. Tam, a well-known blues singer, played regularly in Leith. The 'List' magazine of 2009 relates that the 'legendary vocalist Tam White' played the Leith Festival that year. Tam was a stone mason. In front of the memorial is a disc to Derek 'Dell Boy' Allen, Burrell's father-in-law.

Burrell died suddenly of a heart attack whilst rehearsing in Spain in September 2006; his friend Tam was with him at the time. The sculptor, James Parker, worked with Burrell's widow Kath in designing this memorial. The words inscribed on Burrell's plaque, '*It doesn't get any better than this*', are believed to be his last words; the leaves on it refer to the song 'Autumn Leaves'.

Parker is a Scottish sculptor who has created many interesting designs using slates. His web site recalls his childhood memory of repairing a dry-stone wall with his father. He created his first slate sculpture in 2007.

5.6   Merchant Navy
Honouring sailors of the Merchant Navy

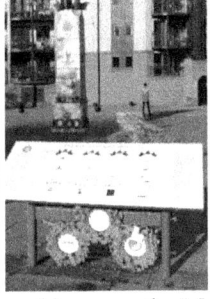
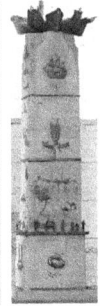

Description: 18 ft tall sandstone column decorated with seafaring scenes in bronze relief, capped with the prows and sails of ships, designed in the form of the top of the Merchant Navy coat of arms
Inspired by: Gordon S. Milne;   Sculptor: Jill Watson
Unveiled: 16 November 2010 by HRH Princess Anne, the Princess Royal
Location: Shore, Leith

It is fitting that Leith, Edinburgh's port, recognizes and honours the Merchant Navy, the many sailors who sail from her shores and the services and training provided by Leith Nautical College. It honours the 6,500 Scottish Merchant Navy personnel who died in World Wars I and II, other conflicts and those who died in service during peace time.

The monument needs to be seen to be appreciated, particularly the detailed scenes of merchant navy personnel, examples shown below. Information about the scenes are on the notice in front of the statue.

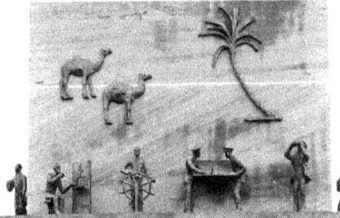

Merchant navy personnel:
Extreme left Engineer
In middle Ships Bridge: radio operator, helmsman, navigators, captain with binoculars;
Extreme right one of the two mooring men ready to catch the mooring line.

The plaque on the monument is inscribed: '*It is a timeless tribute in remembrance of those who died in service for the people of Great Britain*';   and from Psalm 107, '*Lest we forget "They that goe downe to the sea in shippes, that doe business in great waters*"'.

The memorial was commissioned by The Merchant Navy Memorial Trust (Scotland) who raised nearly £200,000 for it. Princess Anne is patron. Leith was chosen as its site as it was Scotland's premier port for over 300 years and Edinburgh's trading base for over 700 years. The site is at the heart of old Leith harbour, opposite what was once the Seaman's Home, now a prominent hotel.

5.7   Vice Admiral John Hunter, 1737 – 1821
Naval Officer, Governor of New South Wales, 1795–1800

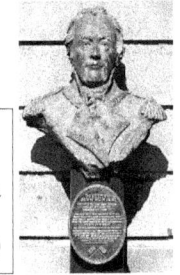

Description: Bust in uniform, mounted on wall
Sculptor: Victor Cusack, Australian   Unveiled: 1994
Donated by: The artist, Mosman Council Australia, Scottish Australia Society
Location: Shore. Behind & to right of Merchant Navy Memorial (*5.6*)

The son of a Leith ship captain, John Hunter was born in Leith. He was second in command of HMS Sirius that founded the colony of New South Wales in 1788. He returned 7 years later to be its second governor, governing with '*sense, duty and humanity*' as noted on the plaque. The Hunter River and Hunter Valley in Australia are named after him.

After arriving in Australia and conducting some explorations Hunter went to Cape Town, South Africa to get supplies, travelling around Cape Horn to the Cape and then back to New South Wales, becoming the first to circumnavigate the world using this route.

Hunter's term as Governor was blighted by the activities of military officers, who, in the delayed period before his arrival, had taken control of the courts and much of the administration, profiting greatly from trade in alcohol. They had entrenched their power to such an extent that, without backing, he was not able to overturn this maladministration. He was forced to return to the UK in 1800. However, his contribution was eventually recognized by the UK Prime Minister who awarded him an annual pension.

Interested in exploration, early in his naval career he explored parts of the West Indies, making charts and plans of Spanish fortifications at Havana. He served in various naval campaigns, including in the American War of Independence.

He spent some of his retired life in Leith and died in London in 1821.

5.8   Sandy Irvine Robertson OBE, 1942 – 1999
Wine merchant, Founder of Scottish Business Achievements Awards Trust

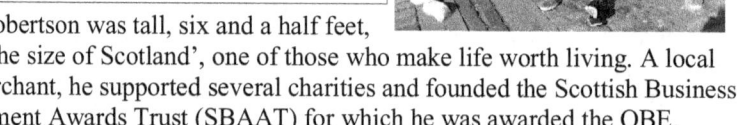

Description: Robertson seated on a wrought-iron bench, his left arm outstretched on its back. He looks out to the water of the old Leith harbour
Commissioned: By his friends
Sculptor: Lucy Poett   Date: 2000
Location: near Merchant Navy memorial (*5.6*).

Sandy Robertson was tall, six and a half feet, a 'heart the size of Scotland', one of those who make life worth living. A local wine merchant, he supported several charities and founded the Scottish Business Achievement Awards Trust (SBAAT) for which he was awarded the OBE.

A popular and sociable man, it is said that he would be pleased with a memorial that allows others to share it with him, a concept included in the sculptor's design. With outstretched left arm he invites passers-by to share the bench. Locals talk of eating their sandwiches with him.

5.9   Hunting for oil
Christian Salvesen PLC and Whaling industry, Leith

Whaling is no longer regarded as respectable, mainly because of previous large scale commercial whaling threatening extinction of whales and cruelty concerns.

However, in the past whaling was a legitimate pastime and it was for many years an important industry. This monument celebrates those positive years of whaling and the sailors who risked life in harsh environments to bring in the valuable source of food and oils wanted by society.

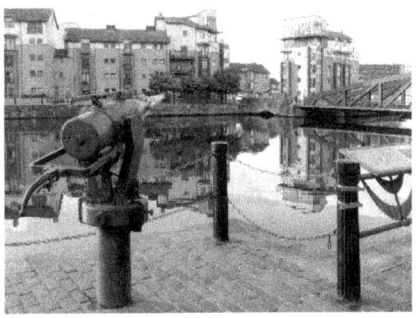

Description: Harpoon from whaling fleet, information board.
Erected: late 20th century
Location: Shore, to left of Merchant Navy Monument (**5.6**)

Leith whaling began in the early 17th century, sailing to Greenland and Arctic waters. It continued till the mid-19th century. In the early 18th century a 'boiling house' was established in Leith in Timber Bush along The Shore for processing whale meat.

The shipping and transportation company Christian Salvesen & Sons established, in the early 20th century, a whaling station in South Georgia, calling it 'Leith Harbour'. By 1911 their whaling fleet, operating in Antarctic waters, was the largest whaling fleet in the world. The industry ceased trading in 1963. After stopping its involvement with whaling the Salvesen became a major transport and logistic company.

The first penguins brought to Edinburgh Zoo were carried by Christian Salvesen's whaling ships, thus making it the first zoo in the world to have and breed penguins.

5.10 Tony Chapman, 1952 – 1999
A sailor who died in the South China Sea

Description: Metal ship's helm, 5-feet high, plaque with inscription and poem.
Sculptor: Unknown;
Unveiled: estimated 1999 to 2000
Location: Rennie's Isle, Leith, across the water from the Whaling Harpoon (**5.9**)

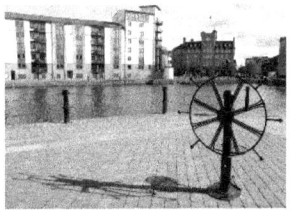

Inscribed: '*In loving memory of Tony Chapman, 1952-1999, who died in the South China Sea, Wife Karen and son Liam*'. On the helm is the poem:

> *How long is a man's life finally? Is it a thousand days or only one?*
> *One week, or a few centuries? How long does a man's death last?*
> *And what do we mean when we say gone forever?*
>
> *A man lives for as long as we carry him inside us,*
> *For as long as we carry the harvest of his dreams,*
> *For as long as we ourselves live,*
> *Holding memories in common a man lives.*

5.11 Reverend Andrew Bell, DD, LLD, FRSE, 1753 – 1832
Education pioneer

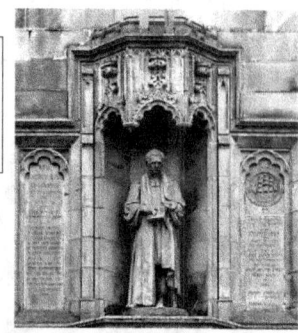

Description: Stone, on wall of the school in Leith
Sculptor: Peter Slater
Date: 1838
Location: Leith, Great Junction Street

The Reverend Dr Bell developed the Madras System of education and founded schools. The Madras system in Scotland was superseded by the education system developed after the late 19th century Education (Scotland) Acts.

He was born and studied in St Andrews, excelling, particularly in Maths. At 21 he emigrated to America to seek his fortune, tutoring children of plantation owners. With savings of £800 he returned to Scotland in the late 18th century, becoming a minister, serving in Leith for 4 years. His next move was to Madras in India with the East India Company. He became Superintendent of the Madras Orphanage that looked after the sons of soldiers. His passion for teaching led him to develop educational systems. There was a shortage of teachers. His solution: teach first the older children, making them then responsible for teaching younger children. The method became known as the 'Madras System'.

Poor health led to his return to Britain in 1797. He started schools, initially in England, using the Madras System. The school in Leith opened in 1835 (after his death) and he also funded, through his legacy, the Madras College opened in his home town of St Andrews. Dr Bell's school in Leith was taken over by the Leith School Board in the late 19th century, becoming a primary school.

The success of his system of education made Dr Bell wealthy. When he died (in Cheltenham, England) he left much of his money to educational developments. Part of the legacy led to the foundation of the Bell Professorships in education at both Edinburgh and St Andrews Universities, the first professorships of education in any English-speaking country.

He was buried in Westminster Abbey.

5.12 Corporal Thomas Peck Hunter, 1923 – 1945
Valiant Royal Marine awarded the Victoria Cross

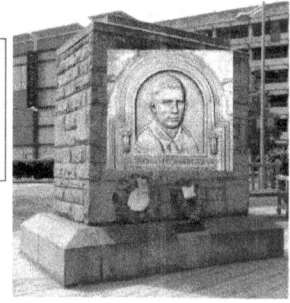

Description: Stone rectangular block with plaque
Sculptor: T.J. Burn;
Date: 1946; Moved to current site 2003
Location: Leith, near Ocean Terminal

The inscription summarises Corporal Thomas Peck Hunter's bravery in action: '*he sacrificed his Life to save those of many of his comrades by his prompt action and fearless courage*'. For this he was posthumously awarded the Victoria Cross (instituted by Queen Victoria, *5.1*), presented to his parents by King George VI at a ceremony at Holyrood

Thomas Hunter was born in Aldershot in England, his parents moving to Edinburgh soon after his birth. He was educated at Stenhouse Primary and Tynecastle High Schools and enlisted in the Home Guard at the outbreak of World War II, joining the Marines in 1942. In April 1845 in action at Lake Comacchio in Italy he single-handedly attacked an enemy position under intense fire, overcoming the enemy, six of whom surrendered, the rest fleeing. This allowed his comrades to reach safety, but sadly he was killed in the action.

5.13 King Edward VII, 1841 – 1910
Edward the Peacemaker, King of the United Kingdom and the British Dominions and Emperor of India

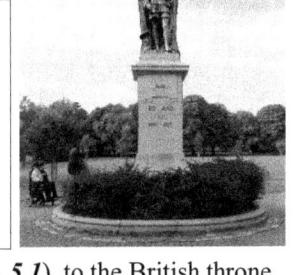

Description: Bronze on stone pedestal, Edward in ceremonial regalia of the Order of the Thistle
Sculptor: John S. Rhind
Commissioned: Leith Town Council, then a separate burgh from Edinburgh
Unveiled: 4th July 1914;
Location: Victoria Park, Leith
See also: Chapter 4, *4.26*

Edward succeeded his mother, Queen Victoria (*1.16, 5.1*), to the British throne in January 1901, reigning till his death in May 1910. His outgoing pleasing personality and the energy and enthusiasm that he applied to his role as monarch endeared him to the country. Her extended family of royalty across Europe gave her mother the nickname 'Grandmother of Europe', which, aided by fluency in French and German, he used to improve political relations across Europe. He was called 'The Peacemaker', ' Peace' inscribed on the monument. But there were underlying tensions between some of the extended family, particularly his nephew Kaiser Wilhelm II of Germany. He helped, in 1907, negotiate 'The Triple Entente' between Britain, France and Russia, cementing their relationships in the face of growing German hostility.

He undertook a successful tour of North America, visiting Canada and then the United States where he stayed with the President. A later successful tour of India followed, where he stressed the importance of treating all people equally, whatever their race or religion.

Ascending the throne as the Anglo-Boer war was ending, he urged military reform, development of a medical service and strengthening of the navy. The military command was redesigned and the Territorial Force and an Expeditionary Force to support France created.

Chapter 6: Around Edinburgh

Selected monuments around the city are discussed. They are arranged by location, starting south of the Royal Mile with the two in Chambers Street near the National Museum and continuing south, then east before looking at a few to the north and west.

6.1 William Chambers of Glenormiston, 1800 – 1883
Publisher, Lord Provost, Edinburgh town planner

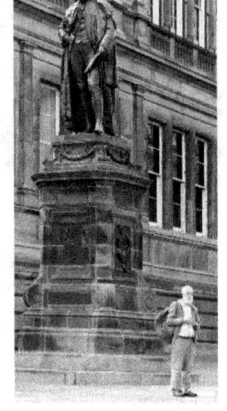

Description: Wearing breeches and Lord Provost's robes and chains, two large books behind him.
Sandstone plinth with 3 copper panels of female figures representing virtues: Literature, Liberality, Perseverance
Sculptor: John Rhind. Panels by Hippolyte J Blanc
Unveiled: 1891, paid for by Town Council
Location: Chambers Street; Location in street moved in 2016

William Chambers, Lord Provost of Edinburgh from 1865-1869, led major city improvements and the restoration of St Giles Cathedral. Through the City Improvement Act of 1866, which followed the 1861 Bailie Fyfe's Close tenement collapse (see Joseph McIver, *4.24*), he led town planning improvements that cleared slums in parts of the Old Town. Several new streets including Jeffrey, St Marys, Blackfriars and Chambers Streets were created, the latter named in his honour and the site of his statue. A successful publisher with his brother, they established a flourishing publishing business, producing a popular weekly journal and some important titles including the Chambers Encyclopaedia.

William was born in Peebles, the eldest son of a rich mill-owning family. The Napoleonic wars (see, National Monument, *3.4*) impoverished the family who moved to Edinburgh. William, an avid reader, accepted an apprenticeship with a bookseller, helping, aged 14, support the family income. His brother Robert, also a keen reader, started a bookshop in a one-room shop in Leith Walk. William joined it at the end of his apprenticeship. An early breakthrough came when they published, with a print-run of 750 copies, 'The Songs of Robert Burns'. They set up a publishing firm 'W. & R. Chambers Publishers'. Five years later they published 'Traditions of Edinburgh'. This was followed by the weekly 'Chambers Edinburgh Journal' (later to be called the 'Chambers Journal of Literature, Science and Arts'). Its success was demonstrated by its 84,000 circulation. When William was about 60, they published the 'Chambers Encyclopaedia', initially in 520 weekly parts at three-halfpence each.

The brothers prospered by taking advantage of modern publishing technologies. Their publishing house was, at the end of the 19th century, one of the largest English language publishers in the world. It later became part of Chambers Harrap Publishers, shutting its Edinburgh premises in 2009. It is now part of Hodder Education based in London.

He was fond of Peebles, opening a museum and art gallery. He was buried there.

6.2 William Henry Playfair, 1790 – 1857
Architect, designed many of the city's 19ᵗʰ century landmark buildings

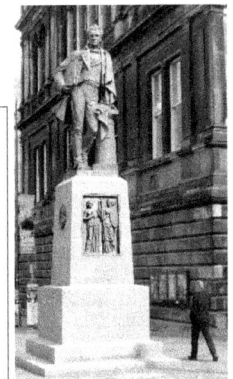

Description: Playfair, bronze, manuscripts in his right hand. On pedestal Edina (Edinburgh, Modern Athens) holds a mirror reflecting the image of Athena, goddess of Athens, on to her.
Sculptor: Alexander Stoddart
Erected: Mid 2016, coinciding with road alterations in Chambers Street. Funded by private individuals, including leading surgeons, National Museums of Scotland, University of Edinburgh and Edinburgh School of Surgery
Location: Chambers Street

One of the great Scottish architects, Playfair's legacy includes many of Edinburgh's iconic buildings including the Mound's two neo-classical art galleries, the 'Royal Scottish Academy' and the 'National Gallery of Scotland'.

An important career breakthrough came when, aged 27, he won the competition to complete Robert Adam's design of Edinburgh University's Old College (near statue). This led to further commissions, designing extensions of the New Town on Calton Hill along Regent Terrace, Royal Terrace and Calton Terrace. On Calton Hill he designed the City Observatory and several monuments: John Playfair, his uncle (*3.2*); Dugald Stewart (*3.1*); the National Monument (*3.4*).

Elsewhere his City works include: the former 'Donaldson's School for the deaf' (now converted for residential use); George Herriot's School; Advocates Library; Royal College of Surgeons; 105 George Street; New College, Mound; Free Church College and Free High Church, which he joined following the Disruption of 1843. Outwith Edinburgh his works include: Dollar Academy, Floors Castle, Spottiswoode House and Lurgan House in Northern Ireland.

His designs have positively influenced Edinburgh's cityscape, its 'Athens of the North' title. The title owes much to the classical Athenian designs he and others introduced, the intellectual thinking of the Enlightenment evoking memories of ancient Athens and an 1822 exhibition by the Edinburgh artist Hugh William Williams of watercolours that compared Athens and Edinburgh.

William was born in Russell Square, London. After his father's death in 1794 (also an architect) he moved to live in Edinburgh with his uncle, John Playfair (*3.2*). He studied architecture at Edinburgh University, spending most of his professional life in the city where he died and was buried in Dean Cemetery.

6.3 Martyrs and Covenanters
Adherents to Protestantism and the Covenant, the Confession of Faith
The covenant declared the sovereignty of Jesus Christ as head of the church. It was based on the Biblical covenant, the personal relationship between God and His people. It conflicted with the power and divine right of the king.

It should be viewed in the context of the Reformation after Martin Luther's 1517 publication of the '*95 Theses*'. These emphasised that Christians are saved by faith, criticising Roman Catholic practices of the time including Papal power and sale of indulgences. Religious divisions then swept Europe; southern countries, France and Spain, remained predominantly Catholic, the north largely Protestant. The British Isles were largely protestant, except for Catholic Ireland, but with strong Catholic adherents, including the monarchy, but forced to accept Protestantism (see Charles II, *4.20*).

The religious conflict was intertwined with political struggles in Scotland involving the largely Catholic-supporting Stuart dynasty with links to the French (Roman Catholic) kings. Scotland had declared for Protestantism in the mid-16th century, led by Knox (*4.14*), with the signing of the Scots Confession of Faith in 1560. Denouncing the Roman Catholic Church, it was adopted by the General Assembly of the Church of Scotland and signed by King James VI, a supporter of Protestantism in contrast to his Catholic mother, Mary Queen of Scots.

However, in the early 17th century the Stuart King Charles I had a different religious outlook and attempted to impose Episcopal worship. He introduced into the Scottish church the Book of Common Prayer in 1637, leading to Jenny Geddes reputedly flinging her chair at the dean in St Giles (Chapter 4). Leaders across Scotland united to confirm adherence to Presbyterians, signing, in Greyfriars Kirk in February 1638, a covenant of adherence to Jesus Christ as head of the church. Copies of the Covenant were distributed throughout Scotland; about 40 copies are known to have been signed. Turmoil continued in both Scotland and England with political and religious rivalries intertwined. King Charles I was executed and the Protestant Cromwell seized power.

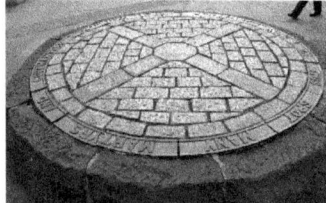

Description: Grey granite stones circle with Cross formed by red granite stones enclosed by a stone wall inscribed: '*Many Martyrs and Covenanters died for the Protestant faith on this spot.*' Plaque lists many of the 300 executed at this spot.
Erected: April 1937; enclosed by wall in 1954
Location: Grassmarket

After the restoration of the monarchy in 1660 King Charles II (*4.20*) denounced the covenants, declaring them unlawful in 1662. A period of sustained persecution followed. Adherents to the Covenant held secret open-air meetings, known as 'conventicles', in the countryside. Many adherents were rounded up and condemned to death, with about 300 executed in Edinburgh's Grassmarket. Conflict was particularly severe in south west Scotland. Robert Woodrow called the period 'The Killing Time' in his 1721 book '*The History of the Sufferings of the Church of Scotland from the Restoration to the Revolution*'. Many regarded them as martyrs, their graves across Scotland including at Greyfriars Kirk.

Near the 1937 Grassmarket memorial an inscribed plinth was erected in 1988: '*This memorial recalls the men and women, nobles and plain folk, ministers, soldiers and others, who were executed at this place and elsewhere in Scotland between 1661 and 1688 for their adherence to the reformed religion and the covenants. The following list, though not complete, gives some indication of the number and also the varied walks of life represented by those executed here in the Grassmarket, at the Mercat Cross in the High Street and at Gallowlee,*

Leith Walk.' Aristocrat and commoner were executed, examples: Marquis of Argyll; Marion Harvie, Bo'ness servant; James Howieson, maltman of Lanark.

The persecution ended in 1688; William and Mary as joint monarchs (William II in Scotland). The 1690 Act of Settlement recognized Scottish Presbyterianism.

6.4 Greyfriars Bobby, 1856 – 1872
Faithfull dog

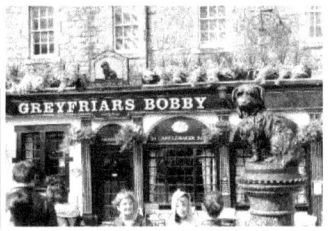

Description: Bobby, bronze, stone plinth
Design by: William Brodie
Unveiled: 15th November 1873
Location: 24 George IV Bridge, EH1 1EN

Bobby, a Skye terrier, belonged to John Gray, a police constable. John died in 1858, buried in Greyfriars Kirk. (Before he died John was looked after by the kindly Dr Henry Littlejohn, the Police Surgeon, later to become Edinburgh's first Medical Officer of Health – see **4.24** and the tenement collapse.) Bobby faithfully guarded John's grave till his death in 1872, 14 years later.

Bobby won Edinburgh's affection. Lord Provost Chambers (*6.1*), a director of the Scottish SPCA, paid for his dog licence. Baroness Burdett-Coutts was so touched that she paid for the statue. The statue's original drinking fountains, upper for humans and lower for dogs, were closed in 1957 for health reasons.

The statue is inscribed: '*A tribute to the affectionate fidelity of Greyfriars Bobby. In 1858 this faithful dog followed the remains of his master to Greyfriars Churchyard and lingered near the spot until his death in 1872*'.

The practice of rubbing Bobby's nose for luck has developed, leading to the shiny nose – compare David Hume's rubbed big toe (*4.15*).

Bobby is an Edinburgh tourist attraction, many flocking to see and be photographed with the dog. Books and films have added to his appeal. In 1981, over a hundred years after his death, a red granite headstone was erected on Bobby's grave, with the inscription: '*Let his loyalty and devotion be a lesson to us all*'. A statue to Bobby was erected in San Diego, USA, with the 2008 statue to 'Bum the dog' in Princes Street Gardens (*1.14*) linking the two statues.

6.5 McEwan Lantern Pillar (William McEwan, 1827 – 1913)
Decorative lamp recognizing the philanthropic gift of the McEwan Hall

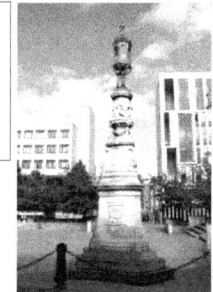

Description: Decorative lantern on Portland stone pedestal
Design by: Sir Robert Rowand Anderson
Erected: 1897
Location: Bristo Square, outside McEwan Hall. The photo shows it in 2009, it was moved, still in the Square, in 2017

After working as an agent in Glasgow and bookkeeper in Yorkshire, William McEwan came to Edinburgh in 1851, starting a brewing firm. Financial success followed, and he entered Parliament as Liberal MP for Edinburgh Central

(1886 – 1900). He was philanthropic, funding the University of Edinburgh's McEwan Hall designed by the architect Sir Robert Rowand Anderson.

The lantern is in Bristo Square, its landscape changed with time. 1897 Photos show the lantern in a triangular plot with vehicular access around it; in the 1960's the road layout changed, with a rectangular plot. The paved area became a popular skateboard venue. In the early 21st century the University embarked on a multi-million pound upgrade of the McEwan Hall and Bristo Square. The Lantern was moved to the south east of the plaza, now a restful relaxing place.

The triangular decorated pedestal has two coats of arms and a figurative group. The coats of arms are of the City of Edinburgh and of William McEwan, the latter being a shield with lion and wheat sheaf and an oak tree.

6.6   International Exhibition of Industry, Science & Art, 1886
An exhibition of industrial developments held in the Meadows

The exhibition was opened on 6th May 1886 by Prince Albert Victor, grandson of Queen Victoria (*5.1*). Over 2.7 million visits were recorded during its 6-month run, ending on 30th October, with a net profit of over £5,000. It covered half of the Meadows' 63-acre estate. A vast temporary exhibition hall housed 20,000 exhibits and accommodated over 20,000 visitors.

Wonders of Victorian engineering and exhibits from around the world were showcased.[1] A memorable exhibit was the '*Old Town Street*', a detailed large scale reconstruction of former Edinburgh buildings. It was described by Alison and John Dunlop (*6.14, 6.15*) in '*The Book of Old Edinburgh: And handbook to the Old Town Street*'. The book described the people who lived in the street, aiming to '*give each house its place in Edinburgh history; to people each, so far as possible, with its old inhabitants*' (quoted from the book's Prefatory notes). Designed by Sidney Mitchell, it showed buildings no longer (at that time) still in existence, not reproducing buildings that were still able to be visited.

The exhibition hall was in a Meadows transformed with gardens, fountain and bandstand. Electrification had recently been developed, enabling the inclusion of a model electric railway and the site's illumination with 3,200 electric lamps – itself an amazing spectacle. James Gowans led the exhibition, for which he was knighted the following year. The exhibition followed the successful London 1851 Crystal Palace exhibition in Hyde Park organised by a royal commission chaired by Prince Albert (*2.1*). He had died before the Edinburgh exhibition.

Some reminders of the exhibition are in the Meadows and other parts of the city, Calton Hill and Nicolson Square.

- **Meadows Sundial, also known as the Prince Albert Victor Sundial**

Designed by James Gowans, it commemorates the Exhibition's official opening by Prince Albert Victor in 1886. It is an octagonal column of six sandstone sections with pedestal and base and large

The Meadows Sundial, Arthurs Seat behind

octagonal top, above which is a bronze armillary sphere.

Below the sphere is inscribed: '*Tak tent o'time ere time be tint*' ('Take account of time before your time is finished').

The red sandstone octagonal top alternates with insignia and names of dignitaries: Coronet of Prince Albert Victor; '*Erected in commemoration of the opening of the International Exhibition by HRH Prince Albert Victor of Wales on 8th May 1886*'; The Arms of Edinburgh; '*The Right Honourable Thomas Clark, Lord Provost of the City*'; Lion Rampant; '*James Gowans, Lord Dean of Guild, Chairman of the Executive Council*'; Castle; '*The Most Honourable Marquis of Lothian K.T. President*'.

The column's sections are each from different quarries: Ballochmyle; Myreton; Redhall; Cocklaw; Cragg; Whitsome; Newton; and the base from Moat.

The red sandstone base is inscribed with texts about the passage of time:
 '*Mark but the hours of sunshine*';
 '*Well arranged time is the surest sign of a well arranged mind*';
 '*Man's days are as a shadow that passeth away*';
 '*Time as he passes us has a dove's wing unsoiled and swift and of a silken sound*';
 '*As a servant earnestly desireth the shadow*';
 '*Time is the chrysalis of eternity*';
 '*Light is the shadow of God*';
 '*Time and Tide wait for no man*'.

- **Whale Jawbones**

The Whalebones formed part of the Zetland (Shetland) and Fair Isle Knitters exhibit, contrasting with their delicate knit-ware crafts. Gifted to the City after the exhibition, they were placed at the entrance of what is now known as the Jawbone Walk. They were placed to form an entrance arch to the path.

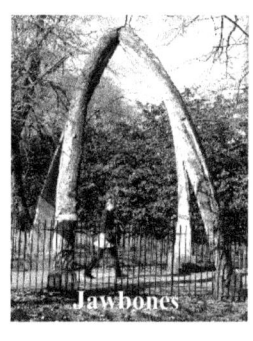

To prevent further weathering they were removed in 2014 for restoration. The photo shows them in spring 2010; currently they have not yet been returned.

- **Masons Pillars, Melville Drive**

Erected in 1886 to commemorate the International Exhibition are a pair of octagonal columns, the Masons Pillars. They are at the west end of Melville Drive, the road through the Meadows. Designed by James Gowans they are built from stones from Scottish quarries. At its top, each pillar has a unicorn holding a flagstaff and shield. The shields bear the city's coat of arms and motto '*nisi dominus frustra*' ('*except with the Lord it will be frustrated*'). Below the unicorns are shields of Scottish Cities and inscriptions to: Thomas Clark, Lord Provost of the City at the time of the International Exhibition; and James Gowans, Architect and Lord Dean of Guild who helped co-ordinate the exhibition.

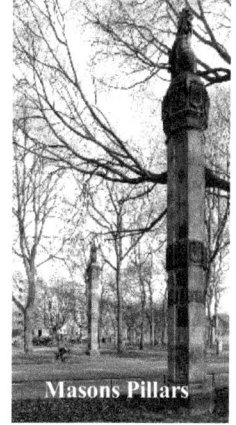

Other pillars in the Meadows:
- East end of Melville Drive: two pillars presented to the city by Messrs T. Nelson & Sons in 1880 in gratitude for the city's support for their publishing firm after fire destroyed their premises in 1876.
- North end of Middle Meadow Walk: a set of pillars erected in 1840s to mark the opening of the Meadows to the public.

- **The Brassfounders Column,** Nicolson Square

A tall square column decorated with coats of arms of England, Scotland and Ireland and of Scottish towns. On its top is Tubal Cain, the Biblical forger of all instruments of brass and iron (Genesis 4:22). It was commissioned for the Exhibition by the Edinburgh and Leith Brass Founders. Designed by James Gowans and the figure of Tubal Cain by John S. Rhind, it won a gold medal.

Brassfounders Column, Nicolson Square

After the 1888 exhibition it was exhibited at the 1908 Scottish National Exhibition in Saughton Park, then gifted to the City of Edinburgh and erected in Nicolson Square where it currently is.

- **Portuguese Cannon,** Calton Hill

A brass Cannon with the Royal Arms of Spain on its barrel, it was cast in the early 15th century. It went to the Portuguese colonies in South East Asia in the late 18th century, then came into the possession of the King of Burma. It was captured by the British during the 1885 invasion of Burma. It

Portuguese Cannon, Calton Hill. At top right is Dugald Stewart (3.1) monument

was presented to Edinburgh where it was exhibited at the 1886 Exhibition. After the exhibition, in 1887, it was installed on Calton Hill.

6.7   Helen Acquroff (Sister Cathedral), 1831-1887
Music teacher, musician, pianist, singer, poet, temperance campaigner

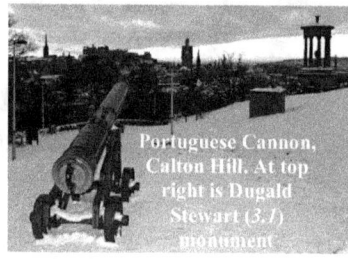

Description: Drinking Fountain within fenced area
Inscribed: Helen Acquroff Sister Cathedral 1889
Erected by members of the I.O.G.T. and other friends (Independent Order of Good Templars)
Location: Meadows, near Whale Jawbones (*6.6*) and Coronation Walk   Date: 1889

Helen (or Ellen or Hellen), was born in Edinburgh, the second of 10 children of John Acquroff, a hairdresser of Russian ancestry, and Sophia Campbell Fletcher from Nairn, Scotland. She was visually impaired form birth, fully blind at 11. She remained unmarried and in 1862 had a son James.

Helen was active in the Temperance Movement. She was given the nickname 'Sister Cathedral' after the publication of an address she gave at Glasgow Cathedral warning of the dangers of intemperance. She wrote poetry and published a book (c1872) of temperance songs under the title of 'Good Templar Songs, &c.' using the name Sister Helen Acquroff, Blind Authoress.

She sang in Edinburgh's concert halls, using the stage name Sister Cathedral. A humorous poem of hers (*'When We Were Bairns Thegither'*) was reproduced in the spring 2016 newsletter of 'Friends of the Meadows and Bruntsfield Links'. Helen writes of a woman addressing her husband ('my ain gudeman') after 40 years of marriage but who had known each other for 60 years since childhood:

'But ah, waes me, it's sixty year | For hand in hand we gaed to chule
Since we kent ane anither | When we were bairns thegither.'

She attended the Blind Asylum School, then in Nicolson Street, later teaching there. She lived with her family at various places in Edinburgh, dying of nephritis aged 55 in 1887.

6.8   James Hutton, MD, FRSE, 1726-1797
Philosopher and Scientist, Father of Modern Geology

Whilst farming in Berwickshire after graduation from Edinburgh James Hutton saw that wind and rain could change landscapes. He studied rock structures, fossil remains, granite veins and rock fragments within conglomerate rocks. Observing the dolerite and sedimentary rock layers at Salisbury Crags helped him develop his theories. A plaque in his honour on the Radical Road below Salisbury Crags now summarises his observations.

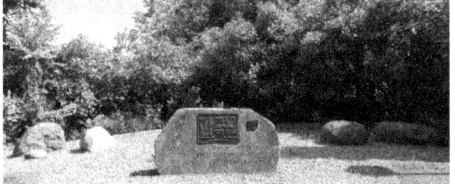

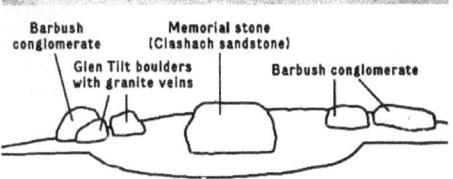

Barbush conglomerate   Memorial stone (Clashach sandstone)
Glen Tilt boulders with granite veins   Barbush conglomerate

He postulated a molten hot interior of the earth whose surface was subject to continuous remoulding, with rocks destroyed and reformed. He suggested that the

Description: Hutton Memorial garden, rock and 5 boulders illustrating themes of Hutton's geological work. Plaque on rock dated 1997
Design: Architects - Crichton, Lang, Willis & Galloway
Date: 2001   Location: St John's Hill

earth was millions of years old, contrary to the then contemporary beliefs of about 6000 years.

His keen observations and insightful deductions led to a scientific approach to geology for which he is now recognised as 'the father of modern geology'.

He also developed theories on rain's formation, based on warmer air's increased capacity to hold water vapour; rain falls when this water-bearing air is cooled.

He presented his findings to the Royal Society of Edinburgh in 1785; he had helped form it. But it was after his death, and thanks to John Playfair (*3.2*), that Hutton's contributions became fully recognized, in particular through Playfair's publication of *'Illustrations of the Huttonian Theory of the Earth'*.

A plaque on the monument recounts that James Hutton lived, from 1770, in a house, 3 St John's Hill, on the site of the current monument. There he '*wrote his epoch-making* **Theory of the Earth** *as well as all his other books and papers'.* Engraved on the memorial rock is Hutton's 1788 sentence: '*We find no vestige of a beginning, no prospect of an end'.*

An explanatory plaque explains: '*Hutton used the presence of granite veins in Glen Tilt to demonstrate that granite is an igneous rock and that it must have been younger than the rocks it penetrated. The granite veins can be seen in the two rocks from Glen Tilt.*' '*The other three boulders are conglomerates from Barbush, near Dunblane, and are full of fragments of earlier rocks, demonstrating the continuity and cyclicity of geological processes.*'

The 18th century was Edinburgh's Enlightenment, Hutton an influential contributor, meeting with leaders, John Playfair (*3.2*), David Hume (*4.15*), Adam Smith (*4.22*) and Joseph Black. John Playfair publicised Hutton's work after his death, giving full credit to Hutton for the innovative thinking.

Hutton was involved in the construction of the Forth and Clyde canal.

6.9   Muschet's Cairn (or Muschat's Cairn)
Commemorates where Nicol Muschet murdered his wife in 1720

Description: Muschet's Cairn is a pile of small cemented boulders. There is no plaque.
Design by: Edinburgh citizens laying stones to remember the awful deed
Date: Original cairn in 1720s. Removed to construct footpath; present cairn 1823
Location: Holyrood Park, Duke's Walk, near Meadowbank entrance

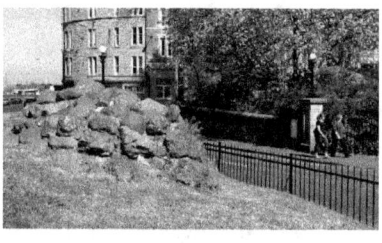

The cairn was erected to commemorate the murder by Nicol Muschet of his wife in 1720 for which Muschet was hanged in the Grassmarket in 1721. At his trial he reportedly said he had simply tired of her. People built the cairn by laying stones '*in token of the people's abhorrence and reprobation of the deed*'[2]. A peoples' monument, erected directly by people reacting to the horrible murder.

Nicol was born in 1695, brought up by his mother '*in the true Presbyterian Principles of Religion*'[3], his father having died whilst he was young. He attended Edinburgh Medical College, becoming a surgeon's apprentice in 1716, but left, leaving town. Returning, he met a young girl, Margaret Hall, marrying her within a few weeks of their meeting. But he rapidly tired of her, accusing her of dubious virtue. He made up his mind to leave her, but, unwilling to pay alimony, looked for alternative ways of ridding himself of her.

A contract to arrange for infidelity was drawn up by a lawyer, co-conspirators including a town magistrate and professor of languages. However, the attempt failed. Muschet was then persuaded to arrange for his wife to be murdered, a relation, James Muschet and his wife Grissel agreeing to carry out the deed. But their attempts failed. So, on a December night, Muschet took his wife into Holyrood Park and, in a gruesome attack, killed her with a knife. Her dead body was found the next day. Muschet confessed and hanged in January 1721.

Sir Walter Scott mentioned the cairn in his novel 'The Heart of Midlothian'.

6.10 Dr Helen Crummy, MBE, 1920-2011
Social reformer, founder of the Craigmillar Festival Society

Helen Crummy, recognizing and wishing to encourage her son's musical ability, asked his school if he could be taught to play the violin. Craigmillar, where they lived, was suffering acutely from post-war depression, with many social problems. In his despair over the problems, the headmaster responded that '*it takes all our time to teach these children the 3Rs, far less music*'. (He was to support Helen in her efforts.) Unwilling to accept this, she galvanised the local mothers' club to stage a 'People's Festival' of music, drama and arts. This was the beginning, in 1962, of the Craigmillar Festival Committee whose continuing success led to official recognition, charitable status and, in 1969, formalisation as the Craigmillar Festival Society.

Her obituary in the Scotsman sums up this amazing leader [4]:

> '*Helen Crummy was one of those rare individuals whose innate modesty concealed an iron determination to change the world for the better, above all for the poor and marginalised. Where some might see the victims of poverty as part of an endemic social problem, she saw the unfulfilled potential of people who, given the opportunity, could overcome disadvantage and find self-esteem.*
>
> '*For her, every child, no matter how poor, was a precious gift; every adult, regardless of circumstances, was worthy of respect, and deserved to be listened to.*'

The obituary concluded by recounting the pause after a concert she had persuaded Yehudi Menuhin to give. The audience, stunned by the brilliant performance, hesitated before applauding. During the pause a voice was heard: '*That wis no bad, eh*'. The Scotsman's obituarist went on to write: '*It is a tribute .. and the very least that could be said of her life, with all its quiet virtuosity. That it was no bad, eh*'.

Her work was recognized with the award of an MBE in 1976 and an honorary doctorate (LLD) by Herriot-Watt University. She wrote several books including 'Let the People Sing'.

Description: Helen Crummy, seated, handing her son the bow enabling him to play the violin. An arch formed by an open door invites: '*Let the people sing*'. On the door are various scenes under the inscription: '*History will be made when the people play their part*'.
Behind the boy is a model of Craigmillar Castle and an open book is inscribed: '*Craigmillar now a fine place to be*' and on the right hand page '*Women tap the creative well*'.
Sculptor: Tim Chalk
Unveiled: 21st March 2014 by Richard Demarco and Helen's grandson
Location: Craigmillar Community Centre, Niddrie Mains Road, EH16 4DS

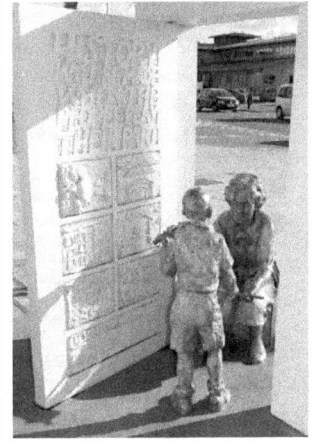

John N. Amoore

Helen Murray Prentice was born in Leith, the eldest of six children. Her father was a watchmaker who started a business first in Haddington and then in Edinburgh. The great depression of the 1930s shattered the family fortunes, forcing them to move to bleak housing in Niddrie. Notwithstanding the widespread social deprivation in the area, their mother ensured that the children were rarely hungry. Furthermore, the children were encouraged to read, a favourite being 'The Ragged Trousered Philanthropist'. The book, by Robert Tressel, is a commentary on society's inequity, which attacks the attitude of some to the poor workers believing that a better life is not for them.

The economic hardship faced by the family forced Helen to leave school at 14 to work. About five years later World War II broke out and she served as a Corporal in the Women's Auxiliary Air Force. This leadership role was to give her valuable organizational experience that she was able to make use of later.

In 1942 she married Larry Crummy, Durham Light Infantry. They had 3 sons.

Helen believed that Craigmillar's children should be given opportunities to flourish and prosper. This led her to request music lessons for her son and the subsequent organization of the Craigmillar Pageant. The pageant celebrated the history of the local area through music and the arts. It included stories about Mary Queen of Scots who had lived in Craigmillar Castle and whose courtiers from France settled in the land to the south – leading to its current name 'Little France'. Her philosophy and approach attracted interest around the world.

In keeping with Dr Crummy's approach of community involvement, Tim Chalk, the sculptor of the memorial, worked with a commissioning group made up mostly of local people who had known Helen. They *'agreed that a monument was probably the last thing that Helen would have wanted, but it was important to all of them that one of their own should have a fitting memorial'* [5]. Tim Chalk, on his website, described the approach to the monument's design [6]:

> *"The Sculpture takes its inspiration from the story of Helen Crummy's request to the school for violin lessons for her son, and how, when this was refused, she and other mothers set about organising musical activities themselves ... and the rest is history. Taking the mother and child playing a violin as the central motif, the sculpture aims to maximise on the symbolic nature of this image and its importance to the Craigmillar Festival Society story. A mother hands her child a bow, providing him with the means to develop his creativity. Standing in a south facing open doorway, sunlight pours through to open up new horizons, symbolised by the image of Craigmillar Castle, the venue for so much local cultural activity, sitting amongst books and clearly visible through the doorway.*
>
> *'THE SHADOW THAT CHARTS THE PROCESS OF CONSTANT RENEWAL – To enhance the feeling of illumination by sunlight (and to provide an effect on all those days when the sun doesn't actually shine!) the shadow cast by the boy is etched into the surface of the plinth – but this isn't just any shadow. Marking the day when the first Craigmillar houses were opened on the 17th September 1930, every year on that date at 12 noon the actual shadow of the boy will fall on the surface of the plinth to correspond with the etched shadow. The etched shadow contains text which explains this.*
>
> *'THE WIDER STORY – To tell the wider story of the Festival Society and the people involved, the surface of the door carries relief panels modelled by local adults and children; very appropriate to a work celebrating Helen Crummy and the Craigmillar*

Festival Society.

'THE INSCRIPTIONS – In addition to the panels, the open door carries the quote 'History will be made when the People play their part', and the arch carries the celebratory inscription 'Let the People Sing', both quoted from the writings of Helen Crummy. Further quotes appear on the pages of an open book lying next to the Castle; 'Craigmillar now; a fine place to be' and 'Women tap the creative well'. All round the edge of the plinth run the words: 'The beauty of Craigmillar lies in the strength of its people'."

6.11 Robert Louis Stevenson, 1850–1894
Author and traveller

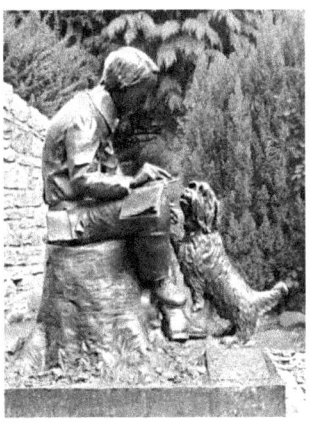

Description: Stevenson as a child, sits on a tree stump, book in hand, 2nd book in pocket, with Cuillin, his Skye terrier. Bronze
Sculptor: Alan Beattie Herriot; Date: October 2013
Location: Colinton, near Parish Church
See also: Chapter 1, *1.11*

This statue and the Robert Louis Stevenson Trail in Colinton recall Robert's many visits to the Edinburgh village of Colinton where his maternal grandfather, Dr Lewis Balfour, was the Minister of the Parish Church.

The statue was unveiled by author Ian Rankin (see 'Edinburgh Award', *4.16*). A Victorian games session for children was organised at the unveiling, recognizing Robert's childhood visits to the area. It shows Robert seated with two books, recalling his statement: *'I kept always two books in my pocket, one to read, one to write in'*, (on plaque at statue, from 'Essays of Robert Louis Stevenson').

A Robert Louis Stevenson Walking Trail was opened a year later between Colinton Village and the Parish Church. It follows the route of the 'Long Steps', beginning at its top through a metal archway inscribed *'The Long Steps: a walk with Robert Louis Stevenson'*.

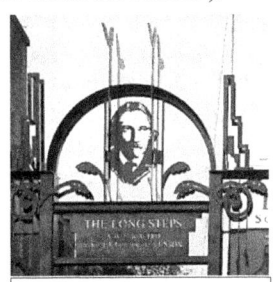

The route is decorated with panels designed by local artist Ian Boyter that are illustrated with verses from Robert's *'A Child's Garden of Verses'*. An introductory panel at the top of the Long Steps recalls that this was an important ancient route in the village and that Robert based many of the poems in the book on his childhood experiences in the village. Panels reproduce some of these poems, starting with *'Summer Sun'* and *'The Moon'* and including *'The Flowers'* and, near the bridge over the river,

The Long Steps, upper part of 'Robert Louis Stevenson Walking Trail'
Date: 2014
Location: Colinton, between village and the Parish Church

'Looking-glass River', inviting us with its words to look down at the river and see how *"Smooth it slides upon its travel"*.

6.12 Twelve Poets at Edinburgh Park
Busts of Scottish Poets

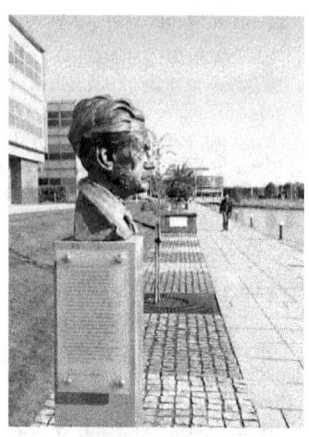

Description: Herms of 12 Scottish poets, each on a plinth, with brief biography and verses from the poet's.
Sculptors: various – see individual herms
Dates: various from 2002 to 2004
Location: Edinburgh Park, near the lochans, shown in the photo with business park buildings to the left

Edinburgh Park is a business park development in the west of Edinburgh, dating from the late 20th century. Public art and literature were included in the planning, with the developers displaying poems in the bus shelters. From this grew the idea of erecting sculptures of Scottish poets, stimulating those who work and visit the area and providing opportunities for sculptors. The business park developer decided to erect a set of 12 herms honouring Scottish literary figures, the poets chosen selected with the assistance of the Scottish Poetry Library.

The term 'herm' originated in 6th century BC Greek art, with the herm, a head, mounted on a plinth. The structures were considered sacred to the Greek god Hermes. They were placed on street corners in Athens.

A second casting of the 12 herms was donated to the Scottish National Portrait Gallery in 2005 who published a book by Ian Wall, Director of the development company responsible for Edinburgh Park: '*Twelve Poets at Edinburgh Park*'. The book describes the thinking behind it with details and photos of each herm.

The poets are listed here by location, starting east-to-west along Lochside Walkway, and then on the north side of the waterway continuing clockwise. The notes about each poet are partly taken from the biographies on the plinths.

- **Hamish Henderson** (1919-2002), sculptor Anthony Morrow; unveiled 2003 by Hamish's widow.
  Whilst serving as an intelligence officer Hamish collected material for his first book, '*Ballads of World War II, in Five Languages*'. The bust biography notes that '*politics, poetry and folksong were inseparable in his life*'. Celebrations of his life leading the 20th century Scottish Folksong Revival were held in 2019, the centenary of his birth. An influential member of Edinburgh's School of Scottish Studies, he valued the communal spirit of song. He '*envisaged a Scotland that was free. Fraternal and joyful*'.

- **Douglas Dunn** (1942-), sculptor Michael Snowden; unveiled 2003 by Dunn. Dunn trained as a librarian, becoming professor in the School of English at the University of St Andrews. He has won many awards for his poetry which often use conversational tone, his strong feelings for social justice always apparent. His biography notes that '*Honesty, fidelity to imaginative truth, and an eye for the telling detail mark his poetry*'. In a moving tribute, '*The intimate lyrics of Elegies*' Dunn mourns in tender verse the loss of his first wife, Lesley. The book won the 1985 Whitbread Book of the Year award.

- **Sorley Maclean** (1911-1996), sculptor Bill Scott; unveiled 2003 by widow. Sorley was born on the Isle of Raasay, studying English literature at the University of Edinburgh. After service in World War II he became head teacher at Plockton High School, leading the Gaelic renaissance in Scotland and preserving its teaching in Scottish schools. In 1943 he published '*Dain do Eimhir*' a collection of passionate poems of love and politics. His '*Reothairt is Contraight/Spring Tide and Neap Tide*' was published in the 1970s, attracting wide acclaim and he received the Queen's Gold Medal for Poetry in 1990. He is regarded as the greatest Gaelic poet of the 20th century.

- **Tom Leonard** (1944-2018), sculptor Alex Main; unveiled 2003 by Leonard. Tom was born in Glasgow, narrating and spreading the city's voices throughout Scotland and beyond. The biography notes that his '*political, aesthetic and linguistic concerns are inextricable. His poetry contrasts different voices, social classes emotional registers, philosophies. It is often funny but fiercely so*'. In his 1995 collection '*Reports from the Present*', he presents powerfully '*the authenticities and indignations which have moved him to act and write*'.

- **Hugh MacDiarmid** (1892-1978), sculptor Anthony Morrow; unveiled 2002
  See also: Scottish Parliament Vigil Cairn (*3.5*); and Stones of Scotland (*3.10*)
  Born Christopher Murray Grieve, he served in the RAMC during World War I and then worked as a journalist. He changed his name to Hugh MacDiarmid reflecting his passionate Scottish nationalism, and he went on to promote the 20th century Scottish Renaissance movement. A member of the Communist Party and a founding member of the National Party of Scotland, he expressed strong views forcefully leading to expulsion from, but later re-joining of both. He was a prodigious poet, fervently expressing critical nationalism. He led the early 20th century revival in the use of the Scots language and is recognized as a leading Scottish literary figure of his century.

- **(Elizabeth Anne) Liz Lochhead** (1947-), sculptor Vincent Butler; unveiled 2002.
  Liz studied at Glasgow School of Art after which she taught art at high schools in Glasgow and Bristol, but was to describe her art ability as terrible. Whilst at Glasgow School of Art she won a BBC Scotland Poetry Competition. Her first collection of poetry '*Memo for Spring*', was published in 1971. She is described as: '*a fresh voice, of women speaking to women, speaking for women*', in '*the predominantly male domain of Scottish Poetry*'; '*She has been a liberating inspiring literary presence*'. She was appointed the Poet Laureate for Glasgow in 2005, stepping down in 2011 when she became Scots Makar (national poet of Scotland), succeeding Edwin Morgan (see below).

- **Edwin Morgan** (1920-2010), sculptor David A. Annand; unveiled 2002
  Edwin was born in Glasgow living there most of his life, except for military service during World War II (serving in the RMAC was a compromise to conscientious objection). His poetry was grounded in Glasgow. He studied at Glasgow University where he became a professor and was Glasgow's first Poet Laureate (1999-2002), going on to becoming the first Scots Makar after

the post of Scot's national poet was established by the Scottish Parliament. His work included translations from a variety of European languages and original work. His '*Sonnets from Scotland*' is described '*as one of the most important works of post-war literature*'. His poetry '*is marked by inventiveness, acceptance of change and an exhilarating energy*'.

- **Iain Crichton Smith** (1928-1998), sculptor Michael Snowden; unveiled 2002
  Born in Glasgow, he grew up on the Isle of Lewis before teaching in schools in Clydebank and Oban. He wrote both prose and poetry but considered himself more naturally a poet, composing in English and Gaelic. In '*Am Faigh a Ghaidhlig Eas? Shall Gaelic Die?*' he pondered the fate of Gaelic's language and culture. Writing with '*lyrical candour and great human understanding*', his poetry '*speculated on the meaning of human existence*'.

- **Norman MacCaig** (1910-1996), sculptor David Annand; unveiled 2004
  Born in Edinburgh and studying classics at Edinburgh University, Norman became a schoolteacher, writing poetry '*marked by elegance, wit and sharp insight*'. The settings of his works were drawn from Edinburgh and from Assynt in the north west of Scotland where he spent summer holidays. Drawing inspiration from the natural world and its '*unempathic marvels*' he was a poet who was '*openly conscious of his act of seeing, of the search to find language adequate to his perceptions*'.

- **Naomi Mitchison (neé Haldane)** (1897-1999), sculptor Archie Forrest; unveiled 2004
  Naomi first pursued a scientific career, publishing a seminal paper with her brother in 1915 on the genetic linkage in mammals. The outbreak of World War I led her to switch to nursing and during the war, in 1916, she married Gilbert Mitchison, then on leave from the Western Front. He entered politics after the war, with Naomi supporting his political career, though, when he was created a life peer in 1964, she objected to the title Lady Mitchison, never using it. Their marriage developed into an agreed open marriage, both having several other relationships, but all her seven children were with her husband. She was a prolific author, completing more than 90 books. Her early novels were prompted by the classics and mythology, with the '*The Corn King and the Spring Queen*' completed in 1931 considered one of her best works. Her writings explored controversial topics, with her guide '*An Outline for Boys and Girls and their Parents*' winning both applause and critical censure, partly because of its lack of emphasis on Christianity. Her controversial '*We have been warned*' explored in frank terms sexual behaviour and had to be extensively rewritten before publication. She also explored Scottish themes including the 1745 Jacobite rising in '*The Bull Calves*' published in 1947. James Watson recognized her scientific work, dedicating his book, '*The Double Helix*', to her [7]. Watson had written much of the book whilst staying with the Mitchison's. (James Watson and Francis Crick won the Nobel Prize in 1962 for their work on DNA.)

- **Jackie Kay** (1961-), sculptor Michael Snowden; unveiled 2004
  Jackie's was awarded the Saltire Society Scottish First Book Award 1991 for

collection of poems, '*The Adoption Papers*', bringing her work to prominence. She published further poetry and, in 1998, a novel, '*The Trumpet*'. Her work has been described as having '*a generous*' humanity, with an '*understanding of the deeply familiar experiences of daughters, mothers, lovers .. filtered through the sensibility of an outsider*'. The biography on the plinth notes that '*she is alert to the register of languages, and to the power of language to make people feel at home or unwelcome*'.

Awarded an MBE in 2006 she became Professor of Creative Writing at Newcastle University, in 2016 succeeding Lochhead (see above) as Makar.

- **William Sydney Graham** (1918-1986), sculptor Anthony Morrow; unveiled 2004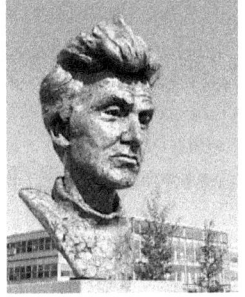
Born in Greenock, Graham left school at 14 to become an apprentice draughtsman, studying structural engineering at Stow College, Glasgow. A bursary to study literature at Newbattle Abbey College in 1938 opened up a new career, and his first book '*Cage without Grievance*' was published in 1942. He spent most of his life in Cornwall, often scraping together a living as he continued writing. His work was not fully appreciated during his lifetime, but subsequently has become more appreciated. The Scottish Poetry Library describes his work [8]: '*His poetry pays close attention to the structure and possibilities of language; he invites readers to explore with him the means to authentic communication in poems of great energy, wit and humanity.*'

6.13 Dr Hugh Dewar, 1866 – 1914
Physician

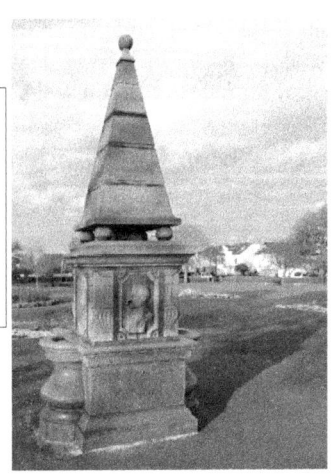

Description: Drinking fountain with obelisk resting on four round balls. The south side has a portrait of Dr Dewar, the north an inscription from the donors
Designed by: T. Currie Bell
Built by: D. Davidson and Son, Edinburgh
Donated by: Patients and supporters of Dr Dewar
Date: 1915
Location: Abercorn Park, Portobello

The monument is inscribed:
'*This fountain has been erected in remembrance of Dr Hugh Dewar, Portobello, by his grateful patients and numerous friends who deplore the loss in the prime of manhood of a kind friend and a skilled and beloved physician. His quiet charity was known to the needy. 1866 – 1914*'.

The monument remembers the tragic death in childbirth of Jane Anderson under Dr Dewar's care. Dr Dewar had graduated from the University of Edinburgh in 1896 developing a large practice in Portobello where he was highly respected. In

1914 he went to Jane Anderson's home to deliver her first child, Jane's mother assisting. Delivery was not straightforward, and Jane died of major blood loss and internal injuries a few hours after the birth of her son. Jane was buried in the nearby Portobello cemetery, remembered on the family headstone (McArthur).

The police suspected medical negligence, charging Dr Dewar with culpable homicide. He continued to practice, but it is thought that, because of self-blame, he committed suicide. A team from Edinburgh University's Forensic Medicine Unit retrospectively analysed the case [9], showing that the forceps used during the delivery had punctured the mother's internal organs, exposing parts of the intestine which Dr Dewar pulled out leading to her death.

The British Medical Journal obituary noted [10]: '*Dr Dewar himself at once reported the death to the authorities, and had he survived to appear in the High Court at the end of this month, expert evidence would have been given as to the nature of the complication, which was .. of a very unusual character*'.

The double tragedy of this event emphasizes the reasons for the late 20th and early 21st century approach that seeks to understand the full reasons for adverse healthcare events. This, rather than a blame-first approach, is crucial to making healthcare safer and to prevent future adverse events occurring. It recognizes that 'to err is human' but that 'to continue to err is devilish', and that consequently to limit the risk of adverse events occurring, equipment and processes must be designed considering 'mistake-proofing', that is, the design helps ensure that the equipment or process is used correctly.

Perhaps this memorial should be considered as a reminder of the risks inherent in medicine, of the adverse events that can and do occur and of how to manage them. It is also a reminder of the tragedies of medical accidents and their effects on all victims and their families. It contrasts the deep respect and affection that patients had for their local doctor with the tragic consequences of the adverse event for Jane Anderson and her family.

6.14 Alison Hay Dunlop 1835-1888
Historian and author

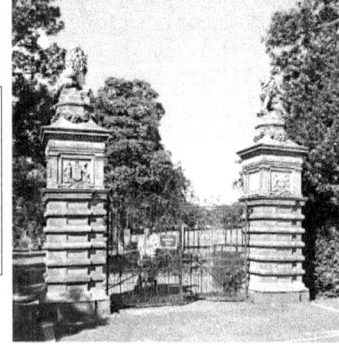

Description: Two classical memorial pillars to Alison Hay Dunlop forming gateway
Design: Sydney Mitchell & Wilson
Commissioned: Alison's brother John Dunlop
Date: 1890
Location: East entrance to Inverleith Park

Alison Dunlop, sister of John Dunlop (*6.15*), was an Edinburgh antiquarian and historian, keenly interested in the life of the city. This led her to write '*Anent Old Edinburgh*' (full title: '*Anent Old Edinburgh and some of the worthies who walked its streets, with other papers*'). Her brothers edited and published it in 1890 after her death. It was the first book to be borrowed from the city's public library when it opened in 1890.

'*Anent Old Edinburgh*' is a collection of stories of Edinburgh life. For example, the first chapter '*Anent Sir Thomas Hope's house*' tells the story of the 'The Hope House' in the Cowgate, built in 1616, to make way for what is now the central library on George IV Bridge. It is more than a description of the buildings and their histories, but with keen focus on 'the worthies' who occupied them, with links to historical events. The early 17th century was a time of religious turbulence and the young Thomas Hope was called upon to defend leaders of the General Assembly of the Church of Scotland who were defying King James VI's attempts to '*crush the Scottish Church*'. Alison describes the trial of the leaders at which the young lawyer '*had brains and a tongue, and he could use both simultaneously. (O rare fair gift!)*'.

Alison also co-authored with her brother John Charles Dunlop (*6.15*) '*The Book of Old Edinburgh: And Handbook to the Old Edinburgh Street (1886)*' to accompany the 1886 International Exhibition (*6.6*) with its reconstruction of an Old Town street. Her brother John was a Joint Convenor of the exhibit.

Alison had a positive optimistic outlook on life, reflected in one of her favourite sayings: '*Ane never kens where a blessing is to licht*'.

She suffered an unfortunate leg accident aged just 10. Sadly, the enthusiastic experiments of various medical experts did not aid recovery. It was during this stage of her life that she was told Border stories and ballads. These excited her interest in folk life, an interest she was to pursue in adulthood, leading to her collections of stories of Edinburgh life.

6.15 John Charles Dunlop, 1833-1899
City councillor and supporter of establishment of Inverleith Park

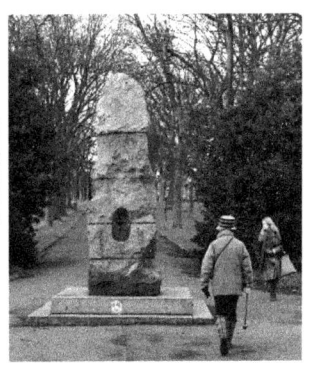

Description: Granite fountain	
Design: William Holt;	Date: 1900
Location: Central position in Inverleith Park	

John Dunlop was a local politician, councillor for St Bernard's Ward, who helped establish Inverleith Park. His sister Alison Dunlop (*6.14*). A fountain roughly carved in a large granite rock, placed at the crossing of the main walkways in Inverleith Park, it was erected in 1900. Inscribed: '*In memory of John Charles Dunlop a magistrate of Edinburgh who died Feb. 4th 1899. This fountain was erected by public subscription 1900*'. It originally had a portrait medallion sculpted by George Webster.

Inverleith Park was purchased by the then Edinburgh Corporation in 1889 for £33,500 and developed into what is now a large park with grand gated entrances and a range of facilities including sports pitches, bowling greens, allotments, a pond (used by a model boat club), wildlife habitat and green fields.

6.16 Queen Elizabeth, The Queen Mother, 1900 – 2002
Queen and Queen Mother

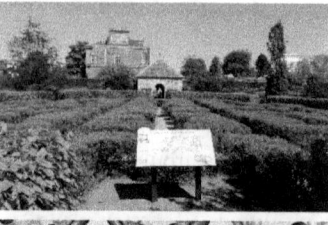

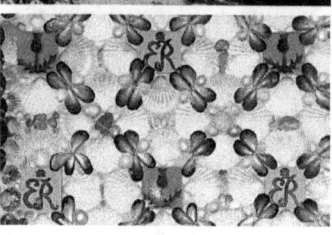

> Description: Memorial garden arranged as a labyrinth, each corner representing a different geographical area of the world. The inner walls of the Pavilion are decorated with sea shells and its ceiling with pine cones
> Designed by: Lachlan Stewart of ANTA Architecture, based on the Eassie Cross near Glamis Castle, the Queen Mother's home
> Opened: 2006 by her daughter Queen Elizabeth
> Location: Royal Botanic Gardens Edinburgh

Queen Elizabeth the Queen Mother, Queen Consort to King George VI, was a much loved member of the Royal Family. She won respect and admiration for remaining in London during the dark days of World War II, being with her people during the blitz and its terrors. She refused to send her daughters to safety in the country saying:

> *'They will not leave without me,*
> *I will not leave without the King,*
> *and the King will not leave'.*

After her husband's death she became Queen Mother, supporting her daughter, now Queen. She was loved by her grandchildren, in particular by Prince Charles. Her life spanned the 20th century, a time of tremendous change.

Her daughter, the present Queen opened the memorial garden and pavilion. Within the pavilion is a bronze portrait of the Queen Mother below which is the inscription: '*This national memorial was created through the generosity of many both in Scotland and further afield to honour a much loved Scottish lady'.*

Garden plaques recognize the many and varied groups for whom she was Patron. Stone paving slabs summarise significant events during each decade of her long life. Her first decade, 1900 to 1909, witnessed: death of Queen Victoria (*5.1*); Coronation of King Edward VII (*4.26, 5.13*); 1st powered flight by Wright brothers; 1st performance of JM Barrie's Peter Pan. In the 1910s World War I is remembered in which her brother died, as is the Russian Revolution and the granting of the vote to women. The 1920s saw the invention of television and penicillin and then through the succeeding decades, with the 1960s seeing man on the moon and the late 1980s the fall of the Berlin Wall.

Plants from around the world are in the garden. The labyrinth is planted with bog myrtle from the Scottish Highlands. The shells and pebbles decorating the pavilion's interior walls were collected by school children from across Scotland and the pine cones are from the four National Botanic Gardens of Scotland.

The chair of the fundraising appeal spoke of a real living memorial, a design that balances the formal and informal and that celebrates a great lady who gave freely of her time for others. Its aim is to inspire people of all ages.

Born Elizabeth Angela Marguerite Bowes-Lyon, she was the youngest daughter and ninth of ten children of Lord Glamis and Cecilia Cavendish-Bentinck. She married the second son of King George V who became King George VI after the abdication of his elder brother Edward VII. As Queen Consort and later Queen Mother she devoted her life to the people of Britain and the Commonwealth, earning respect, admiration and love.

6.17 Organ and Tissue Donors
A tribute to Organ and Tissue Donors for giving life to others

Description: A 'wilding' garden offering a space of peace and calm, of quiet reflection, for donors and recipients. Within a wooded area is a dry-stane Taigh (Gaelic, house) with turf roof. A Font contains 'offering' pebbles gathered from Scottish beaches.
Designer: Alec Finlay, working with Donors, Recipients and healthcare professionals
Date: 2014   Location: Royal Botanic Gardens

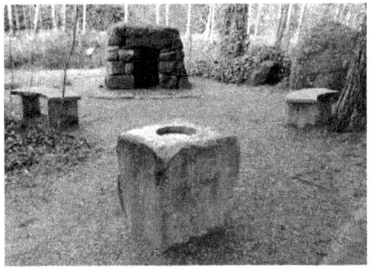

The National Monument for Organ and Tissue Donors in Scotland was made for '*the dead, the donors and their families, and those who are alive today through the gift of donation. Organ and tissue donation touches many people: as an act of giving that passes between the dead and the living it speaks to our values as a culture.*' (Words of its designer, Alec Finlay, inscribed on the information panel at the monument.)

Two circular verses inscribed around the Font and Taigh basins, respectively:

'nothing that ends in a gift ends in (nothing)';
'light of those taken from the (light)'.

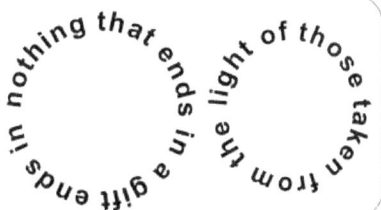

The designer described the memorial and its development on a website:
http://www.alecfinlay.com/taigh.html

6.18 King James V, 1512-1542
King who sometimes travelled in disguise

King James V, King of Scotland, liked to travel disguised as a commoner, calling himself the 'Gudeman of Ballengiech' ('gudeman' means landlord or farmer, Ballengiech the nickname of a road near Stirling Castle).

Crossing Cramond Bridge alone and in disguise, James was attacked by five men. He attempted to defend himself with his sword. A farm labourer, seeing a solitary man attacked by five, stopped threshing corn and ran to support the victim, attacking the five with his flail upon which they fled. He took the victim

John N. Amoore

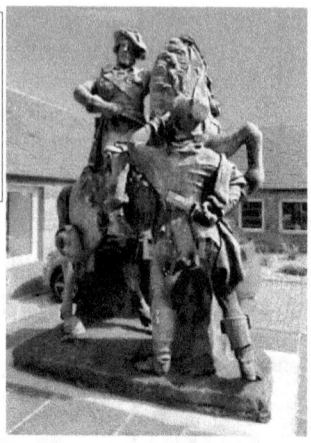

<table>
<tr><td>Description: King on horseback confronted by knife-wielding man. Inscribed: 'James V attacked at Cramond Brig A.D. 1532'
Sculptor: Robert Forrest.　　　　　Date: c.1836
Location: Braehead Mains, off Queensferry Road, near Cramond Bridge</td></tr>
</table>

to the barn, washing the stranger's wounds with water and towel.

The king, still disguised, asked his name and wishes. John Howieson replied he would like to farm his own land. Meet me at Holyrood in a week's time, asking at the Palace door for the Gudeman, responded the disguised king.

A week later John duly appeared at the Palace door, asking to see the Gudeman. The king, now in fine clothes, met John who was still unaware that this was the king. The king showed him around the Palace, John in awe. Would you like to meet the king, the king asked John? *'But he will be angry with me'*, said John. *'No'* replied the king, *'let us go into that large room to meet him'*. *'How will I know which is the king'* replied John. *'The king will not take off his hat'*.

So they entered the room and John saw all taking off their hats, remarking *'they have all taken off their hats'*. He then realised that only he and the Gudeman still had their hats on. Then the king revealed himself. John was given Braehead farm on the condition that he provide a towel and basin to wash the king's hands if he ever passed the bridge. And years later, when King George IV (*2.4*) visited Edinburgh, John's descendant appeared with basin and towel.

James V, son of James IV and Queen Margaret, daughter of Henry VII of England, was born at Linlithgow Palace in 1512, receiving the titles Duke of Rothesay and Prince and Great Steward of Scotland. Aged 17 months, following his father's death at the Battle of Flodden Field, he was crowned king at Stirling Castle. Regents ruled Scotland till James was 12. However, shortly afterwards James was held as a virtual prisoner by his stepfather, Archibald Douglas, Earl of Angus. James escaped after three years captivity, assumed the throne and exiled the Douglas family. He improved Stirling Castle and the Palaces at Linlithgow, Falkland and Holyrood. He built up the royal fleet, sailing to Orkney and Lewis to show his presence and hold courts of justice.

The Auld Alliance between France and Scotland was renewed by the Treaty of Rouen in 1517. Its main purpose was to agree mutual military assistance and aid, but also provided for James V's marriage, then only 5, to a daughter of King Francis I of France. In 1536 James sailed to France, marrying Madeleine, the King's daughter on 1st January 1537. However Madeleine was in poor health and died that July, soon after arriving in Scotland. Within a year James married Mary of Guise, whose only surviving child from their marriage was Mary, born in 1542 at Linlithgow Palace, who was to become Mary Queen of Scots. James died a week later.

James V supported Catholicism, persecuting outspoken Protestants. By this time Henry VIII, now king of England, had broken from the Catholic Church and tried to persuade James to close Scottish monasteries, seizing their wealth. James refused. The Pope sent James a sword and hat, praying that James would be resolute in loyalty to the Catholic Church.

Following his mother's death war broke out between England and Scotland in 1542. An early victory by the Scots at the Battle of Haddon Rig was followed by a serious defeat in November at the Battle of Solway Moss. Soon afterwards James V fell ill, dying on 15th December.

6.19 Captain Eric Melrose 'Winkle' Brown, 1919-2016
British Royal Navy Test Pilot flew 487 different aircraft, more than any other pilot. Most decorated pilot in the history of the Royal Navy

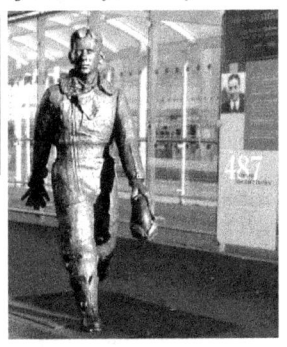

Description: In pilot's uniform, striding forward. Plaques behind describe his achievements
Funded: Pilots of Edinburgh University Air Squadron
Sculptor: David Annand   Unveiled: Duke of York, July 2018
Location: Edinburgh Airport

Eric Brown was born in Leith, his father, a pilot, taking him flying before he was 10. Later, in 1936, on a trip to Berlin for the Olympics, Eric met Ernst Udet, a former WWI pilot. Sharing a love of flying, Udet took young Eric flying. Udet asked Eric two favours: to learn German and to fly. Eric proceeded with both, studying German at the University of Edinburgh and joining its flying unit. Selected to a student exchange programme he was in Germany in Sept 1939 when war was declared. Briefly imprisoned, within three days he was escorted out of the country.

Short at 5ft 7in, his Naval colleagues nicknamed him 'Winkle'. He credited his survival of air disasters to his small size which gave him the ability to curl up.

He started war service in the Royal Navy Volunteer Reserve, flying from a small aircraft carrier, HMS Audacity. He survived hypothermia overnight after it was sunk in December 1941. His bravery and skill under enemy action whilst on the carrier earned him the Distinguished Service Cross. Seconded to the Royal Canadian Air Force he escorted US Air Force planes over France. His carrier-landing expertise led him to train pilots and to join the Farnborough team testing new planes and carrier-landing techniques, becoming Chief Test Pilot. Whilst there a German cruise missile attack injured his wife and destroyed his home.

He helped the US Air Force assess aircraft. In 1944 he was awarded the MBE for 'outstanding enterprise and skill' testing aircraft.

As the war ended Brown was asked to recover German aircraft developments. This he did, overseeing the surrender of a Luftwaffe base and its 2000 troops before the Allies arrival a day later. He was asked to help interrogate the commander and assistant of the newly liberated Bergen-Belsen concentration camp, remarking later that 'two more loathsome creatures it is hard to imagine'. He went on to test captured German aircraft and then assisted with the developments of British aircraft. Later he helped the re-emergence of the German Air Force and its integration within NATO. He took command of what became RAF Lossiemouth in 1967, retiring in 1970 and was awarded the CBE.

His achievements include flying the greatest number of different aircraft (487) and carrying out the most carrier landings (2407). He wrote several books and articles on flying, including his autobiography '*Wings on my sleeve*'.

He remained active in retirement, flying till 1994, lecturing and being President of the Royal Aeronautical Society. Much of his retirement was spent in West Sussex. His wife whom he had married in 1942 pre-deceased him in 1982.

6.20 James Watt, 1736-1819
Inventor, Steam engine design, Enabled the Industrial Revolution

Description: James Watt, seated, head down looking at large sheet of papers on his knee. Sandstone
Sculptor: Peter Slater
Unveiled: 1854 Adam Square, 1990 in current location
Location: Heriot-Watt University, Riccarton (1990). Moved in 1874 to new Heriot-Watt College in Chambers Street, Adam Square having been demolished to make way for Chambers Street.

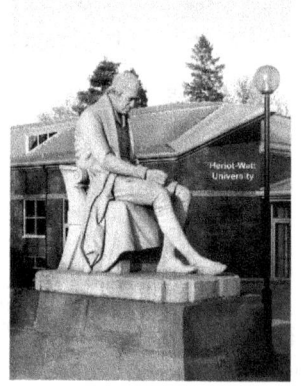

James Watt improved the design of steam engines by introducing a separate condenser, with major efficiency gains. He went on to develop it to produce rotary motion. These developments made possible the Industrial Revolution.

James was born in Greenock, his father a shipwright and shipowner, he was educated mainly by his mother. Interested in engineering rather than Latin and Greek, at 18 he went to London to study instrument-making, returning after a year to Glasgow intent on setting up in business. Denied entry by the trades-guild, he was fortunate to get work restoring astronomical instruments donated to Glasgow University. This led three professors to invite him to set up an instrument workshop. In 1763 he was asked to repair a steam engine. He critically assessed it, realising its inefficiency. With financial support (firstly John Roebuck in Boness, later from Mathew Boulton in Birmingham) he solved the design and fabrication problems. Boulton and Watt formed a successful business that led steam-engine manufacture for many years, Watt becoming very rich. Adam Smith (*4.22*) met Watt writing: '*It was a real philosopher only who could invent the fire engine, and first form the idea of producing so great an effect by a power in nature which had never before been thought of*' [11].

During his lifetime he received many honours including an honorary doctorate from Glasgow University and Fellowship of the Royal Society of Edinburgh, as well as accolades from continental countries. The 'watt' as the unit of power was adopted by the British Association for the Advancement of Science in 1889, and in the International System of Units (SI system) in 1960. He was one of the first seven to be listed in Scottish Engineering Hall of Fame in 2011. Around the UK several statues were erected in his honour, such as this one in Edinburgh. There is a copy in the National Museum of Scotland in Chambers street.

Heriot-Watt University bears his name and that of George Heriot, goldsmith to King James VI. It grew out of the 'Watt Institution' named after him. The 2019 bicentenary of his death was celebrated with exhibitions and talks, further testimony to his enduring legacy.

6.21 Sir David Brewster, 1781-1868
Scientist, author, father of modern experimental optics

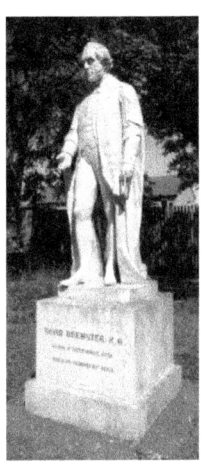

Description: Brewster standing on pedestal, book in left hand, right hand out-stretched
Sculptor: William Brodie   Date: 1877
Location: Kings Buildings, University of Edinburgh

Sir David Brewster is best known for his studies on optics, the polarisation of light, light spectra, including analysis of Newton's theory of colours, and the reflection and refraction of light. His studies on the effects of compression of crystals led to his discovery of photo-elasticity. His invention of the kaleidoscope, although popular, brought him little wealth because of inadequate patent protection.
His interest in photography led him to improve the stereoscope.
His admiration for Isaac Newton led him to study Newton's works and publish a detailed biography of Newton.

He was appointed Principal of St Andrews University in 1837 and in 1859 Principal of the University of Edinburgh, a post he held till his death. He was a founder member and enthusiastic supporter of the British Association for the Advancement of Science.

David Brewster was born in Jedburgh in the Scottish Borders, his father the rector of its grammar school. Educated at the University of Edinburgh, he had wished to be a church minister, but he did not relish the public speaking required of a preacher. Whilst working as a scientist his faith remained important to him and he supported the Free Church of Scotland and its breakaway from the Church of Scotland in 1843 (see Dr Thomas Chalmers, *2.2*).

Brewster is remembered by this statue in the Kings Buildings area and by having one of the streets there named after him. Many famous scientists and engineers are associated with Edinburgh University's College of Science and Engineering based at the Kings Buildings; several of them are honoured by the names of streets and buildings on the campus including: Charlotte Auerbach; Thomas Bayes; Alexander Graham Bell, Max Born; James Hutton; Nicholas Kemmer; Marion Ross; Robert Stevenson.

John N. Amoore

Chapter 7: Memorial plaques on benches, trees and flowers

Donated benches add amenities to parks and gardens whilst honouring people and events. Across the city benches have plaques giving interesting insights into people who have lived or passed through Edinburgh. Most record people deeply missed but still remembered and loved, some with dates, perhaps with a brief summary of those remembered, others with simple timeless messages. Some recall events in people's lives, others simply acknowledge how the scene was important. Benches have been donated to remember events or important anniversaries, both of people and of organizations.

Whilst most plaques remember those who have died, some recall happy events in people's lives. For example: *'To my dear wife Jessica Susan Pacey; For our wedding on 1st May 1978, And for all our days in our beloved Scotland'*. Many acknowledge fondness and continuing love for Edinburgh: *'Gifted by Mary and Stephen Surrey who love this city, 1987'*; *'In appreciation of the delights of Edinburgh, Maureen MacLellan'*.

Some are beautifully simple, inscribed: *'In loving memory of ..'* followed by the name or names of those remembered. On a bench on Portobello beach: *'Sandra Duthie loved sitting here eating ice cream. Ashley would have loved it too.'* Several remember with poetry, often inspiring: *"In memory of Dougie Love, 'Mr Fitba', 1920 -2006. Just cast your eyes across the Meedies. Then think of football and wee heidies. And picture kids, some big some small. Hear Dougie's shout to 'Pass the ball. And help your mates in time of strife, Not just in games, but throughout life '"*. It paints a picture of games on the Meadows and a spirit of comradeship, of helping one another.

The benches open up and transform the urban landscape into living areas, inviting us, encouraging us to stop and enjoy the moment, the environment, the scene. To eat a snack or lunch, escaping from the office confines, to meet a friend, to read, or simply to give ourselves time to rest and to be still, to enjoy and experience the area around us. The inscriptions add to the rich tapestry of the city. Ponder and enjoy. Graham Clark [1] in his series of 42 'Benchmark' photographs writes of the memorial benches highlighting *'ordinary lives'* and *'commemorating loved ones'*. *'The benches form a collective memory of the city and its people. Individuals, both locals and visitors who have loved a particular spot, died young or in tragic circumstances are remembered.'*

There are hundreds of gifted benches with plaques. Those noticed at different times vary with the seasons and mood, or simply as we glance on passing by. Many described here are along Princes Street or in its gardens, though similar themes will be found in benches throughout the city. The included examples introduce the many and varied messages. Not all are on benches; in some gardens, as we have seen in Chapter 1, *1.15*, trees and flower beds have been planted in memory of people and organizations, with plaques providing details.

The positions of benches sometimes change; positions described here were when recorded by me. The words have been transcribed as on the plaques. However, punctuation has been added to clarify where the text has been reproduced on the same line whereas on the plaque phrases were on different lines.

7.1 Princes Street and its gardens

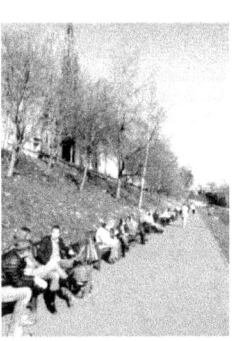

Fondness for Princes Street and its gardens

- In loving memory of dear Isabelle Grant McKenzie who found in these gardens companionship and peace
- To the memory of Hugh McGregor Sanderson who found peace and pleasure in this park. Presented by his loving wife and son
- In memory of Charlie (Cockburn) who loved to feed the birds in these gardens
- To Eliza Jane Ferguson, A very special wife and mother. A seat in her favourite place forever. Alex and Toots.
- In loving memory of James and Johan Brebner. They enjoyed many hours in this garden. Daughters – Effie Tapling, Peggy Walsh
- In memory of my husband Ex K.O.S.B. Peter Pepper, aged 61; who loved this city and these gardens. 'Promise kept Pete darling', Mae and family
- In loving memory of my grandfather, Alexander Gould Smith, 1861-1942, who loved this beautiful scene. (Gladys Gibson Armour)
- In loving and everlasting remembrance of Charles Doward Farquhar, 1890 – 1960. A lover of music and this grand scene.
- In loving memory of my dear husband who loved the peace and beauty of these gardens. William T.H. Cairns, 23 June 1910 – 22 March 1962
- For Ethel Mary Christina Cumming of Ealing. London. W.13. She loved flowers and she loved this city. At rest. 25th April, 1967
- Tarry awhile and enjoy this grand scene, Nancy and Cameron Dey, 1971
- Janie Cumpstie Drever who loved Princes Street. Died 28 August 1975
- Gifted by Ragmar Wilhelmsen in loving memory of his wife Frances Trower, Died Norway 1990. Who when young spent many happy hours in the gardens

Remembered for their contributions

- Presented to the City of Edinburgh by the Edinburgh branch of 'The Royal Scottish Country Dance Society' in memory of Helen Addison, leader of the Scottish Country Dance sessions in these gardens for many years.
- In memory of Tim Wright whose Scottish Dance music was heard so often in the gardens. Gifted by his wife and sons.
- In memory of Rev Allan B. Cameron MA BD STM, the Piping Hot Scot, a help to all in need. He proved Romans 8. From the Scottish patriots and friends world wide.
- In loving memory of Catherine Anne Hamilton Bruce MBE, Founder of the Trefoil school for handicapped children, 1940. For all the wonderful help and love she gave to so many people who will always be grateful. From Grace with love.
- A loving remembrance of Gertie Gitana, Music Hall Artiste. 'There's an old mill by the stream, Nelly Dean'. (*Gertie Gitana, from Staffordshire, born 1887 died 1957; seat presented by her husband during the 1959 Edinburgh International Festival. Gertie sang this favourite song, Nelly Dean, several times at the Empire Theatre. Nelly is sometimes spelt Nellie.*)
- In loving memory of Al Fairweather, musician, composer, arranger and artist. 12 June 1927, Edinburgh, 21 June 1993. 'If music be the food of love, play on.' Fiona.

Memories of weddings and married life

- To my dear wife Jessica Susan Pacey. For our wedding on 1st May 1978, And for all our days in our beloved Scotland
- For Heather J. Pascoe (neé Harwood-Nash), with fond memories of our wedding at Upper Canada College in Toronto, Canada, 20 November 1988, with love from Paul
- In memory of our dear parents and their 55 years of married life. John Gibson (18 Aug 1895 – 25 Aug 1975), Mary Elizabeth Gibson (17 Dec 1898 – 3 Oct 1976). Who became engaged in Edinburgh

John N. Amoore

Happy times in Edinburgh and Scotland and to the Scots

- Gifted by John and Elizabeth W Burnett. For happy memories of this lovely city.
- In appreciation of the delights of Edinburgh, Maureen MacLellan
- In appreciation of many happy days spent in this lovely city, Alexander Robertson and Margaret Hindmarsh Munro
- Donated in memory of happy college days 1922 by Ada E Colley (neé Halford) of Newport, Gwent.
- To the memory of Nora and Bill Thompson of Castle Bromwich, Birmingham, who spent many happy holidays in Scotland
- In memory of 'Geof' (Charles Geoffrey Crownshaw) and the many happy times spent together in this city. Gifted by his friend
- In loving memory of Elizabeth and William Fraser Young who loved Edinburgh so well. From their daughter Irene
- Dedicated to the everlasting memory of my husband and our father Neil Greer, who was so proud of, and dearly loved his 'Hame toon Auld Reekie'. By his entire family and friends, may God grant him eternal rest
- In loving memory of my dear wife Elizabeth Paris Mitwich, 23 Mar 1915 – 20 Aug 1980. Remembering the many happy days we enjoyed together in 'Auld Reekie' our home town. Known to our friends as Bette and Joe.
- Donated by Mrs Lorna Waddington. "Rest awhile in this beautiful city".
- In memory of Katherine L.W. Reid, M.A., who loved this city
- Joan Clark, 1882-1964, Citizen of Edinburgh, Presented by her daughter Meg
- In memory of Harry Gegg, 1909-1990, who so loved Edinburgh. From his wife, family and friends
- In loving memory of Catriona MacNaughton, 21 October 1926 – 19 March 2013. Catriona loved Edinburgh and Scotland.
- In loving memory of my dear wife Nan Cranston Burrell who was so proud of being an Edinburgh citizen. Presented by her husband John Burrell.
- A salute to Edinburgh – a lovely capital. A salute to the Scots – a memorable people. James and Teresa Fucini, U.S.A.
- Gifted by Mary and Stephen Surrey who love this city. 1987
- To the memory of Muriel Pain who loved this city. Given by her daughter
- To the memory of James Black who lived in and loved Edinburgh. Donated by his cousin Christine Burns, Glasgow 1987

Thinking of others who will enjoy the bench

- Donated by Joseph N. Mitwich to the visitors and citizens of Edinburgh that they may rest and enjoy the ever changing scene.
- In memory of my dear wife Isa Sweeney Porteous Hunter. Presented by Bob and family. May all who sit here be content and happy
- In memory of Thomas and Christina A. Scott in grateful appreciation of the seats presented by others

Beautifully simple inscriptions

- In loving memory of Ella and Walter Fraser
- In memory of William Little Macrae
- For Helen Murchison Lane, 'Queen of Balmy-Gröt'
- Dedicated to our old scotch mither, Margaret MacCallum Evans, Your loving daughters
- Le Bolt – Keating
- In memory of Alison Mary Johnston Himsworth
- In loving memory of Mr and Mrs John Young McBain gifted by their family
- For Léan Scully who made a festival of this city
- In loving memory of Martin Healey Gomnaes
- In ever loving memory of our dear Mum and Dad, Norah and David Malcolm
- In loving memory of Kathleen Lightbody Mead. Daughter Mary Ann Wallace

- In memory of Annie Shanks Orr (Nan). Gifted by her sisters.
- In memory of loving caring parents, Alex and Mary Stewart, Sloan Street, Leith
- In loving memory of Alice Ferguson Allan, dedicated teacher of the young.
- Gifted in loving memory of Mrs Daisy Lawson, by a few friends 1963
- In memory of my beloved mother, Marion Swift Young, February 1965
- In loving memory of Annie Forbes Dallas Burn 1894-1981
- In memory of Bill and Jenny Allan, (1903-1979) (1904-1983). With love
- Mary Marshall George 1900-1987. R.I.P.
- Paul Sheen, 1962 – 1992, No regrets
- Margaret Ann Park, 1958 – 2004, Rest and Dream

Families remembered on benches

Husband and wife both remembered, two separate plaques on the same bench, the second speaking of them now together again 'in the city they both loved'

- In loving memory of John Brodie Muirhead, born Edinburgh 26th May 1918, passed away 20th June 1986. Treasured memories of a devoted husband, father and grandfather. Sadly missed
- Also in loving memory of Agnes Purdie Muirhead, who passed away 7th December 2013. Wife of John Brodie. United once more in the city they both loved.

On neighbouring benches

- In memory of our father Thomas D Cant who died 2-8-91, aged 83 years
  In memory of our mother Georgina M. Cant who died 11-2-93 aged 85 years.
- In memory of a much loved brother Roddy Cant who died 30-9-90, aged 55 years
  In memory of a much loved brother Norman Cant who died 21-3-93, aged 55 years
  In memory of a much loved brother Kenny Cant who died 20-12-2012, aged 73 yrs.

Two plaques on the same bench

- In loving memory of John Burrows, born 1920 – died 1985. Always remembered
  Also his dear wife Jessie Fraser Burrows (Janet), born 1919– died 2009. Always remembered
- In loving memory of our parents Mr and Mrs George Renwick.
  Also with sad regret their son George Renwick and his beloved daughter Celia of Toronto who both died December 1990. Sadly missed by their families.

Those remembered will not be forgotten

- Too dearly loved to ever be forgotten: Margaret H. Bryce and James C. Bryce. Born in Edinburgh, Died in Toronto. Feb 8 1925 – Nov 4 1979 and Oct 24 1918 – Oct 22 2010. A remarkable and lovely lady and a kind and wise gentle man. Presented in loving memory by daughter Trish and son-in-law Attila Soti.
- In loving memory of Lettie Scott (nee Meechan). A dearly loved wife and mother, Born 15-4-31 died 13-3-83. 'Alive in our hearts forever.' Gifted by her husband Bill and daughter Valerie.
- This seat is bequeathed in memory of Thomas McDiarmid by his wife Jeane and daughter Diane. 'Ne Obliviscaris'. *(Never forget)*
- In Memory of 'Farquie', Archibald Noble Farquharson, Died 30th December 1977, Late of Kuala Lumpur, Malaya and Wick, Caithness. 'To be remembered by those we loved is not to die'
- In loving memory of our dear parents, Robert and Peggy Aitken. Worthy of Everlasting Remembrance.
- In memory of our beloved daughter and sister Fiona Alexandra Reith, 1971-2010. You will be in our hearts forever. Dad, Mum, Kirsty and Alistair.
- Robert Wilson Daly Winning, 1943 – 1991. The seasons will pass with coming time but his memory will weather all.
- In memory of Katherine Heppenstall (Dingwall), 1933 – 1999. A true and loving smeddum wife of Horace. Forever missed. Lynda, Martin, Gillian & Cristina *(smeddum = vigour of intellect)*

Special words of fondness for those who died young

- In loving memory of our beloved daughter Katrina Morrison, flight hostess Air New Zealand, died 28 Nov. 1979, Mount Erebus, Antarctica, Age 24

John N. Amoore

- Dr Julian Roebuck, born 4 Sept 1964, died tragically 24 Jan 1990. Beloved elder son, admired brother and great friend. He achieved and gave so much, and asked for so very little. So many joyful memories, for ever. Chris, Martyn and Stuart
- In memory of Pamela Scott, Research Assistant, Edinburgh and South East Scotland Blood Transfusion Service, Presented by her colleagues and friends (29th Sept 1949 – 11th Aug 1970)
- In loving memory of Yvonne Louise Byers (nee MacDonald), beloved wife of Gary, daughter of Joseph and Maureen, sister of Karen, Fiona and Allison, 6-12-1965 – 22-8-1997, aged 31 years.

Links with other monuments

- *The Reverend (Dr) Thomas Guthrie (1.3)*
  In loving memory of Charles John Guthrie, Q.C. (Lord Guthrie), Son of the Rev. Thomas Guthrie, D.D. Presented by his daughter Anne R. Priestman, 23 December 1964
- *Royal Scots Greys (1.4)*
  In memory of Col., The Rt. Hon. Walter Elliot. P.C., M.P., C.H., M.C., M.B., CH.B., F.R.S., F.R.C.P., LL.D.. Medical Officer 1914 – 18. Presented by fellow officers of the Royal Scots Greys
- *Scottish American War Memorial in Princes Street Gardens (1.9)* Presented by the Mississippi Valley Conservation Authority, Ontario, Canada. In memory of Dr R. Tait McKenzie, Surgeon, Physical Educator and Sculptor. Born in Canada of Scottish parents, 1867–1938. Commissioned to sculpt the Scottish American War Memorial in Princes Street Gardens
- *Falklands Memorial Garden (1.8)*
  Remembering with love and pride 2nd Engineering Officer Paul A Henry G.M. Died 8th June 1982 aboard R.F.A. Sir Galahad at Bluff Cove – Falkland Islands.
- *Norwegian Brigade (1.10)* Presented by the Norwegian Scottish Association 17th May 1996
- *Royal Scots (1.13)* Dedicated to the memory of Major Adam Lothian T.D. 1920 – 1998. By members of the 8th BN. Section, The Royal Scots Regimental Association
- *Sir Walter Scott (1.21)* The Lothians and Border Horse Yeomanry. In memory of the men of this regiment who gave their lives for their country in the South African, and both World Wars. Sir Walter Scott served as Secretary and Quartermaster when the Regiment was raised in 1797.
- *The Spanish Civil War (1.23)* In memory of those who left this city to serve with the International Brigade in the Spanish Civil War. Edinburgh City Labour Party
- *Hugh MacDiarmid (1892-1978), born C.M. Grieve, better known by pseudonym. See 'Stones of Scotland' (3.10) and bust at Edinburgh Park (6.12):* Donated by the 1320 club in memory of Dr C.M. Grieve (Hugh MacDiarmid), Poet and Nationalist

Groups have donated benches

- Presented by Boots the Chemists to commemorate their Jubilee in Scotland, 1902-1952
- Presented by Thos. Cook & Son Ltd. 126 Princes Street. 1952
- Presented by the New and University Clubs on their amalgamation, 1953
- Presented by the members of The Berlin Philharmonic Orchestra, August 1st 1961.
- Presented by the General Assembly of Unitarian and Free Christian Churches to mark the occasion of their annual meetings in the city, April 22nd – 25th 1963
- Presented by the Institute of Medical Laboratory Technology to mark the occasion of the Jubilee conference held in Edinburgh 11th to 18th August 1962.
  > *Also on the bench is a plaque commemorating the Institute's centenary,*
  > *its name having changed by then.*
  To commemorate the Institute of Biomedical Science centenary celebrations 1912 – 2012
- *Two plaques on a bench remember Soroptimist International, a global volunteer movement working to transform the lives of women and girls – www.soroptimistinternational.org)*
  Presented to the city by the Soroptimist Club of Edinburgh, 1962
  In celebration of 85 years of Soroptimist International of Edinburgh, 6th of December 2012
- Presented by the Edinburgh and Lothian's Baptist Association on the occasion of the Centenary of the Baptist Union of Scotland, 1869 – 1969. Jesus said 'come unto me and rest'
- Presented by Edinburgh Festival Voluntary Guides Association on the 25th Anniversary of Edinburgh International Festival, August 1971.

- Presented by The Rugby Football Union, In Commemoration of the Centenary of the First International Rugby Match ever Played, Scotland v England, at Raeburn Place on 27ᵗʰ March 1871
- In affectionate memory of Kenneth Charles Murray Mackay, honoured Past President of the Clan Mackay Society. His enthusiasm led to the First International Gathering of the Clans in Scotland in 1977. He played a key part in the extension of the international gatherings of the Scots, first to Nova Scotia, to the United States of America and to Australia. He lived to see his dream come true and to participate in the strengthening and developing of closer links among the world-wide family of the Scot.
- Presented by Edinburgh Beatles Appreciation Society, John Lennon 1940 – 1980, Dr Winston O'Boogie *'Bless you wherever you are'*
- Presented by Royal Mail International Letters to commemorate the meeting in Edinburgh of the European Posts Commission, January 1989.
- Presented by the guests of the Fireworks Ball held at 7 Castle Street on 31 August 1995. Hosted by Trafalgar House Property Ltd.
- Presented by the Boy Scouts Association of the City of Edinburgh & Leith to commemorate the Centenary of the birth of the founder, Lord Baden-Powell of Gilwell and the Jubilee of Scouting. (The top wooden beam of the bench is inscribed: '1857 B-P 1907 B-P 1957')
- On the occasion of the fiftieth anniversary of the closing of United States Air Force Security Service operations at RAF Station Kirknewton, Scotland 1952 – 1966. The RAF Kirknewton Alumni Group affectionately dedicates this seat to the citizens of Scotland and especially the people of Edinburgh for their warm hospitality and friendship which has endured over the years since. Presented March 1, 2016. *'Freedom is best, I tell thee true, of all things to be won'*, William Wallace (*4.2*).

Several have poetic verses

Words of Robert Burns beneath a plaque presented by United States Air Force, R.A.F. Kirknewton

'Tho I were doomed to wander on,
Beyond the sea, beyond the sun,
Till my last weary sand was run,
Till then – and then – I'd love thee!'
Robert Burns

In memory of Margaret Maitland Carson (Peggy), 18-2-1927 - 25-8-1999
Dearly loved wife of William TL Carson and mother of Mhairi, Lloyd and Reid

'I absorbed from birth as now I know,
The whole earth
Through her jaunty spirit.'

May Lillian Davenport Mackenzie,
1910-1979
'I once was lost, but now I'm found'
28 - 12 - 1984

In cherished memory of
Mhairi C. Carson,
24-5-1952 - 22-6-1985

From her Mother, Father,
Lloyd and Reid

'Stones weep though eyes were dry,
Choicest flowers soonest die.
Their sun oft sets at noon
Whose fruit is ripe in June'

In memory of
Thomas Marshall MPS
Husband of Eileen
Father of Eileen, Sheelah and Maureen
Father-in-law of Victor and Grandfather of
Nadia, Antonia, Vincent and Paul.

'And the birds sang round him,
o'er him'
'Do not shoot us, Hiawatha'

In loving memory of Angus and Martha McPhee Presented by their daughters 'as life goes swiftly past rest awhile in quiet meditation'	In loving memory of Susan Montgomery Woods 1888 1960 William J. Woods 1890 1968. 'The kiss of the sun for pardon, The song of the birds for mirth, One is nearer God's Heart in a garden, Than anywhere else on Earth.'
Murray Brett Johnston, 1964 – 1982 'When all the words have gone There's the thoughts to carry on Leave it all behind And spread your wings' 11-12-1984	*Often used in gardens without crediting the source. The verses are from the poem 'God's Garden' by Dorothy Frances Gurney (1858-1932).* *These verses are also inscribed into the wood on another Princes Street Garden's bench.*

7.2   New Town

St Andrew Square

- In gratitude to all those who gave their lives in the 2nd World War, that I may live in Peace and Freedom. '*A man's a man for a 'that*'. Tack så mycket. Carl-Axel Lindgren, Karlstad, Sweden
- In memory of S/LDR J.R. Savage R.A.A.F. 1916 – 1948. Nina
- In memory of René Lauener (1916-1993) who liked to sit down
- Treasured memories of my loving sister Margaret Waddell, 1933-1998. Stay and rest awhile
- Donated by the Guardian Royal Exchange Assurance Group on the occasion of the 50th Anniversary of their building at 13 St Andrew Square. 1939-1989
- Remembering J.C.H. who was often tired

Shandwick Place

- Jan Cameron, 03/09/21 – 14/12/00, Never a wallflower, always a rose
- Annie Hardie (1895 – 1993). Her warm welcome made her home at 18A Atholl Crescent (1941-72) a focal point for the family.
- In memory of Marjory Middleton MBE, FRAD. 1908 – 1985. Teacher, choreographer, Founder member of Edinburgh Ballet Club, Director of the Scottish Ballet School. She inspired generations of dancers
- Sarah H. Pearson and Gerould R. McWane, of Milan, Ohio, met here Nov 1929 and were married Aug 1934. Presented by their sons Col Pearson D. McWane and Dr. John W. McWane.
- John Reynolds (Buchanan), 06/11/86 – 04/09/00. Forever smiling
- In memory of Nicol Gifford Kilgour, Director of The Heart of Midlothian Football Club 1948-1964, Chairman 1954-1960, President of the Scottish Football League 1964. Presented by his friends.

Stockbridge

- In loving memory of my daughter Anne Ramage 1957–2000. The world is a lesser place without you. Dad

7.3   Calton Hill

Happy times in Edinburgh

- For my beloved husband, Percy Rosen, 1931 – 1998, Toronto, Canada. In remembrance of the joy we shared in Edinburgh
- In memory of Doreen Archibald, 1908 – 2003 and her husband Hugh Archibald, 1904 – 1985 who loved Edinburgh
- In loving memory of John Hobart Sands of Martinsburg, West Virginia, who loved this place and found peace here.

> 'For all the raindrops that fall
> those will be our tears.
> For all the snow that lays
> That will be our arms.
> For all the wind that blows
> that's us whispering 'we love you'.
> And when the sun shines warm and bright
> That's how we'll think of you.'
>
> Our Dad, William Meikle Forsyth
> Son of
> Mary Meikle & Andrew George Forsyth

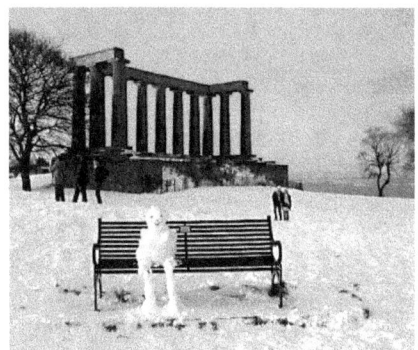

Birthday wishes

- To honour my loving wife and partner Jean Nicholson Medley on her birthday, July 19th 2002. Tim Medley, Jackson, Mississippi, USA

In memory

- Remembering John and Annie Lovell and their children Annie, Alex, Johnny, Cathy, Dick, Violet and Sarah. R.I.P.
- In memory of my beloved mother, Violet Smail 1941 – 2002. Thank you for loving me. I think about you all the time, Heather
- In memory of young James

7.4   Royal Mile

- Presented by Edinburgh Old Town Association to celebrate its 20th anniversary, 1976 – 1996.
- In memory of William and Jean Stuart, devoted members of St Giles for many years
- Jon Carr (Jonathan), you will always be in our thoughts. Your family, friends & colleagues.
- Presented by Brian and Louise Caine & brothers and sisters to honour their dear parents Jack Levey (jeweller) and wife Josephine, and Charles Caine (Poole's cinemas) and wife Rose – Rest awhile –
- In loving memory of David Downie Haig, born Edinburgh City Chambers 1903, died Dec 1983, and his dear wife Margaret, born 1903 – died July 1988. Dearest parents of Dorothy.
- In memory of Highlander Scott McLaren (4th Battalion, The Royal Regiment of Scotland) who died on 4th July 2011, aged 20 at Nahr-e-Saraj, Afghanistan.
  'It is in truth not for glory, nor riches, nor honours that we are fighting'
- With loving thoughts of our Mum and Dad, Granny and Grandpa, Catherine (Katie nee Dolbear) Robertson, 1919-1998, James (Jimmy) Robertson, 1912-1998.
  In life our inspirations and now our guiding stars, Janette, Sylvia, Jim, Catherine and families.
- In loving memory of our dear Mum and Dad, Harry and Isa Holt, lately of 123 Canongate. Donated by their loving family.
- In memory of George Allan Young F.M.A, Superintendent of the City Museums from 16th July 1946 – 15th November 1971.
- In memory of our loving mother Cathie Jane Hopes (neé) Mackie. Canogotian 1912-1997. Presented by her family Richard, Douglas, Irene, Liz

Edinburgh Castle

- Burma Star Association (Scottish Area). In memory of our comrades.
  'When you go home tell them of us and say: 'For your tomorrow we gave our today''.
- Old Contemptible's Association, Edinburgh Branch. In memory of our comrades

- In loving memory of Charles Innes. 7th Oct 1931 – 7th May 1997. To Edinburgh city he was proud to belong, and sang its praises with his favourite song, 'The Royal Mile'. Presented by his wife and family
- In memory of Captain John A. Maclellan MBE, Queen's Own Highlanders (1921 – 1991). The first Director of Army Bagpipe Music. Placed here by the Piobaireachd Society.
- In honour of Admiral of the Fleet, The Earl Mountbatten of India, KG, PC, GCB, OM, GCIE, GCVO, DSO, FRS. 1900 – 1979. Given by Mrs. Mary Nicholson to the Scottish National War Memorial

Near Holyrood Palace at the foot of the Royal Mile

- To commemorate the 150th anniversary of The Church of Jesus Christ of Latter-Day Saints in the British Isles 26th July 1987. On the morning of 19 May 1840, Orson Pratt, an early apostle of the church, climbed to the top of Arthurs Seat in Holyrood Park and in mighty prayer dedicated the country of Scotland for the preaching of the restored Gospel of Jesus Christ.

At the top of the Mound, below the Assembly Hall

- This seat is the gift of the widow of Thomas Bryson Corbett of Avonholme, Glassford, Lanarkshire in gratitude for many happy years. He found himself happiest in communicating happiness to others. 1894- 1975.
- In loving memory of my dad, Willie Raitt (1897 – 1976). 'Raitts Progress' of Edinburgh Evening Dispatch. Caroline Kaart Raitt
- In memory of Nancy Watson Simpson, died 15.12.67. Presented by her husband John and sons Alasdair and Robbie of Motherwell.

7.5   Leith

- Lest we forget. To the memory of + James McDonald +, Master Mariner and late L.D.C. Rigger. Also his sons (M.N. and shore workers) late of 10 Shore, Leith. Also his son-in-law James Webster (M.N.) Late of Leith Docks. And to the seamen of this port who gave their lives in the two world wars.
- To the memory of Captain William Christopher Brodie, Master Mariner, who, for many years sailed out of the Port of Leith, and of his wife, Mary Charlotte Irvine.
- In loving memory of William (Bill) Morrison (Nov 1916 – Jun 2012) and Isabella (Bunty) Morrison (Jan 1923 – Sep 1999). Lifetime Leithers through birth and marriage. Resting together in the arms of the angels.
- In loving memory of '*Always a Leither*'. David F. Bell.
  Treasurer of Leith Victoria Boxing Club 1949-1990. Chairperson, Leith Community Centre 1988-1990. Vice Chairperson, Leith Community Association 1988-1990. Member of the Edinburgh Masonic Club. Gifted by his family and friends in gratitude for all his work and friendship in Leith

7.6   Around Edinburgh

Meadows

- Jack's resting place
- In memory of Margaret Chisholm (1931-1999) who loved to walk with her dogs in the Meadows. With love, Lynda, Ross and Neil
- In loving memory of my husband and soul mate, Alan Anderson. A wonderful person, father and friend, truly missed and loved forever.
- In loving memory of Showman William Newton Taylor, 1921 – 1998. Remembered for his steadfast support and kindness. Presented by the Meadows Festival Association, June 1998.
- Death will always bring darkness, but where there is love, there is light. Thank you for sharing your light with us. Danny Martin. Enjoy the view. Love from all your friends. *(On a separate plaque on same bench his parents remember their young son in a poem – see box below)*

To our darling precious angel boy,
Daniel David Martin
1991 - 2012

Those we love don't go away
They walk beside us every day
Unseen, Unheard, but always near
Still loved still missed and very dear.

Forever Young Son
Love Mum and Dad xxxx.

- As a tribute and in fond memory of Jackie MacFarlane, Edinburgh's 'Mr Jazz' who died in 1993, age 73 years, this seat was presented by his friends, fellow artistes, and fans.
- David S Drummond, 1960 – 1968, Beloved son
- Margaret Rose Jackson, 10.04.1944 – 01.06.2001, A Wonderful Woman, Well Remembered
- *Attached to the wall railings near Middle Meadow Walk*
'Don't be shy give it a try'. In memory of Big Issue seller John White who sold at The Meadows for 8 years. He will be greatly missed by all in the local community 1946 – 2014.
- In loving memory of Tony Ferguson, who died on the 5th July 2001 aged 27. A very special and unique character who will be remembered always by his family and many friends.
- Tom R. Brodie, He never forgot his beautiful Edinburgh, presented by his loving family, 1997
- In memory of Scot Simpson. An Edinburgh man

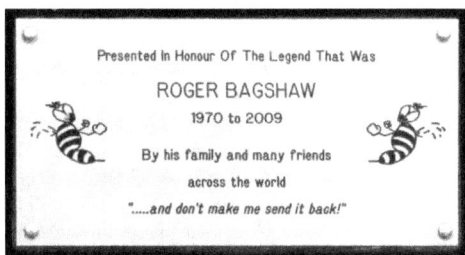

Presented In Honour Of The Legend That Was
ROGER BAGSHAW
1970 to 2009
By his family and many friends
across the world
"…..and don't make me send it back!"

In memory of Dougie Love,
'Mr Fitba', 1920 -2006.

Just cast your eyes across the Meedies.
Then think of football and wee heidies.
And picture kids, some big some small.
Hear Dougie's shout to 'Pass the ball
And help your mates in time of strife,
Not just in games, but throughout life'.

Messages from different nationalities

- In the memory of Amparo Jose Zapater Colomer, 19-3-1963 – 13-8-2005. Please stars tell my sister I love her, Tell my sister I need her, Tell my sister my love for her will never die. Hasta luego, te quiero, tu hermano. (*The last phrase, in Spanish, means: 'see you later, love you, your brother'.*)
- Jacques TURNIN, Toulouse – France.
- Emil Kozok, (1920 – 2006). With love from his family and friends
- In loving memory of Yulia Solodyankina (24.09.1990 – 10.01.2014). A wonderful daughter, remembered with love by her family and friends.   В память о Юлечке
- In loving memory of Patricia M.A. Couch, 4-5-30 to 19-9-08. From Aboyne to Edinburgh, And loved every minute of it.
- Thomas Arthur Fredrick Walker, Born 12/10/1936 Died 25/12/2007. A Southsider from the Pleasance. Every day was a bonus.

Saughton Park, Winter Gardens,
Flower beds

- In loving memory of Colin. So little time, so many memories. Mum, Dad, Roddy & Ross
- In loving memory of Christina Mealyou who loved these gardens 1929-2007

John N. Amoore

- Here lies a Kiwi Scot, Always remembered, never forgot. In loving memory of Hector McDonald Hudgell. 1914-1999
- In memory of Kathy & Harry Campbell, Lovingly remembered

Benches

- Remembering Paula. From family and friends at Edinburgh Airport
- James Dignall Deans, Master Joiner, 1929-2008. 'Haud Forrit'
  (*'Haud' is a Scots word for hold; 'forrit' is Scots for 'forward'. The expression 'haud forrit' means to continue to keep well, to improve. Haud is also used in the sense of celebrate, observed.*)
- 2004. Stenhouse Whitson Community Centre. In remembrance of members and friends past and present
- In loving memory of our parents Alexander (Sandy) and Annie C. Walker, 9.11.1908-24.10.1996 5.01.1913-25.04.2005. Who loved this park
- Rest awhile in the memory of Lizzie and Rab Hamilton, our dear mother and father. The family
- From family and friends in loving memory of Mrs. Nellie Milne, aged 90. Resident of 25 Murieston Crescent, 1954-1984
- This seat was presented to Edinburgh Town Council in memory of Mable Manson McQuade. Gifted by her daughter 25th February, 1969
- In loving memory of Eunice Barrie, died 27th April 1965. Gifted by her mother
- Treasured memories of my loving husband Duncan Y. Heron. Goodnight sweetheart until tomorrow. Love you always, Jane
- In memory of our parents Isabella and Hugh Cuthbertson who loved these gardens
- In loving memory of Jock and Kathleen Crawford, 1914-1968   1916-2004. And their daughter Margaret 'Maggie G' Glass 1943-2015. Who loved these gardens. From all the family xxx

- . *On the same bench*
  - In memory of Les Wilson, a dearly loved husband and dad. Donated by Irene and Ross.
  - In memory of Ina Cooper, died Glasgow aged 86 years. Dearly loved mother of Irene, Margaret and John

Corstorphine

- (*At Parish Kirk*) In memory of David Salton JP. Elder of this Kirk, Chairman of Corstorphine Community Council who loved Corstorphine and they him. His beloved wife Penny.
- (*Corstorphine Hill*) In loving memory of Catherine Keeble, beloved wife of Jack and sister to Isobel. Who never forgot walking her dog in these woods
- (*Corstorphine Hill*) In loving memory of Stuart and Isobel Mair, who lived locally for many years and had happy memories of walks in these woods

Inverleith Park

- In loving memory of Sharon Addison. '*We're all of us stars. We're fading away. Just try not to worry. You'll see us some day.*' May your smile shine on from Swansea to Edinburgh. Love from Col. Your family and friends.
- Elma G. Wilkie, 1929-2009. The best Wife, Mum & Grandma.
  Don't cry because you miss me, but smile because you remember me.
- Tom Yarrow, 02/01/87 – 19/05/99. Thank you for 12 years of love, cuddles, music and laughter – now with your daddy in heaven. Our love for you never ends. Mum and Ross xxxx
- In loving memory of James Alexander Brown 1913-2006. Married for 8 years to his beloved Dutch wife, Lineke
- In memory of Ellen Conway 1929-2008. Ellen loved Edinburgh. We hope this beautiful city gives you as much pleasure as it did her.
- In loving memory of Jamie Alexander Cockburn 1985-2009. A Wonderful Son, Brother, and Friend. '*The Love we give away is the only Love we keep.*'

- James Barlow 1968-2010. Beloved Son, Grandson, Nephew, Cousin, Friend & Team-Mate. A Life Less Ordinary
- In memory of my parents who loved this park. Violet Mary Forrest 1929-2015. Scott Forrest 1925-1996
- William Gordon Darroch 02/09/1928 – 01/05/2015. Beloved husband, dad and granddad. Sorely missed. Forever loved.
- Mr George Thomas Cook (Stockbridge) 12.05.1938 – 20.10.2015. George loved this park, his family and friends will sit here and have their own memories of a wonderful man. Loved and missed by all who knew him.

Cramond and Silverknowes

- In loving memory, Stevie Barnes. Let the good times roll.
- In Loving memory of Jean and Douglas Dallas. Two Special People Very Much Missed.
- In memory of David Drysdale who loved to walk here with his dogs Cher & Ruby and find time to stop for a blether with his friends.
- For Bill Findlay whose family remember him with love.

> In loving memory of Sarah Beaney
> 1976 – 2005
>
> 'Do not go where the path may lead,
> go instead where there is no path and leave a trail ....'
>
> That was you Sarah.
> Full on energy and bounce and always ready to 'play'.
> You touched so many lives and will always be missed.
>
> An angel taken too soon

- In Loving Memory Barbara H Fulton, 1938 – 1997. Always loved, Always in our Thoughts
- In memory of Lilian (Lil) Gladstone, née Robertson, 1931 – 2015. Who loved this place and Cramond. Till we meet again, Andrew (Andy)
- In loving memory of Bill and Jean Porter. Your smile is on our lips. Love from your children David, Moira & Janet
- In memory of Miss Kathleen Scott-Muir, late of Silverknowes, Edinburgh
- In Loving Memory of our beloved and sadly missed dog, Sheba. And also the family dogs, Whisky, Tanya and Hamish. This was their favourite place. Loved always, Susan & Gary Matthews & Family.

Newhaven

- In memory of Jean Brown. She lived a lot and she laughed a lot. From her friends
- Newhaven Fisherwomen's Choir. 1927 – Golden Jubilee – 1977. Presented by Charles Addison
- Angus G. Flockhart. Presented by the Port O'Leith Motor Boat Club in appreciation of his many years of service to the Club
- Society of Free Fishermen (Foundation 15th century0. In consideration of the early origins and unique history of the Society of Free Fishermen of Newhaven.
- In memory of James Noble Hall *Lost North Atlantic WWII.* 1912 – 1941. William Hall *Lost over Germany R.A.F. WWI* 1918 – 1941. Andrew Stevenson Hall *Respected Artist and Tradesman of Newhaven and Trinity.* 1915 – 1984
- In memory of my Grandparents and Father. Boris Lyon Hall. *Lost at Sea 1800.* James Hall *Trawler Skipper 1831-1897.* Thomas Hall *Trawler Skipper 1879-1938.* Thomas Hall *Trawler Skipper, Mine Sweeper Skipper WWII and Skipper of the Forth Ranger 1915-1986. My Late Brother* Tom Hall 1943-2012. To all the Halls who earned their living from the sea. When the sun sets on Newhaven they will be remembered
- In loving memory of Magnus Carnie Young who was lost at sea August 6th 1968. Gifted to the people of Newhaven by his wife, son and daughter
- In memory of William (Bill) Liddle. Died 24th December 1996. Departed to be with Christ
- Presented by Wullie Merrilees tae "His Auld Friends" at the Fit O' The Walk. Settle Doon an Ca Canny

Portobello

Abercorn Park

- In loving memory of Ellen Cunningham 1921-2002. '*You have gone but the tears live on.*' Donated by her loving partner Tom and her loving daughter Loretta. So sadly missed.
- Erected by Betty L. Gemmell in loving memory of her parents Mr. and Mrs. John Gemmell and her sister Grace and her dear friend Bobby Cowan.
- Mrs. Frances Gibson 1904-1989. '*She so loved this place.*' From her loving daughter Myma and family.
- With treasured memories of our Mum and Dad, Ian (1917-1997) and Nan (1918-2004) Hogg. With our love Ian, Joan, David and family.
- In loving memory of Lizbeth Melville who loved Portobello.
- In memory of our late managing secretary, Andrew Wilson Monteith. From Employee's Welfare Association, Portobello Co-operative Society Ltd.
- In loving memory of J. Stewart Smith, 7.11.1931 – 31.12.2011. Fondly missed by wife Margaret, daughters and grandchildren. '*Today is a gift, embrace it.*'
- Happy memories of this place. Henry and Molly Wanless, 1941-2006 1940-2008. Together forever hand in hand. Always in our thoughts. Philip, Craig and Karen
- In memory of George and Mary Davidson. From their late son George. "Sit and rest your weary bones"

Portobello Beach and town

- Sheilagh Mary Nisbet Dance, 1947 – 2016.
  'May all who rest upon this bench feel the warmth and love our mother gave to us. Love you to the Moon and back' Andy, Chelle & Jill
- Sandra Duthie loved sitting here eating ice cream. Ashley would have loved it too.
- Treasured Memories of George Clifford Handren and his faithful friend Rusty.
  May those who sit here appreciate the Promenade as much as he did.
  Donated by his Wife Jessie, Daughter and Family
- In loving memory of Jackie Cairns. A 'Porty' boy. From 18 June 1928 – 25 October 2004.
- In memory of Eddie Guinness. '*Gone down to the sea again*'
- In loving memory of Edith A. Johnson who died 15 February 1988. Presented by her husband Peter, daughter Evelyn and son Bruce. '*We shall remember while the light lives yet and in the night time we shall not forget*'
- In memory of our dear mother Sarah McDonaugh (nee Nelson) 1940 – 2010 and our dear father Thomas McDonaugh 1930 – 1996. The bench commemorates them both and the happy summer days we spent together at our favourite spot on the beach, just a few feet from here. Happy timeless moments, never forgotten. Leslie, Karen and Gaynor *xxx*
- This seat is placed here in loving memory of our Parents, Alex and Fay Nisbet, well known of Portobello, 'now together forever'. '*The memory of a good person is a blessing*'

Joppa

- In loving memory of Ella and Tommy Flockhart. '*Their special place*'
- Our dearest Dr Ann M. Rathie Guldberg (1938 – 2006). Always with us.
- On the same bench two plaques side by side
- Loving memory of Eddie Smeaton 13.12.1931 – 17.02.2006. Honorary President of the Kids Taxi Outing. Forever in our hearts
- With Love, Appreciation and Gratitude to our parents Walter Thomson 28/07/1910 – 11/11/1994 and Winifred Thomson 25.10.1900 – 09/01/1973
- Precious memories of Paul Joseph McElroy (13th Nov 1952 – 28th Sept 2008) A loving son, brother, uncle and friend who loved music and people. '*A beautiful mind and a gentle soul*'
- Precious memories of Maureen Anne McElroy (4th June 1959 – 26th May 2003) A loving daughter, sister, aunt and friend who lost her life in a tragic road accident. '*A free spirit with a heart of gold, who's loving light shines on*'

Chapter 8: Gathering the Monuments Together

What do the monuments reveal about Edinburgh and its citizens? Do they evoke particular themes? What is a monument? Why have monuments? Who should be honoured? These and other thoughts will be explored in this concluding chapter.

Before investigating it is worth reflecting on the importance many have for remembering those who have gone before them. The continuing importance of one monument illustrates this: annually, on Remembrance Sunday, crowds gather around the Hearts memorial to honour the football team's World War I sacrifice (*2.13*). Early in the 21st century the monument was removed to lay tram tracks. Although there was no monument at which Remembrance wreaths could be placed, faithful followers attached wreathes to the temporary fencing at the scene. The monument was removed, but the memory, and the importance of upholding it, remained. (The monument has been returned.) And of course wreaths are laid at many war memorials, the Stone of Remembrance (*4.17*), the Falkland War (*1.8*) and the Scottish American War (*1.9*). On anniversaries flowers are attached to park benches (Chapter 7), keeping memories afresh.

The 'living' nature of monuments is shown by many who flock to Greyfriars Bobby (*6.4*), keen to be photographed with the faithful dog. Those who rub David Hume's toe (*4.15*) keep the myth that this will bring them luck – despite what the rationalist Hume might think of the practice! (Caution: rubbing can cause damage.) Wojtek's monument has become popular, many stopping to photograph themselves with the bear, children climbing onto it. The National Monument (*3.4*) is active in its 'unfinished' state, enabling people to climb up on to it, enjoy the views – and have their photographs taken.

Several themes emerge when reflecting on the monuments, literature and the human striving for freedom are two of those discussed over the next few pages.

Literature

Edinburgh is a city of literature, disseminating ideas through the written word. Literature is important for developing and sharing ideas, for entertainment and enjoyment. Scottish Enlightenment leaders, Smith (*4.22*), 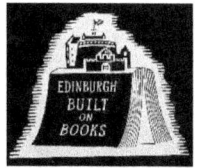 Hume (*4.15*) and Stewart (*3.1*) used it to circulate their ideas. The 'Stones of Scotland' (*3.10*) depends on poetry, thoughts put into verse by MacDiarmid and Ransford. Sir David Lyndsay's words of 1554 on a Makars' Court paving slab (*4.13*) reminds us that books are required for well-being '*Lat us haif the bukis necessare to common weill*'. His statue is on the Portrait Gallery (*2.10*). Popular fiction by Stevenson (*1.11* and *6.11*) and more recently by Rankin and Rowling (Edinburgh Awards, *4.16*) entertain people of all ages across the world.

In 2004 Edinburgh became the first UNESCO City of Literature. The monuments testify to literature's importance in the city's life. Those involved in its various aspects are remembered: writing itself; dissemination through printing and publishing; making it available through shops and libraries. The monuments dominating its central hub, Princes Street, honour literary figures, that to Scott (*1.21*), the world's tallest to a writer, perhaps the best known. Other literary figures along the street are Black (*1.20*), Wilson (*1.19*), Allan Ramsay (*1.5*) and Dean Ramsay (*1.1*). Stevenson is remembered in Princes Street gardens (*1.11*) and elsewhere in the city, including Colinton (*6.11*).

The famous Royal Mile honours literati. The Edinburgh Award (*4.16*) at the City Chambers off the Royal Mile was first awarded to two authors, Ian Rankin and JK Rowling (2007 and 2008, creators respectively of the Inspector Rebus and Harry Potter fictional characters). Paving slabs in the Makars' Court (*4.13*) off the Lawnmarket are inscribed with quotes from Scottish literary figures. On the Canongate is 'Edinburgh's Poet', Robert Fergusson (*4.25*). Scotland's Poet, Robert Burns, is remembered on Calton Hill (*3.9*) and Leith (*5.2*). His advice that we be objective when viewing ourselves: '*O wad some Pow'r the giftie gie us to see oursels as others see us*' is amongst the inscriptions on the exterior wall of the Scottish Parliament on the Canongate. Other phrases on the outer wall of Scotland's legislative seat: the Proverb '*Say but little and say it well*' a reminder to politicians and public alike; Mary Brooksbank reminds of the struggle against poverty and inequality '*Oh, dear me, the warld's ill-divided. Them that work the hardest are aye wi' least provided.*'

Literature abounds throughout the city. In the mid-2010s artist Astrid Jaekel produced a Rose Street 'Poem of the Season', Burns' 'Red red rose' featuring one year. She illustrated George Mackay Brown's poem Beachcomber on Rose Street panels, one for each of its Monday to Sunday verses. Brown was a 'Rose Street Poet', frequenting its pubs, as was Norman MacCaig, verses from his poetry also on the street. Poetry on bus shelters in Edinburgh Park developed into its Twelve Poets (*6.12*). The 'Processions' is a set of five Meadows murals by Astrid Jaekel and poet Rachel Woolf. The Middle Meadow Walk panel is from Muriel Spark's 'The Prime of Miss Jean Brodie'. The Vennel leading from the Grassmarket was re-named 'The Prime of Miss Jean Brodie Steps' in Spark's honour in the centenary of her birth.

Writers require publishers and printers. Adam Black (*1.20*) established the publisher producing Scott's Waverley Novels. William Chambers (*6.1*) and his brother founded 'W. & R. Chambers Publishers'. Allan Ramsay (*1.5*), himself a poet, developed Edinburgh's first lending library.

Some authors are remembered by characters from their books: Stevenson by two characters from 'Kidnapped' (*1.11*, Glasgow Road); Sir Arthur Conan Doyle by his famous detective Sherlock Holmes (*2.15*, Picardy Place).

But many literary figures nave no monuments. Susan Ferrier, a 19th century novelist, has none. Nor does Carolina Oliphant, Lady Nairne, a practitioner of what she called '*this queer trade of song-writing*'. Perhaps as important as Burns, but largely anonymous because of late 18th and early 19th century norms. Several of her songs remain popular: '*Charlie is my darling*', '*Will ye no come back again*' and '*The Hundred Pipers*'. Her work remains her memorial.

Literature gives joy, hope, opens up new ideas and fresh views, enriching our lives. Uplifting, it reminds us to be positive, to live life to the full. Robert Louis Stevenson offers encouragement on the plaque in Drummond Street (*1.11*): '*..how I hoped I should possibly write one little book. And then now – what a change!* (Text in full in section *1.11*.)'

Enlightenment and the quest for freedom

Literature is a key tool in humanity's striving for a better quality of life,. The National Library of Scotland heralded their 2019/2020 exhibition on the Enlightenment with the phrase: 'Ideas that Shook The World'. With strong links with philosophical developments on the European continent the 18th century literati, the literary intelligentsia, led Edinburgh as the City of the Enlightenment. The were supported by the fermentation of ideas springing forth from the mix of people of all walks of life in its crowded 18th century Old Town. Paradoxically, the cramped living conditions became a fertile ground for developing thoughts and ideas, expanding people's visions and horizons. This was supported by social meeting in coffee houses, clubs, oyster bars and pubs, in the absence of space and lighting in homes.

Alexander Brodie [1] cites two essential features of the Enlightenment:

- firstly '*its demand that we think for ourselves*', questioning, enquiring, not bowing to the views of authority figures or institutions;
- secondly, an environment that tolerates, in fact positively encourages the freedom to think individually.

These don't imply that 'questioning' will not face criticism, but that the environment welcomes and encourages the cut and thrust of new ideas, even if unpopular. The cut and thrust refines evolving ideas. Some ideas will be vigorously opposed, such as experienced by Hume (*4.15*) when he challenged existing concepts, even to the extent of blocking his career. But despite disagreements, the atmosphere enabled new and controversial views to be expressed. Hume, Smith (*4.22*) and Hutton (*6.8*) were able to explore and express original thoughts in philosophy, economics and geology.

At its core the Enlightenment is part of the on-going quest to enhance the quality of life, the on-going act of creation, the universal desire for freedom, physical and of expression. 'Liberty, Equality, Fraternity' cried the 18th century French Revolution. Scotland did not experience that violent revolution, but its history is marked by strivings for political and religious freedoms, bringing war and unrest. These strivings continue. The French Revolution's rallying cry links liberty, equality and fraternity. Focussing on liberty alone leads to conflicts between vested interests. Embedding liberty with equality for all, a common fraternity, leads to a truer deeper liberty. Hamish Henderson recognized this, envisaging '*a Scotland that was free. Fraternal and joyful*' (Twelve Poets, *6.12*). '*Fredome is a noble thing*' wrote John Barbour in 1375 (Makars' Court, *4.13*).

'Friends of the People' (*3.8*) obelisk thrusts up through the clouds, symbolic of the struggles for freedom.

On Calton Hill, visible from Old and New Towns, is the tall 'Friends of the People' (*3.8*) obelisk. It thrusts upwards, piercing the sky, a visual reminder of this quest for freedom. At his 1793 trial for agitating for universal franchise Thomas Muir verbalised his convictions inscribed on the monument: '*I have devoted myself to the cause of THE PEOPLE. It is a good cause – it shall ultimately prevail – it shall finally triumph.'* They were opposed by the political elite, leading to banishment to Australia. Amongst their opposition was Dundas, his tall St Andrew Square monument (*2.6*) ultimately overshadowed by the obelisk (*3.8*). Muir's prophecy was fulfilled, though universal franchise had to await the 20th century. A plaque was added in 2019 in the Vennel to Bessie Watson, an Edinburgh suffragette.

Freedom requires freedom from tyrannical rulers. George Buchanan's pioneering 16th century treatise *'De Jure Regni apud Scotos'* ('The law of kingship among Scots') discussed the balance of power between ruler and ruled. A Makars' court (*4.13*) paving slab summarizes his assertion that *'it is right that the people confer power on whom they please'* (translation of *'Populo enim jus est ut imperium cui velit deferat'*). Not the divine right of kings, it is the people who confer power. Rulers have obligations to the ruled who have the right to remove rulers who fail to serve the people. This principle underlined the Declaration of Arbroath. The king has obligations; if Robert the Bruce *'should give up what he has begun, and agree to make us or our kingdom subject to the King of England or English, we should exert ourselves at once to drive him out as our enemy and a subverter of his own rights and ours, and make some other man who was well able to defend us our King'*. These words precede the words from the Declaration inscribed on the Royal Scots monument (*1.13*).

The search for freedom, for having opportunities, lies at the heart of much human endeavour, personal and national. At the personal level, extending to the local community, is the example of Dr Helen Crummy (*6.10*); the design of her monument sums up her beliefs, verbalised in her obituary in the Scotsman [2]:

> *'Helen Crummy was one of those rare individuals whose innate modesty concealed an iron determination to change the world for the better. ... Where some might see the victims of poverty as part of an endemic social problem, she saw the unfulfilled potential of people who, given the opportunity, could overcome disadvantage and find self-esteem. For her, every child, no matter how poor, was a precious gift; every adult, regardless of circumstances, was worthy of respect, and deserved to be listened to.'*

She channelled her strong positive views into constructive action, demonstrating in practice her saying inscribed on the monument's open door: *'History will be made when the People play their part'*. Her inspiring leadership built on her belief that *'The beauty of Craigmillar lies in the strength of its people'*.

Guthrie (*1.3*) saw the unfulfilled potential in the poor and often thieving youth. He believed that education and proper feeding could transform the lives of the young beggars who resorted to petty theft, often to bring money home to parents who resorted to alcohol to free themselves from oppressive grim lives. He put his thoughts into action with 'Ragged Schools' offering hope and a future.

Recognizing the needs of the vulnerable and poor, particularly of the healthcare needs of women, triggered Dr Inglis (*4.23*) to act. She had already shown pioneering determination to advance women as doctors. But more was required, women deserved equality, prompting her support for the suffragettes and votes for women. She channelled her expertise, care and compassion to provide practical health care for women, particularly the poor and destitute, opening the women's Hospice on the High Street, in those days very deprived (c.f. *4.24*).

The outbreak of World War I was to see another side of her character. Concern for the healthcare plights of wounded soldiers and a determination to show that women can respond led her to form 'The Scottish Women's Hospitals' to care for wounded soldiers. Her enormous contribution was soon appreciated and recognized in continental Europe, particularly by the Serbian people, but sadly not initially in Britain, though the 2017 centenary of her death and funeral was an opportunity to redress this earlier lack of recognition.

Improving living conditions improves lives. Patrick Geddes (*4.11*) recognized the profound effect of the physical environment in which people live, leading to his pioneering urban planning based on enhancing the life-style of a city's inhabitants. Lord Provost William Chambers had earlier acted on the appalling state of much of the Old Town in the mid-19th century, passing the 'City Improvement Act' of 1867 (see *4.24* and *6.1*).

At the individual level many strive for equal rights. Burns reminded '*that man to man the world o'er shall brithers be for a'that*' (Makars' Court, *4.13*). Nan Shepherd emphasized personal freedom: '*It's a grand thing to get leave to live*' (Makars' Court, *4.13*). As individuals we must allow ourselves that freedom, a freedom to live the life we have been given. (These words were reproduced by the Royal Bank of Scotland on its 2016 £5 note, with a portrait of Nan.)

The popular Scottish cry for liberty has often been associated with independence from England, particularly the battles of King Robert the Bruce (*4.1, 2.10*) and William Wallace (*4.2, 2.10*). The Cairn (*3.5*) recalls the late 20th century fight for a Scottish Parliament. Its return was celebrated in the 'Stones of Scotland' (*3.10*), with poetry by Hugh MacDiarmid and Tessa Ransford. Whilst some call for independence, other have looked for balance between independence and interdependence. Sir Walter Scott (*1.21*), who proclaimed, '*This is my own, my native land*' (Makars' Court *4.13*), was proudly Scottish whilst at the same time seeing benefits in the interdependence of the nations of the United Kingdom.

Religious conflicts illustrate how the desire for freedom by one group can lead to domination, suppressing other views. The Covenanter's (*6.3*) monument reminds us how movements that should be about love for fellow children of God get usurped into tyranny. The Scottish Protestant reformation was led by John Knox (*4.14*) supported by leaders such as George Buchanan, fiercely opposing Roman Catholicism and its leaders such as Cardinal Beaton. The religious conflicts were intertwined with political rivalries. It is worth reflecting on the politico-religious conflicts that led King Charles II to have two wedding ceremonies on the same day, one private, one public (*4.20*). Not even monarchs had '*leave to live*'. Behind these religious clashes were political ambitions and the desire for power. Today there is much greater understanding and respect between religious denominations. It is fitting that the former adversaries, Knox and Buchanan on the one hand and Cardinal Beaton on the other, now stand side-by-side on the outer wall of the Scottish National Portrait Gallery (*2.10*).

The search for freedom, or is it power, by one group often enslaves another.

Those admiring the 78th Highlander regiment (*4.8*) monument on the Castle Esplanade may marvel at the soldiers' heroism, mourning the loss of life in the Indian Mutiny; but in India it is known as the First War of Independence. Similarly, imperial aims and access to the wealth uncovered in the South Africa gold fields brought conflict between the British and Boers; the Anglo-Boer War (*1.4, 1.17, 4.6*) was called the 'Freedom War' by the Boers. It is appropriate here to mention the 'Woman and Child' statue (*2.14*) recognizing the search for freedom from the Apartheid laws that the black people of South Africa had had to endure and the eventual equality under law achieved towards the end of the 20th century. Closer to home is the fight for freedom in the Spanish Civil War (*1.23*), the poem on the monument strongly expressing the feelings.

Monuments recall the campaign to abolish slavery. Six Scots who died in the American Civil War fighting with Abraham Lincoln to abolish slavery are remembered on Calton Hill (*3.6*). Livingstone (*1.22*) also worked to end slavery.

This brief view of monuments highlighting quests for liberty recalls the 1320 'Declaration of Arbroath' (Royal Scots (*1.13*)): '*It is not for glory or riches, neither is it for honour that we fight, but it is for the sake of liberty alone, which no true man loseth, but at the cost of his own life*'. Nicola Benedetti receiving her Edinburgh Award (**4.16**) spoke of it as a gift, '*a reminder of our place in a lineage of contributors to bettering life for ourselves and for others*'.

Military

Whilst not dominating the city's monuments, many are associated with wars. The last erected in 2018 all have military themes: Scottish War Poets (see Makars' Court *4.13*); General Maczek (*4.18*); Captain 'Winkle' Brown (*6.19*). The Portrait Gallery (*2.10*) includes military leaders on its external walls: Field Marshall John Campbell; Admiral Duncan; General Abercromby.

The late 18th and early 19th centuries Napoleonic wars are remembered by Nelson's triumph at Trafalgar (*3.3*) and Wellington's defeat of Bonaparte at Waterloo (*1.24*). The impact of the decades of war with France that ended at Waterloo is less appreciated now, but the phrase '*The Ever Memorable Year*' on Regent Bridge (*2.18*) requires pausing for thought. Why was '1815' the ever-memorable year? It ended two decades of war in which many Scots died. Scottish regiments played a major role with parts of Edinburgh Castle transformed into a prison for French prisoners of war. At the 1815 Battle of Waterloo both the allied and French soldiers showed many acts of valour. The seizing of the French Standard by Ensign Ewart is remembered by his memorial on the Castle Esplanade (*4.4*) – and by a pub at the start of the Lawnmarket. The relief that war had given way to victorious peace prompted the decision to build the National Monument (*3.4*). But early enthusiasm waned as economic realities and funding priorities changed and the monument was never completed. Its incomplete state arguably serves as a better monument.

The two Calton Hill monuments to the Napoleonic wars have forward-looking as well as remembrance messages. Nelson's monument (*3.3*) was erected by the grateful citizens of Edinburgh not simply to celebrate Nelson, but '*by his noble example, to teach their sons to emulate what they admire, and, like him, when duty requires it, to die for their country.'* The National Monument (*3.4*) similarly looks to the past and future: *'A Memorial of the Past and Incentive to the Future Heroism of the Men of Scotland.'*

The military campaigns known as the South African or Anglo-Boer War in what is now the Republic of South Africa feature in many monuments: Royal Scots Greys *1.4*; Black Watch, *1.17;* The Scottish Horse *4.6* (raised in South Africa for the war)*;* and the Gordon Highlander's Plaque on the Castle Esplanade. It is perhaps surprising that this war, fought thousands of miles away on another continent, should be the focus of so many military memorials. Valerie Parkhouse [3] suggests that the *'flowering of popular patriotism'* in Britain in the late 19th and early 20th centuries may have contributed to the large number not just in Edinburgh but throughout the UK. She compares their relatively large numbers to those to the earlier Crimea and Napoleonic Wars.

Earlier the different British and Boer perspectives of the wars (there were actually two Anglo-Boer Wars) have been mentioned, the Boers referring to the Freedom War, their freedom at stake. Both sides suffered heavy losses: estimates put the British military losses at over 20,000 dead and a further 23,000 injured; the Boers and their followers suffered 45,000 to 50,000 deaths in the concentration camps, approximately 20,000 of whom were black Africans; the financial cost estimated at over £200 billion in today's money.

Edinburgh monuments remember those who died in the Great War (World War I), World War II and other conflicts, most not included in this book, in particular the Scottish National War Memorial in the Castle. Amongst those included are the Stone of Remembrance on Edinburgh's Royal Mile (*4.17*) and the memorial to the close relationship between Scotland and the USA in Princes Street Gardens (*1.9*). The patriotic duty that major conflicts trigger is exemplified by the Hearts War Memorial (*2.13*) at Haymarket. The Italian part of World War II is remembered by two monuments, the Wojtek monument in Princes Street Gardens (*1.7*) and the Manuscript of Monte Cassino (*2.16*) on Picardy Place.

Amongst individual war heroes honoured is Captain 'Winkle' Brown (*6.19*). But he was more than a war hero, taking air flight to new levels through his test flying of novel aircraft. Equally importantly, his life story tells of the futility of war, how it pits friend against friend.

Women in monuments

Women's contributions are under-represented by city monuments. Queen Victoria is at the foot of Leith Walk (*5.1*) and on the Royal Scottish Academy (*1.16*). Dr Helen Crummy is sculpted in a delightful memorial symbolising many of her contributions (*6.10*). Catherine Sinclair is remembered by the gothic spire north of Charlotte Square (*2.9*) and Susannah Alice Stephen by the parakeet and trug (*4.12*) off the Lawnmarket. Queen Elizabeth the Queen Mother is honoured by a memorial garden (*6.16*). The 19th century author Alison Dunlop has a memorial gate at Inverleith Park (*6.14*). Women are in group monuments: exterior statues on the National Portrait Gallery (*2.10*); Edinburgh

Park's Twelve Poets (*6.12*); recipients of the Edinburgh Award (*4.16*); and phrases from women authors on the Makars' Court paving slabs (*4.13*). On Festival Square off Lothian Road a statue of a mother, her child and a shanty shack remember those who suffered under South African apartheid (*2.14*). The small number of monuments to women poorly reflects their contributions.

The plaque to Dr Elsie Inglis on the High Street (*4.23*) is included, 2022 gave the welcome news that approval for a monument to her has been granted. Plaques in general are not included in this volume; those to women in Edinburgh are included in the website of monuments to women in Scotland (http://womenofscotland.org/memorials).

Susan Ferrier (1782-1854), the Edinburgh author as popular in her life as Sir Walter Scott deserves greater recognition.

Animals in monuments

It has been suggested that Edinburgh has more monuments to dogs than to women, but this is not strictly true. There are only two monuments specifically to dogs, those to Greyfriars Bobby (*6.4*) and Bum (*1.14*). Greyfriars Bobby (*6.4*) is well loved and important because it honours and reminds us of the strong bond between pets, particularly dogs, and their human companions.

Another such bond is remembered in Corstorphine Parish Kirk's graveyard. It has a rough-hewn rock headstone to John Foord, a '*sheepherd who departed this life Feb^Y the 15th 1795 aged 75 years*'. He died, frozen by a snowstorm, while tending his sheep on Corstorphine Hill, his sheep dog faithfully remaining with him. Legend has it that his rock headstone was the rock at which he was found lying dead. Some reports suggest that after John was buried his dog stayed at his grave, others that the dog also perished in the snowstorm. The relationship is remembered in the graveyard, the dog's grave close to John's. The dog's headstone is a small stone carried down from the hill to the kirkyard. There are other 'Bobbies' whose faithfulness is known only to their human companions.

It is thus not surprising to see statues of famous people with their dogs. Maxwell, the brilliant physicist, is shown with his Irish terrier, Toby (*2.5*). Famous writers have their dogs with them, Sir Walter Scott with Maida (*1.21*) and the young Robert Louis Stevenson with Cuillin, his Skye terrier (*6.11*).

Similarly, there is a bond between humans and horse. Several monuments include horses, but, within Edinburgh itself, there are none explicitly to horses. Monuments with horses include: Royal Scots Grey (*1.4*); Wellington riding Copenhagen (*1.24*); Prince Albert (*2.1*); and Sir John 4th Earl of Hopetoun (*2.6*). Earl Haig is on horseback (*4.10*), Charles II is triumphant on horseback (*4.20*) and James V is on horseback being attacked by a man carrying a knife (*6.18*).

The beehive and bees on Patrick Geddes' monument (*4.11*) symbolise his views on people linking with nature, a relationship of nature central to urban planning followed by Susannah Alice Stephen and seen in her monument (*4.12*). This relationship should be at the heart of town planning: those responsible for our cities should keep this in focus as they decide how to manage city developments.

The close relationships between humans and animals is illustrated by the statue to Wojtek and the Polish forces (*1.7*). The mural summarises the story of the baby bear bartered for food, then nurtured by the soldiers and subsequently enrolled in the army, embarking for the Italian front where it carried ammunition. After the war the bear settled in Scotland and finally Edinburgh.

Monarchs

Edinburgh is the capital of a country ruled by monarchs and it is thus not surprising that several monuments are of Kings and Queens. King Robert the Bruce, King of Scots and fighter for independence, has a statue at the entrance to Edinburgh Castle (*4.1*) and the Scottish National Portrait Gallery (*2.10*). Several other monarchs are on the exterior wall of the Portrait Gallery including King Malcolm III and his saintly wife St Margaret. Its east wall has a statue of Mary Queen of Scots with two of her advisers. More recent monarchs remembered are Queen Victoria (*1.16* and *5.1*) and her son King Edward VII (*4.26, 5.13*). The oldest exterior monument in Edinburgh is to a King, Charles II (*4.20*).

Scientists

Edinburgh, home to universities and research institutes, has fostered famous scientists, some with monuments: Sir James Young Simpson (*1.2*); James Clark Maxwell (*2.5*) and also an India Street plaque in recalls his birth; John Napier of Merchiston, the inventor of the logarithms and the geologist, James Hutton have statues on the Portrait Gallery (*2.10*); Hutton has a memorial garden (*6.8*), his impact enhanced by John Playfair (*3.2*) publicising his work; James Watt (*6.20*) pioneering engineer, developer of the steam engine that enabled the Industrial Revolution; James Braidwood (*4.21*) is remembered for pioneering a scientific evidenced-based approach to fire-fighting; Sir David Brewster (*6.21*) is remembered for his insights into optics; Professor Peter Higgs, Nobel Laureate, is amongst those honoured with the Edinburgh Award (*4.16*).

A monument dedicated to NHS staff who sacrificially worked through the Covid-19 pandemic was unveiled in October 2022 in the Royal College of Surgeons. Sculpted by Kenny Hunter it has 4 life-size figures of clinicians. But not all have been honoured: Should Mary Somerville, honoured on the Royal Bank of Scotland's £10 bank-note, have a statue recognizing her scientific achievements? What about Nobel Laureate Dr Joseph Black?

Engaging with monuments

Monuments can be viewed as static reminders of the past. However, we can engage in monuments, perhaps even transforming what they represent.

David Hume (*4.15*) advocated realism, arguing against superstition. However, his Royal Mile monument has a big toe polished bright from the myth that rubbing it brings good luck. Greyfriars Bobby's nose (*6.4*) is rubbed, showing affection for the dog and his story. Traffic cones have a way of being added to monuments, with Wellington (*1.24*) and Prime Minister Gladstone (*2.11*) sometimes embellished. Spectacles have been added to one of the boys on the Gladstone statue. Queen Victoria (Leith, *5.1*) is sometimes given a necklace.

Those planning the National Monument (*3.4*) envisaged a grand building, but only its west pillars were built, derided as Edinburgh's disgrace. What was completed is now something that residents and visitors enjoy, the challenge of climbing it, a place for fun. Rather than a grand building Edinburgh is blessed with a monument with opportunities for the living. Not a disgrace; arguably the disgrace would have been building over more of Calton Hill, destroying the wonderful green space that we can still enjoy. In a 2019 poem, 'The Unfinished Monument' Ledingham wrote of it recognizing, acknowledging our own personal incompleteness (Hunter, Ledingham, see Bibliography).

This author suggests re-interpretating Dr Dewar's (*6.13*) monument. It was built to honour the doctor, respected by many patients despite the tragedy. It should also honour the patient who died, but also should remind us of the tragedies of medical adverse events, the need to learn from mistakes, to prevent repetitions.

Some statues seem designed to be interacted with, for example climbing onto Wojtek (*1.7*). Its enduring appeal is shown by flowers regularly placed there.

Monuments look back, reminding us of the past. Many are not forgotten monuments to the past, but regularly remembered, with wreaths and flowers laid at anniversaries. But some were not erected simply to remember the past. Several have continuing messages. Amongst these are those that convey messages of co-operation between peoples and communities: the Scottish-American War Memorial (*1.9*); the Canine Connection linking San Diego's 'Bum' (*1.14*) and Greyfriars Bobby (*6.4*). And the messages to future generations of Nelson's Monument (*3.3*) and the National Monument (*3.4*).

Monuments are often viewed as remote, figures high above street level, their stories largely unknown (a reason for this book). When Edinburgh Collective opened its new gallery on Calton Hill in November 2018 the artist Klaus Webber in '*Nonument*' describes monuments as '*large, heavy, reactionary, stiff and ideologically burdened*'. In contrast, can lessons for design be learnt from those to General Maczek (*4.18*) and Sandy Robertson (*5.8*): benches with statues, inviting passers-by to sit, sharing a moment with the person honoured.

Does a city, does Edinburgh need monuments?
What do monuments add, what benefits do they give? Do they improve the aesthetics of the city? Should those they commemorate be remembered?

Edinburgh's natural landscape has been transformed by individuals, groups and society. Their legacy is the buildings, streets, parks, gardens and open spaces of our city. A recent monument was to William Henry Playfair (*6.2*). Undoubtadly a major contributor whose architectural talents hugely benefited the city. But is a statue warranted? Are not his buildings sufficient monuments? Perhaps the buildings should be. However, whilst many admire his works, most could not name him as the architect. Is this a good reason for erecting the statue? Pointing to their educational value, Turnbull recounted Professor Blackie comments during the 1870s discussions motivating for David Livingstone's statue (*1.22*):

> "*If Edinburgh were filled with statues this would stir the minds of strangers in a way no guidebook could.*" [4]

But there is another point of view. When Robert Louis Stevenson (RLS, **1.11**,

6.11), was approached to support a proposal for erecting a monument to the author R.M Ballantyne, RLS apparently responded: '*Mr Ballantyne would, I am sure, be vastly more gratified if we added to the prosperity of his wife and family than if we erected to him the tallest monument in Rome*'. [5] Ballantyne, who died in Rome, was a childhood hero of RLS.

Who should next be remembered with a monument?
In late 2022 the most recent monument to a named individual was that to Ken Buchanan (**2.17**). Shortly afterward 'Your last breath' by Kenny Hunter was unveiled in tribute to the clinicians who saved countless lives during the Covid pandemic. The statue of 4 clinicians was placed in the grounds of the Royal College of Surgeons in Nicolson Street.

Who next, where should it be sited and how to decide? Should cities have strategic development plans, guidelines and forward-planning for monuments? Or should it be left to popular requests and the persuasive power of influential leaders? There are arguments for and against each approach. The collective diversity that creates the character of a city, notably seen in the medieval Old Town, can lead to a rich mix of who are honoured if the process is left to individual enthusiasm. But it can overlook important contributors to the city.

Why should one person be honoured and another not? These are not new questions and apply not just to monuments. Robert Louis Stevenson, writing in the Calton Hill chapter of his '*Edinburgh: Picturesque Notes*' published in 1878 (reprinted by Albyn Press Ltd in 1983 under the title of 'Picturesque Old Edinburgh') raised this question about Calton Hill: '*The scene suggests reflections on fame and on man's injustice to the dead. You see Dugald Stewart (3.1) rather more handsomely commemorated than Burns (3.9). Immediately below, in the Canongate churchyard, lies Robert Fergusson, Burn's master in his art..; and if Dugald Stewart has been too boisterously acclaimed, the Edinburgh poet, on the other hand, is most unrighteously forgotten.*' [6] When Stevenson wrote this in the 19th century there was no monument to Robert Fergusson; this was corrected in the early 21st century when the Friends of Robert Fergusson commissioned his monument, erected in 2004 (**4.25**).

The choice of whom to include was faced by those planning the 12 herms (**6.12**). Ian Wall, in the foreword to his book '*Twelve Poets in Edinburgh Park*' (published by National Galleries of Scotland, 2005), summed up the dilemma: '*As to why these twelve? There is no formal 'rhyme or reason' particularly as we took a wide view of the nature of poets' contribution to Scottish life; the discussions about who should be in and out were stimulating and enjoyable and any one of us would want to bring in other poets*'. Not random choices, but healthy decision making, recognizing the validity of other conclusions. Should those approving future monuments satisfy themselves of '*the nature of (the subject's) contribution to Scottish life*'?

Several names of those deserving a monument are raised. Calls have been made to recognize the injustice done to women killed for alleged witchcraft, more prominent than the Witches Fountain (**4.9**). Edinburgh was the centre of the 18th century Scottish Enlightenment with prominent figures such as Hume (*4.15*), Smith (*4.22*), Hutton (*6.8*) (Father of Geology) and Playfair (*6.2*) all remembered by monuments. But not all: Robert Adam, the prominent architect of Georgian Edinburgh; nor Adam Ferguson, the Father of Sociology, author of 'History of Civil Society'; nor the pioneering medical officer of health, Dr Henry Littlejohn (see *4.24*, Joseph McIver); nor the chemist Joseph Black. And does the simple plaque to James Craig on a seldom travelled side street do justice to his inspired design for the New Town (*2.8*)? Or does his legacy live on in the classical design of this part of Edinburgh, with no need for a monument? There is no street monument to Lord Provost George Drummond for his vision and driving force leading to the New Town. Drummond also established the Royal Infirmary in the 18th century and chairs in medicine at the University. Are the National Portrait Gallery (*2.10*) and Wells Court in Dean village sufficient memorials to John Richie Findlay.

Realistically, not all who have helped create the Edinburgh we know – and those continuing to do so – can be remembered by monuments; neither space nor funds permit. The Edinburgh Award scheme (*4.16*) is an excellent unfolding story of those contributing to the city.

Who should be honoured next? Should there be a period of reflection with '*stimulating and enjoyable discussions held*' as to who should merit it? It is worth reflecting that the first years of the 21st century have proportionally seen more monuments erected than in any period of the last two centuries (one fifth of the monuments in this book were erected between 2000 to 2019, surpassing the prolific years of monument installations in the 19th century.

Why the need to remember? What is the role of monuments?
The 2016 Edinburgh Arts Festival took for its theme the title of Horace's Ode 3.30, '*More lasting than Bronze*'. Referring to his writings Horace boldly stated:
> '*I have created a monument more lasting than bronze and loftier that*
> *the royal structure of the pyramids, that which neither devouring rain,*
> *nor the unrestrained wind may be able to destroy. I shall not wholly*
> *die*' but will continue to be newly arisen so long as my words are read.

Ramsay's (*1.5*) burial plaque in Greyfriars kirkyard records similar sentiments:
> '*Tho here you're buried, worthy Allan,   For while your Soul lives in the Sky,*
> *We'll ne'er forget your canty Callan;   Your Gentle Shepherd ne'er can die.*'

These remind us that we don't require physical monuments to remember people or events. The references to the power of the written word is very appropriate for Edinburgh, the first UNESCO City of Literature.

Plaques on benches in parks and along streets and paths (Chapter 7) point to the need for tangible ways of honouring and remembering people, places or events that have touched their lives. This urge to keep loved ones alive and present is expressed in phrases like '*Too dearly loved to ever be forgotten*' and '*To be remembered by those we loved is not to die*'.

Another way of remembering pioneers is shown by the honouring of the 17th c physician Sir Robert Sibbald. In 1670 he and Andrew Balfour started a 'physic garden' near Holyrood Palace to grow medicinal plants. This it did, but also became popular as a pleasant and attractive place to walk and relax. Forward to the 21st century when the Royal Botanic Garden Edinburgh continues its important scientific botanical role and is also a pleasant, attractive and quiet place to walk, to enjoy and to be at peace. The 2021 Floral Clock (**1.6**) celebrated the 350th anniversary of the garden. Sir Robert has a bust in the Royal College of Physicians and is being honoured by the Sibbald Walk, part of the early 21st century development of New Waverley to the north of the Canongate. Is not this as fitting a memorial as a physical statue?

Street names honour people and events. Streets and buildings at the Kings Buildings, Edinburgh University's College of Engineering and Science, honour men and women engineers and scientists (see *6.21*, Brewster, for details). Lord Cockburn, 19th century lawyer, judge and literary figure noted for promoting heritage-sympathetic development is remembered by Cockburn Street.

Some are remembered by the names of organizations. An example: Mary Erskine (1629-1707) is remembered by the school that bears her name. Mary became a successful businesswoman following the death of her two husbands, establishing a foundation in 1694 to educate the daughters of Edinburgh burgesses, establishing the Trades' Maiden Hospital, later named the Edinburgh Ladies' College, then, in 1944, renamed the Mary Erskine School, one of the oldest girls' school in the world. She was a remarkable pioneer.

The Royal Bank of Scotland honoured 4 women on its first four polymer banknotes: Nan Shepherd; Mary Somerville, Kate Cranston and, in 2021, Flora Stevenson, also with a school named after her.

And it is worth noting that James Watt (*6.20*) is more widely remembered and honoured by having the unit of power named after him, than by his monuments.

How long will a monument last, how long is it relevant?

Monuments suffer decay not lasting forever. The 10 monuments project restored 10, including Charles II (*4.20*) whose supporting structure was ageing. The Jawbone Arch (*6.6*) in the Meadows had to be removed for restoration, at the time of writing still not returned.

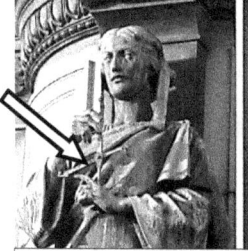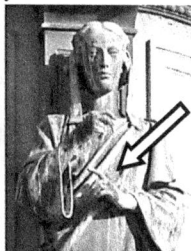

'Measure' with (left) and without (right) measuring instrument (*2.11*).

Details on monuments also suffer from damage and ageing. Gladstone's monument (*2.11*) includes six allegorica l figures representing his virtues. The 'Measure' figure had, up until the early 21st century, a measuring instrument in her hand. This has been damaged and is no longer there. The Duke of Buccleuch and Queensberry's monument also had six allegorical figures representing some of his virtues (*4.19*). The author noticed in early 2018 that one of the allegorical figures was missing; despite detailed investigation no information on the missing 'virtue' has been found. James Watt's statue has lost the instrument on his hand (*6.20*). The bayonets on the rifles of the soldiers on the Black Watch monument (*1.17*) had been damaged and had to be restored. However, whether through natural damage or vandalism, several soldiers' rifles remain (at the time of writing in 2021) damaged.

In recognition of his granting a Royal Charter to the Royal Infirmary of Edinburgh (RIE) in 1736 a statue of King George II was placed in front of the old Infirmary in 1759. It was moved to Lauriston Place when the RIE moved

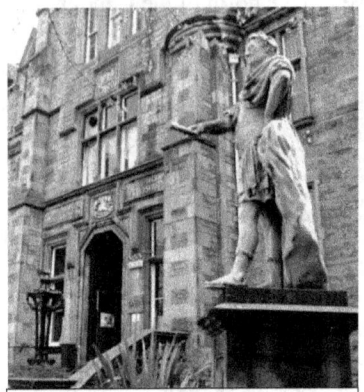

from Infirmary Street in the late 19th century, the statue placed to the right of the main entrance. However, when the RIE moved in the early 21st century to Little France the statue was too fragile to be moved. Pending restoration, it was moved to the National Gallery of Scotland.

Town planning change may move monuments, sometimes to nearby sites as with Chambers's monument (*6.1*) in 2016. At other times the move is to very different locations, for example the move of the monument to Gladstone (*2.11*) from its original location in St Andrew Square to its current location in Coates Place.

King George II at Royal Infirmary of Edinburgh, Lauriston Place, 2003.

Some early 'Boots' buildings had statues of locals, that in Princes Street had: Sir Walter Scott (bottom left), above it John Knox and then Robert the Bruce; top right William Wallace; below it George Wishart and bottom right Robert Burns; top central Bonnie Prince Charlie and Jacobite followers (architect Michael Wayne Treleaven). Demolished in 1965 as part of redesign of the street.

The Floral Clock (*1.6*) is renewed every year, its commemorative theme changing. The annual re-creation involves designing, planting and maintaining.

When to remove a monument?
Changing socio-political views can lead to demands to remove monuments. Some are toppled following forcible deposing of leaders. Across the world monuments are removed as popular opinion deems the person or views no longer acceptable. Edinburgh examples include demands to remove Dundas's monument (*2.6*) and the 2018 removal of the Princes Street Gardens plaque to the freedom campaigner and Nobel Laurette Aung San Suu Kyi (*1.15*) following concerns about her role in the 2017/2018 Rohingya refugee crisis.
Some removals are more curious: An editorial in the British Medical Journal (25 Mardh 2010) questioned the removal of Edward Jenner's Trafalgar Square monument (erected with the support of Prince Albert in 1858), but removed after Albert's death, contrasting the honouring of men who killed with those who served to save.
An alternative approach is to retain and explain controversial monuments, reflecting new views on the person commemorated.

What to include in a compilation of monuments?

The compiler of any list of monuments must decide what to include, what to exclude. This requires asking and answering questions: what is and is not a monument? What do we mean by monument? Distinctions will need to be made between works of art and works designed or considered to be in remembrance of people or events. This concept of a monument as a work designed to remember people or events is the basis on which this author decided what to include and exclude. In general buildings designed for a particular purpose, although named in remembrance of a particular person or event, are excluded. One exception is the bridge on Regent Road (*2.18*) built to span the chasm between the growing New Town and its expansion onto Calton Hill. It is included to draw attention to 'The Ever Memorable Year', recalling the nationwide relief at the ending of the lengthy and costly Napoleonic Wars.

Works of art are excluded, two examples being the Ross Fountain and Brodie's statue representing the 'Genius of Architecture', both in West Princes Street Gardens. In Chapter 1 these are mentioned as landmarks, to identify them, but noting that they are excluded from the list of monuments. A redevelopment of Princes Street Gardens commenced in 2017. As part of this the Ross Fountain was removed for repair, partly to restore its water fountain that had not operated for several

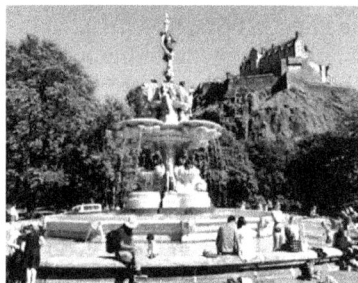

Ross Fountain, water flowing, 8th July 2018.

years. It also involved repainting and some sculptural restoration. The renovated fountain was re-installed in 2018, flowing water restored.

Examples of other urban art excluded are the statue of Alexander and Bucephalus in the courtyard of the City Chambers on the High Street (Chapter 4) and 'Dreaming Spires', the sculpture of two giraffes in Picardy Place.

Allegorical statues on the exterior of buildings, many associated with the original purpose of the building, are excluded. Notable examples are the six representing Navigation, Commerce, Manufacture, Science, Art and Agriculture on the skyline of the former Bank of Scotland in St Andrew Square, formerly the British Linen Bank. These were by the 19th century sculptor A.H. Richie. Similarly, on what is now 'The Dome' in George Street but was originally the 'Commercial Bank' are Caledonia flanked by Prudence, Agriculture, Commerce, Enterprise, Mechanical Science and Learning. On the Royal College of Physicians in Queen Street Hygeia is flanked by Hippocrates and Aesculapius. At the west end of Princes Street at the foot of Lothian Road is the Caledonian Hotel, opened in 1903 to serve the then Princes Street railway station. Statues of women on the hotel's front represent Engineering, Agriculture, Commerce and The Arts. These reflect the hotel's origin at the terminus of the Caledonian Railway line, part of the developing trade-transport network. Also on Princes Street, but to the East, on the exterior of Jenners are several caryatids. The 1930s St Andrews House Scottish Government offices on Regent Road are adorned with statues representing government departments of Health, Agriculture, Fisheries and Education, and of Architecture and Statecraft. The statues of historical figures on the exterior of the National Portrait Gallery along both Queen Street and North St Andrew Street are included (*2.10*) but the allegorical statues are excluded, such as the recently replaced statue of Clio, the Greek muse of history, centrally on the roof above the main entrance.

More difficult was the decision to exclude the smaller statues on the Scott Monument (*1.21*), as was that to exclude the statues on the west end of St Giles – though John Knox's statue is mentioned (*4.14*).

Monuments and statues within buildings are excluded, for example the many statues in the Scottish National Portrait Gallery, including that of Robert Burns originally within the Calton Hill (monument *3.9*). Another building containing an impressive number of statues is Parliament House on the High Street, notably those of leading legal figures from the 18th century that include Henry Dundas, 1st Viscount Melville (who also has a statue in St Andrew Square – Chapter 2, *2.6*) and the mid-18th century statue of Lord Forbes of Culloden, believed to be the oldest marble statue in Scotland. These are all excluded.

Monuments within cemeteries are excluded, with three Calton Hill exceptions (*3.6; 3.7; 3.8*). The Scottish-American Civil War monument (*3.6*) is included; it honours the striving for freedom (in this case abolishing of slavery in the USA); its Abraham Lincoln statue is significant. David Hume's mausoleum (*3.7*) is included because of what its design says about the man, its prominence still visible from the Royal Mile, and the contradiction between his atheism and the Christian inscription reflecting the beliefs of his relative also buried there. The Martyrs Monument (*3.8*), also called the Monument to the Friends of the People, is included; it is not a burial spot; rather it recalls the belief in universal freedom (exemplified in the right to vote) of the five men for which they suffered banishment. The soaring obelisk exemplifies the spirit of soaring high above prevailing views to a higher status for humankind.

The scope is limited to Edinburgh. Monuments in neighbouring towns such as Musselburgh, Penicuik, Dalmeny and South Queensferry are thus excluded.

Ultimately a decision has to be made, a decision which may be subjective but which the compiler must be able to justify.

Concluding remarks

Edinburgh is the product of its rich history, geological and social, and by those whose work and lives have formed the city. Its history is not complete, but continues to develop. Its monuments reflect aspects of its history. The list of monuments is not complete, but changes, with requests for new monuments to honour and remember people important to the development of the city and its inhabitants. Together all the monuments, seen and unseen, like the stones of Scotland (*3.10*), are gathered together, and together form an important part of the city we know and cherish.

Index

Guide to Edinburgh Monuments

References and Bibliography
End notes by chapter
Chapter 1

1. Quotations from the preface to the 22nd edition.
   https://archive.org/stream/reminiscencesof00ramsmiss_djvu.txt
2. http://www.thereformation.info/revthomasguthrie.htm
3. Page 1725 in David Radcliffe 'English Poetry 1579 – 1830: Spenser and the Tradition.
   http://spenserians.cath.vt.edu/TextRecord.php?textsid=33958
4. Page 99 in Allan Foster, The Literary Traveller in Edinburgh
5. Edinburgh Evening News, 2nd February 2019
6. http://whc.unesco.org/en/list/728/
7. Page 1 of the Introduction by John Skelton to the 1876 publication of 'The Comedy of
   the Noctes Ambrosianae.
   https://archive.org/stream/comedynoctesamb00skelgoog#page/n14/mode/2up
8. Lord Cockburn, writing in September 1832 on hearing of Scott's death. Rosemary
   Goring 2021. 'Bonnie Scott-land'. Historic Scotland, Spring 2021: 26-30.
   https://www.electricscotland.com/culture/dates1-f.htm
9. Walter Scott, first sentence in Chapter Two of 'Waverley'

Chapter 2

1. Youngson A.J. The Making of Classical Edinburgh. Edinburgh University Press, 22
   George Square, Edinburgh. ISBN 0 7486 0446 4. 1993 Edition
2. Carl Becker, The Heavenly City of the Eighteenth Century Philosophers, page 34
3. Leading article. The Times, page 29, Saturday, August 24, 2019
4. William Wilberforce's description: Asa Briggs. 'The making of modern England 1783-
   1867: The Age of Improvement.' (1959), pp 148-149; Wikiepidia.org
5. http://the-lothians.blogspot.co.uk/2012/05/triumphal-visit-of-king-george-iv-to.htm.
   See also: 'A narrative of the visit of George IV to Scotland in August 1822'.
6. www.nationalgalleries.org
7. Chambers Robert. Traditions of Edinburgh, 1824 (1996 Edition, page 8
8. Edinburgh Evening News, 15th August 2022

Chapter 3

1. www.scottishphilosophy.org/dugald-steawrt.html
2. Brown, Iain Gordon. David Hume's Tomb: a Roman mausoleum by Robert Adam.
   Proc. Soc. Antiq. Scot. 121 (1991), 391-422.
   www.northernmirror.com/pdf/121_391_422.pdf
3. To Robert Louis Stevenson by Dillon and MacCaully; ascribed to George Barclay by
   Iain Brown – see footnote Chapter 3.7
4. https://www.rcs.ac.uk/news/beethoven-burns-and-the-folksong/

Chapter 4

1. Robert Louis Stevenson. Picturesque Old Edinburgh. Albyn Press Ltd, 1983. p28
2. Wikipedia.org/wiki/Patrick_Geddes http://www.scottishphilosophy.org/dugald-
   steawrt.html
3. Michael A Thomas, 'Obituary: General Stanislaw Maczek', Independent, 16/12/1994
4. Dianne King. Personal correspondence (page 371 in book she co-authored with Ray
   McKenzie 'Public Sculpture of Edinburgh', vol 1, Liverpool University Press, 2018)
5. James Grant. Old and New Edinburgh. Volume I, page 176, 1st column
6. Women of achievement http://womenofscotland.org.uk
7. Lost Edinburgh: Tenement collapse 1861. Scotsman, 24th June 2014
8. Page 69 in Allan Foster, The Literary Traveller in Edinburgh

Chapter 5

1. James Grant. Old and New Edinburgh. Volume III, pages 184, 186
2. Dr Robert Anderson, Edinburgh Magazine, December 1786, as reported on: http://www.sath.org.uk/edscot/www.educationscotland.gov.uk/scotlandshistory/jacobit esenlightenmentclearances/robertburns/burnsmap/writersmuseum.html

Chapter 6

1. David Mclean, Scotsman 15 April 2013. www.scotsman.com/heritage/people-places/lost-edinburgh-edinburgh-international-exhibition-1886-1-2895307 (accessed 30th January 2017)
2. https://en.wikipedia.org/wiki/Holyrood_Park
3. Anon http://strangeco.blogspot.co.uk/2013/12/nicol-muschet-murder-by-committee.htm
4. Scotsman.com/news/obituaries/obituary-dr-helen-crummy-mbe-social-activist-1-1755037. 18 July 2011
5. Personal correspondence with Tim Chalk, August 2016.
6. https://www.chalkworks.com/news/The-Helen-Crummy-Memorial-Sculpture--Let-The-People-Sing-/
7. Robin McKie, The Guardian, Sunday 9th December 2012: DNA pioneer James Watson reveals helix story was almost never told.
8. www.scottishpoetrylibrary.org.uk/poetry/poets/w-s-graham – accessed 28th Jan 2017.
9. Simpson MA, Squires TJ, Busuttil A. The *case of Jane Anderson, Portobello, 1889-1914*. Journal of the Royal Society of Medicine, 2000, volume 93, pages 646-648
10. Obituary, British Medical Journal, 1914; 1:947. (25th April 1914)
11. As quoted by James Buchan, page 276 in 'Capital of the Mind' – see Bibliography.

Chapter 7

1. Graham Clark, Benchmark series of photographs of memorial benches. http://grahamclarkphotographer.com/Benchmark-exhibition(337233).htm; Accessed 2nd October 2018)

Chapter 8

1. Brodie, Alexander. 2001. The Scottish Enlightenment, Berlinn Ltd.
2. Scotsman.com/news/obituaries/obituary-dr-helen-crummy-mbe-social-activist-1-1755037. 18 July 2011.
3. Parkhouse, Valerie B. 2015. Memorializing the Anglo Boer War of 1899 – 1902: Militarization of the Landscape, Monuments and Memorials in Britain. Matador, UK. ISBN 978-1780884011
4. Turnbull, Malcolm, 1989. Monuments and Statues of Edinburgh. Chambers mini guides. ISBN-10 0550200509, Section on the statue of David Livingstone
5. Foster, Allan. The Literary Traveller in Edinburgh. Mainstream Publishing Co., 2005
6. www.undiscoveredscotland.co.uk/usebooks/stevenson-edinburgh/chapter08.htm

Bibliography

The internet: The internet provides much useful information on the monuments of Edinburgh and the people and events that they represent. Popular search engines open the information stored. Some of the websites that were found to be useful in compiling this material are listed below.

- Edinburgh Places, with information on several people remembered in monuments: http://www.edinburgh-places.co.uk/folk/oldfolk - entries on John Knox, David Hume, Elsie Inglis, Adam Smith, Robert Ferguson etc. For example:
  David Hume: http://www.edinburgh-places.co.uk/folk/oldfolk/david-hume.htm
  John Knox: http://www.edinburgh-places.co.uk/folk/oldfolk/john-knox.htm

Elsie Inglis: http://www.edinburgh-places.co.uk/folk/oldfolk/elsie-inglis.htm
- Edinburgh City Council website on monuments:
  www.Edinburghmuseums.org.uk/venues/monuments
- Historic Environment Scotland: https://canmore.org.uk
- Historic Environment Scotland (John Playfair *3.2*):
  http://portal.historicenvironment.scot/designation/LB27826
- Wikipedia website of Edinburgh monuments:
  https://en.wikipedia.org/wiki/list_of_public_art_in_Edinburgh
- Wikipedia website – general queries: https://en.wikipedia.org
- Monuments to women in Scotland: http://womenofscotland.org/memorials
- Details on Scott Monument, including its many statues of characters from the Waverley
  novels on the monument (*1.21*):   https://sites.scran.ac.uk/scottmon/index.htm
- BBC website on writers:
  http://www.bbc.co.uk/scotland/arts/writingscotland/writers/robert_fergusson

Books: Several books have also provided very useful information.

Berry E. 1990. **The Writing on the Walls**. The Cockburn Association, Edinburgh

Buchan, James. **Capital of the Mind. How Edinburgh Changed the World.** Berlinn
Limited, 2007.

Cant, Malcolm. **Villages of Edinburgh, An Illustrated Guide. Vol 1.** Malcolm Cant Pub.,
Edinburgh, 1997

Gifford, John, Colin McWilliam and David Walker. **The Buildings of Scotland,
Edinburgh.** Yale University Press, 2003 edition.

Gillon, Jack & Paul McAuley. **Monumental Edinburgh.** Aberley Pub., Gloucestershire,
UK, 2015.

Harris, Stuart. **The Place Names of Edinburgh**, Steve Savage, 2002

Hunter, Gordon and Don Ledingham. **Edinburgh Revisited**. Hunter-Ledingham, Selkirk,
TD7 4NT, Scotland, October 2019. www.edinburghrevisited.co.uk

McHardy, Stuart & Donald Smith. **Scotland's Democracy Trail.** Luath Press Ltd,
Edinburgh, 2015.

McKenzie, Ray, Dianne King and Tracy Smith. **Public Sculpture of Edinburgh**, volumes
1 and 2. Liverpool University Press, November 2018,

Peyton, Jane. **Looking Up in Edinburgh.** Wiley Academy, 2004

Smith CJ. 1978. **Historic South Edinburgh**, Volume 1. Charles Skilton Ltd., Edinburgh

Tait, Gillian. **111 Places in Edinburgh that you shouldn't miss.** Emons Verlag GmbH,
Germany, 2016.

Turnbull, Malcolm, 1989. **Monuments and Statues of Edinburgh**. Chambers mini guides.
ISBN-10 0550200509

The author

John Amoore has lived in Edinburgh for nearly forty years, increasingly interested in and
attached to it and its history. The city has a wealth of detail and he never tires of walking its
streets, uncovering new and previously unseen aspects.

Amongst the wealth of the city, John observed the monuments and wanted to know who
they represented. Monuments were revisited many times, often with camera in hand.

This started John on a journey of exploration, a journey of discovery, finding out more
about the monuments and the people behind them. The journey continues. This book
represents a stage in the journey, a journey that he hopes the reader will join.

www.ingramcontent.com/pod-product-compliance
Lightning Source LLC
Chambersburg PA
CBHW071303220526
45468CB00001B/255